D0374401

EMBRACING OUR SELVES

Voice Dialogue Manual

EMBRACING OUR SELVES

Hal Stone, Ph.D.
and
Sidra Winkelman, Ph.D.

Devorss & Company, Publisher
P.O. Box 550, Marina del Rey, California 90294

ISBN: 0-87516-553-2
Library of Congress Catalog Card Number: 85-70722

Printed in the United States of America

DEDICATION

To the Seekers . . . .
Past . . . .
Present . . . .
and Future . . . .

ACKNOWLEDGMENTS

We wish to thank the multitude of people in our lives who have contributed their insights, their wisdom, their support and their love to each of us individually and to both of us collectively.

We would like to give special thanks to our many colleagues, clients and program participants around the world who have enriched and supported our work.

Hal Stone, Ph.D.   Sidra Winkelman, Ph.D.

EMBRACING OUR SELVES

CHAPTER I

A NEW VISION
OF CONSCIOUSNESS

The Introduction to Our Selves

THE AWAKENING

Once upon a time there was a tiger who was about to give birth. She was out hunting for food for herself and for her soon-to-be-born cub, when she came upon a herd of goats. She gave chase. Even in her pregnant condition, she managed to kill one of the goats, but she, herself, died as she was giving birth to a male cub. The goats, who had run away, returned when they sensed that the danger was over. They discovered this newborn cub and adopted him as part of their herd.

Over the next few years, the tiger cub grew up in the goat community. He bleated like a goat, smelled like a goat, and ate vegetation like a goat. In every respect, he behaved like a goat, except that underneath, as we are well aware, lived the tiger that he was. All went well until one day an older tiger came into the neighborhood where the goat herd dwelled and attacked one of the goats and killed it. All the goats ran away except our tiger/goat. He saw no reason to run away, of course, since he sensed no danger.

Our older tiger was a veteran campaigner, but never in his life had he been in as much shock as he was when he stood before the tiger cub who was now no longer a cub. There stood a full-grown tiger who smelled like a goat, bleated like a goat and in every way had the disposition of a goat. Since he was of the older generation, and not of a particularly understanding nature, our older tiger grabbed the young one by the scruff of the neck, dragged him to the water and showed him his reflection in the water. This made little impression on our friend because he couldn't make any proper connections about the meaning of this reflection. So our older tiger determined upon another course of action. He dragged the young tiger back to the place where he had made his kill. There he ripped a piece of meat from the dead goat and shoved it into the mouth of our young friend.

The reader may well imagine the shock and consternation of the young tiger. He gagged and tried spitting out the raw flesh, but the older tiger was committed to his teaching task and made sure that the tiger cub swallowed this new food. When he was sure it was swallowed, he shoved in another piece of meat and this time there was a change. Our young tiger allowed himself to taste the raw flesh and the warm blood and he ate this piece with gusto. When he finished chewing, the young tiger stretched and then, for the first time, let out a powerful roar, the roar of the jungle cat. The two tigers then went off together into the forest.

Heinrich Zimmer tells this story in the opening of his

book, *The Philosophy of India*. He calls it the "roar of awakening." What is this "roar of awakening?" It is the discovery that we are more than we think we are. It is the discovery that we have taken on identities that incorrectly or inadequately define our essential beings. It is as though we have been dreaming and suddenly we awaken from the dream, look around ourselves and become aware of a totally different reality.

Let us return to our tiger/goat. Up until the time when he meets the older tiger, he thinks that he is a goat and he experiences the world as a goat would experience it. His reality is that of a goat. We outside observers are aware that this goat-like perception of reality gives him a chance to experience only a fraction of his total being; that he is capable of many other perceptions, emotions and activities. We might say that he has been living his goat "self" and that the older tiger awakens him to his essential being, the tiger that he really is.

We are all raised as goats, in a symbolic sense. We are all raised in cultures and families where we are trained to think, feel and see in specific ways. Since this is all that we know, we naturally assume that the world around us is as we perceive it. This is our reality. We assume that the self we know is the only one there is. For instance, if a man is raised in a family that worships the mind, and if this man identifies with the mind as his primay source of information regarding the world, then he is in the same situation as our tiger/goat. This man will know nothing of his "other" nature. He will know nothing of his imagination, of his deeper intuitions, of the reality and validity of his feelings. He will not have access to the information available from these

other sources. Furthermore, he will be denied the richness and pleasure that this "other" nature could bring
to him.

THE CONSCIOUSNESS PROCESS BEGINS

The moment of awakening is often a very special time
in one's life. It may come in a waking state, it may be
the result of a dream or it may occur during a meditation. It is always accompanied by a heightened awareness, a sense of new perspectives. Thus the consciousness process begins.

For example, Marilyn, a woman in her thirties, has
spent her life identified with the role of "mother." She
has treated everyone as a mother would treat a child.
She has taken care of the world. This is her "goat
nature," caring for the world. She enters therapy and
has the following dream. It comes at that moment of
awakening when Marilyn begins to separate from her
maternal nature, when she begins to awaken from the
sleep that she thought was reality.

Dream of Mother Identification

Sounds have become acute. There is so much noise and
confusion I cannot rest. I finally become fully awake
and I look about me. It is as if I were in a strange house
and yet I know that it is my house and that I have lived
in it for a long time. There is a mirror across from my
bed and I glance at it. I am horrified to see that I have
grown old while I slept. The noise is deafening and I
go out to try to find where it is coming from. As
I reach the kitchen door, I realize it comes from there.
Around the kitchen table are many people, some

young, some older by far than I am. They are all dressed in children's clothes and are waiting to be fed. They see me and begin to pound their bowls on the table and call "mother" to me. I see my priest across the room with his back to me, and I think surely he can explain this to me, but as I approach him he turns around and I see that he is wearing a bib and is holding his bowl too! I run back to the door to leave and, as I pass the table, I see my parents there, wearing bibs like all the rest. I reach the door as a man comes in. I know him to be my husband, although he is not the husband I had when I went to sleep. He makes a pass at me and I feel relieved, thinking at least he doesn't think I'm his mother. When I look at him, however, he is wearing knickers and his face is the face of a child. I think that this is a nightmare and I run and shut myself in my room in order to wake up more fully, but I know I am not asleep. I ask myself over and over again: "What have I done while I slept?" Ray comes into the room (Ray is a therapist in the city where she lived). I think that surely he can help me to understand this, but he is crying because he has hurt his knee and wants me to bandage it.

This dream clearly shows Marilyn's moment of awakening. Until now, the only reality that she has known has been the computer program of "Mother" (her goat nature) into which she was locked at an early age. The dream image is so poignant—she has grown old while she slept and, during this sleep, everyone around her has become a child needing nurturing. But now Marilyn is awake and she is separating from her identification with this Mother part of herself. She is looking at herself and her surroundings through newly opened eyes and thus is beginning to ask questions and to search for something different. She is curious. She wants to discover what exists within her, other than this Mother, and to move toward the fullness of her being. Much as our tiger/goat discovered his tiger part, Marilyn, too, will discover parts that she has not known before.

The "roar of awakening" is not always a roar. It may be a roar when it applies to our tiger parts, to our sexuality, or our anger. There are, however, a multitude of parts to be discovered which are quite different from these. Ralph, a successful, hardworking, rational man 62 years of age, has the following dream. It is a dream of discovery.

Dream of the Hand in the Earth

I am walking on a country road. Suddenly I hear a noise; it sounds like a cry. I look down and, to the side of the road, I see a hand sticking up from the earth. I am shocked and I run to the hand and start digging there. I dig deeper until I unearth the body of a child three or four years of age. He is barely alive. I start to clean him off and I hold him to me.

In this dream, the awakening comes as an unearthing of something that was buried long ago. It is the Inner Child. Ralph had spent his life identified with parts of himself that pushed him toward great success financially and politically. Something was missing from his life. He had never known a real intimacy with others. In this dream he begins to deal with that intimacy as he makes the remarkable discovery that a very important part of himself has been buried. The buried child is the part that carries his vulnerability, his fear of the world, his feelings of isolation and his fear of abandonment.

This child was "buried." This self was fully repressed at the age of three or four.

Sometimes the process of awakening to what lies within us is presented to us as a journey. This is a very common motif in dream symbolism. A fifty-year-old woman who is at the start of her voyage of personal discovery, has the following dream.

Dream of the Journey

I have to embark on a journey. I have to go alone. No one can help me. This is a thing I have to do for myself. My husband would do it for me if he could, but this is a thing that each person has to do for himself. It is a long way home.

Here the unconscious portrays the newly developing consciousness process as a journey. It is a journey that each one of us must take alone. Our loved ones cannot do it for us. It is a long and often difficult way home, for in order to come to know our essential being, it is necessary to travel through a multitude of selves.

After becoming aware of her strong maternal identification (see Dream of Mother Identification), Marilyn begins to realize that she has also been identified with her Rational Self. She takes up meditation and this practice precipitates experiences that are different from anything that she has known before. For example, one night she has a dream with a very religious flavor. It is an upsetting dream because spirituality is not a legitimate part of her "goat nature" (rationality). The following experience occurs in this context:

Vision of Writing

I awakened from a dream feeling very disturbed. I could not go back to sleep so I went down to the living room. I lit a cigarette. The kitchen light was on, throwing a shaft of light into the living room, so I did not turn on any other light. Our living room rug is sand colored and the path of light from the kitchen door illuminated it. I was idly looking at this portion of the rug when it suddenly seemed filled with writing. We have a clear plate glass top on the coffee table and I thought that perhaps a letter was lying on it and the light had somehow projected the writing onto the rug. There was no letter on the coffee table and so I moved the coffee table away, but the writing remained. I then tried to rub it out with my foot, thinking that the children had been writing in the nap of the rug with their fingers. Still it persisted and I sat back down to try to read it. I could not read it and I thought: "Whoever you are, please show me what you are trying to say." The words then appeared singly. When I couldn't read one of them and felt confused, the word reappeared on the rug at once. This occurred each time I felt the confusion. It no longer seemed a rug of sand color, but sand, itself, with the words etched deeply into it. These are the words I can recall:

> You meet yourself not yet. You must love your life. Find a mind whose hope is a light to light the way for your soul. I gave you Mary (the figure in the dream from which she had awakened and from which her disturbance arose). Why have you not hoped? Now you have begun again. Put love next to hope and follow them to your Self. The voyage has begun.

I closed my eyes and thought that this is crazy. I am imagining this. Writing cannot appear on a carpet. Something said to me: "Can you throw stones at those who will not see?"

I opened my eyes and the writing was gone. I got up and looked closely at the space where it had been. I felt it must have left some mark because it had not been written on the surface but with a depth as if it were actually written in sand. There was not a trace. I was angry with myself because I had not accepted it at once and thus had lost some of the words.

In our original tiger story, the roar of awakening is the discovery of our basic instinctual nature. We must become what we are. The process of becoming fully what we are is what the consciousness process is all about. Our male dreamer, Ralph, discovers the lost little boy of his own childhood who must be reclaimed. Here, with Marilyn, we discover a radically different kind of energy—what we would call spiritual or transpersonal energy. The vision initiates her into a different reality. She is asked to find a new kind of mind, one that can light the way for her soul. The voice of her spiritual nature brings such a different kind of teaching from what she has known until now! In effect, she is being asked to develop new ways of thinking that are more compatible with the realities of these spiritual energies that are emerging. The consciousness process is filled with such surprises.

In contrast to Marilyn, Jane is working on the issue of empowerment. Her awakening to the consciousness process comes about during psychotherapy. She has learned how to be powerful in the world, but she has done this at the expense of her inner child and her basic instinctual reactions. She is introduced to the Inner Child in a Voice Dialogue format (which will be discussed in detail in the next chapter) and the child is allowed to speak and become real for one of the first times since Jane has been an adult. By doing this, she becomes aware of the child, and thus separates from it. She is now better able to care for it. Within a few nights she has the following dream.

Dream of the Lion

I am in a room and there is a small lion. I rush to the door, quite terrified, and open it and push the lion out. I come back into the room, breathing a sigh of relief, when I see another, much larger, lion. I am terrified and I rush to the door to open it, but the lion gets there first, preventing me from opening the door to either get it out or leave it behind.

This dream is very much like our tiger story. This time, however, it is a lion that our dreamer must face. She cannot escape her lion. It grows and becomes more powerful. It is an aspect of herself that can no longer be ignored. By facing this lion and learning to use its energies, she will have available to her the power of her instincts. With this power, she can successfully care for herself, and in particular, can successfully care for the child. This is true empowerment. True empowerment means that our vulnerability is available in relationships in a conscious way, and that our instinctual energies are also available to function protectively. In this way, the energies are balanced. One need not behave in any particularly assertive fashion. One is quite naturally in a position of power.

HOW THE PARTS DEVELOP

We have referred to the fact that we are made up of many parts. These parts have been referred to in many different ways by many different people. They have been known as the many 'I's, selves or partial selves, complexes, multiple personalities, and, more recently, as energy patterns. We use the latter term throughout this book because it more clearly points to the dramatic animating qualities of these selves, as they enliven us, causing us to think, feel and act in a variety of ways. The concept that we are made up of different parts is sometimes difficult to understand. Some people object to this idea. They argue that this kind of theory fragments the personality. We feel that it is already "fragmented" and that our task is to become aware of this fragmentation or multiplicity of parts so that real choice is available in our lives.

These contradictory feelings are apparent in all of us at one time or another. The higher the emotional stakes, the more likely we are to have differing sets of feelings in any given situation. Think of the woman whose only child is leaving home. On one side, we see her feelings of relief: "I wish she'd hurry up and move out. I'm so eager to have the house to myself." On the other side, we see her feelings of loss: "I wish she wouldn't go. I wish she would stay and keep me company forever. She's such fun." Or think of a man who is offered a promotion to a key leadership position. Needless to say, one part of him is overjoyed and looks forward to the challenge, the authority and the excitement. Another part regrets the loss of comraderie that necessarily accompanies this move up from the ranks.

Now let us see how the parts or selves develop. We start with a newborn infant, a unique human being. This infant comes into the world with its own genetic make-up which determines its physiology (and some of its behavior) and with a specific quality of being which is all its own. We call this unique quality of being the

essence level of the individual. (Ask any woman who
has had more than one child. Each child is different in
utero, and at birth this difference in essence is even
more apparent. It is as individual as a fingerprint.)

At this essence level, the infant is quite defenseless,
totally vulnerable, and dependent upon the adult world
for its survival. However, along with this basic and
unique essence level energy, the infant also has the
potential to develop any energy patterns or selves that
one can imagine, the sum total of which will be the individual personality we soon come to know. It is now
that the armoring of this vulnerable condition and the
development of the personality begins.

The infant learns that he or she must establish some
measure of control over the environment, otherwise
things can be very unpleasant. This development of control over the environment is what the development of
personality is all about. Personality develops as a way of
dealing with vulnerability. The stronger the personality
that develops, the farther away the child moves from
vulnerability and its essence level reality. It loses contact
with its own unique way of being as it learns to be
powerful.

How does this process work? How does the child become more powerful? The child learns, for example,
that the mother is very happy when baby smiles. Now
baby may enjoy smiling, but soon this will be overrid-
den by the knowledge that smiling brings about certain
consequences. By the same token, going to the toilet
soon becomes a cause célèbre as a system of rewards and
punishments is established in relation to the acts of
urination and defecation. Similarly, aggression is either
rewarded or punished. It may become a means of mastering the world or it may be treated as negative or anti-
social behavior.

In some instances, the child might try to establish some measure of control over the environment by retreating into fantasy. Daydreams can then become a core factor in the personality. A young boy whose parents separate develops a fantasy that he is in a submarine deep under the sea. He spends increasing amounts of time there and so tries to make himself feel better. Objectively speaking, he is obviously retreating from pain. On another level, he has found a way of dealing with his extreme vulnerability. In contrast, another child finds that success in school is the key to mastering his environment and protecting his vulnerable parts, and so he develops his ambitious side and his pleasing parts.

Thus, in our developmental process we are rewarded for certain behaviors and punished for others. Some parts are strengthened and others are weakened. We learn our lessons well and we develop "personalities." It is strange to think that personality is actually a system of sub-personalities (parts) that takes us away from our essence level being at the same time that it brings us control—and thereby power—in the world.

In fact, one of the earliest parts of our personality to develop is one that watches over us. It is like a giant computer mechanism. It is constantly looking to see what dangers lie lurking around us and how it can best protect us from them. It incorporates parental and societal injunctions, and so controls our behavior to a large extent by establishing a set of rules that it feels will ensure our safety and our acceptance by others. It decides how emotional we can be. It makes sure we do not act foolishly or in ways in which we might embarrass ourselves. We call this self the Protector/Controller and it is the primary energy pattern that lies behind many other parts. It will utilize, for example, the energies of the Rational Self and the Responsible Parent as a way of keeping control of the environment. When most people use the word "I," they are in fact referring to this Protector/Controller. For the vast majority of us, this Protector/Controller energy is the directing agent of personality. It is what many people think of as an Ego.

We see then how, in the development of personality, different energy patterns serve to make our sojourn on earth a more successful one. The problem is, of course, that we gradually begin to lose our essence level reality. This is a sad state of affairs, for without it our whole system of relationships is affected. If we are no longer in touch with this essence level of being, then it is not our deepest and most vulnerable self that is involved in relationships. Instead, it is a group of sub-personalities, watched over by the Protector/Controller, that determines our feelings and behavior. Thus, there is always a vague fear that if the other person *really* knew what we are like, he or she would abandon us. But *we* don't know what we are really like!

We can see, therefore, how important it is to learn about the sub-personalities that operate inside us. If we do not know what they are, then we are in the position of having different sub-personalities driving our psychological car, with us sitting in the back seat or, worse yet, hiding in the trunk. It becomes a matter of great importance to discover what these parts are, and how they operate within us. This journey of discovery is the unfolding of the consciousness process.

It may seem like a strange idea to think of our car being driven by different parts of us, each one demanding its turn. Yet, be assured that this is exactly the situation. We have usually been well conditioned so that by the time adulthood is reached, and generally long before, we have lost all connection to essence level reality. As has been suggested, we no longer know who we are or what we feel. Our snakes and lions have long been buried, and we only know them by momentary lapses. We may fall into rages periodically and not know why. It is easy to forget about them because "that really wasn't me," that felt like killing. It was just an aberration.

Our lions and tigers often emerge when we drink and the Protector/Controller dissolves a bit in the alcohol. For example, a very quiet controlled man would fly into rages and use terrible language to his wife when he drank. This went on for years. The therapist suggested to her that she record her husband's remarks during one of his inebriated diatribes. She did this and played it back to him. He was in a state of shock when he heard the tape. He couldn't believe that it was he who was saying those things!

Let us see how these lions and tigers get buried in the first place. A young child, Kevin, four years of age, is playing outdoors. He runs into the house because another child has hit him. The mother responds very protectively. She says something like: "Johnnie is a mean boy. Why don't you stay with me and keep me company." She has not helped her son deal with his instinctual life. She has never dealt with hers, and so it is that she cannot support his natural aggressions.

That night, Kevin has a nightmare. He wakes up screaming that there is a lion in his room. His mother comes in and comforts him and assures him that there is no lion, that it was "just a dream." So he goes back to bed and soon there is the same nightmare and he awakens screaming again. This time the mother turns on the lights and, together, they look under the bed and in the closet. Thus, she demonstrates fully that there is no lion.

When this happens enough times, soon there is no lion. First, Kevin is protected from dealing with the issue of his natural aggression. Then, the natural aggression appears in a dream in the form of a lion. Since he has denied the lion in his life, and his mother has supported this, the lion in his dream becomes his enemy. Next, the reality of the symbolic life is denied. Since the mother has never learned to honor the dream, to honor the symbolic life, how could she do otherwise? So it is that early in his life the Protector/ Controller in Kevin becomes much stronger and becomes a directing agent that makes sure that Kevin stays away from children who are aggressive. He either becomes a a victim to these children, or begins to play with children who, themselves, are no threat to him.

Kevin grows up and becomes a trial attorney. He is filled with anxiety in the courtroom situation. Why is this? What fills him with such dread when he is faced with an attorney on the other side who is unscrupulous? His own lion is stirred deep inside his loins. He does not realize this, however. He just feels uncomfortable as this part of him (that his mother disowned in herself and helped him to disown in himself) is activated deep in the unconscious.

Without his lion available, Kevin feels vulnerable. There is a child within him who feels endangered. He also does not know about this inner child. He lost contact with this child a long time ago, for unlike Peter Pan, *he* grew up. His "psychological car" was driven at times by his Inner Pusher, at times by his Pleaser, at times by his Frightened Child and at times by his Inner Critic who always was willing to let him know how inadequate he really was.

At night he would often have dreams of great violence, but, after all, they were "only" dreams. From our perspective, Kevin's evolution is a perfectly normal and natural one. He has no Awareness level operating, and so there is no Aware Ego that could drive his car in accordance with the rules that would suit his essential being. Instead, it is driven by his sub-personalities (an amazing array of characters) exactly as is the case with the vast majority of us before we awaken from our waking slumber.

As we have said before, one of the primary issues in the evolution of consciousness is the discovery of these sub-personalities and how they are operating inside of us. Before we approach the issue of the discovery of these parts, and how we go about learning more about them, it is necessary to pause to describe a conceptual structure that will be referred to over and over again in this book. Our approach to the exploration of parts is based upon this conceptual structure or definition of consciousness and related terms. It is to these definitions that we now turn.

THE NATURE OF CONSCIOUSNESS

In approaching the definition of consciousness, we start with the basic idea that consciousnes is not an *entity*. It is a *process*. What we will be defining, therefore, is not consciousness but the consciousness process. We will be calling it consciousness, but we are not talking about a condition of being. As far as we are concerned, one does not become conscious; consciousness is not simply something that we strive to achieve. Consciousness is a process that we must live out—an evolutionary process continually changing, fluctuating, from one

moment to the next. As we refer to consciousness in the
coming pages, it will be important to keep this kinetic
aspect of the process in mind.

The consciousness process evolves on three distinctly
different levels. One level is that of Awareness. The second level is that of the *experience* of the different parts,
sub-personalities, or energy patterns. The third level is
the level of the Ego.

What is Awareness? It is the capacity to witness life in
all its aspects without evaluating or judging the energy
patterns being witnessed, and without having the need
to control the outcome of an event. It is often referred
to in spiritual and esoteric writings as the "witness
state" or "consciousness". In these writings, it is seen
as a position of non-attachment. It is neither rational
nor, conversely, emotional. It is simply a point of reference that objectively witnesses what is.

This Awareness level of consciousness must be clearly
differentiated from the energy pattern that we call the
Protector/Controller. The Protector/Controller is subjective in its observations. It is always deeply concerned
about our impact on others. It always has a specific goal
in mind. It is generally quite rational and very much
determines what we perceive and the way we think and
behave. In contrast, the Awareness level is simply the
silent witness, observing in an objective fashion. Most
meditative systems are trying to help develop the
Awareness level of consciousness. It is a non-action
reference point. It does not do anything except witness.
In the traditional psychological systems, this Awareness
level would be related to the concept of pure insight.

The second aspect of the consciousness process is the
experience of the energy patterns. We see everything in
life as an energy pattern of one kind or another. These

particular energy patterns relate to our own internal states, be they physical, emotional, mental or spiritual. The energy patterns may vary from a vague feeling, or a barely discernible sensation, to a fully developed part or sub-personality. Let us show you what we mean by this.

A man is angry. He is raging inside, or he is expressing his rage for all to see. We would say that he is identified with, or overcome by, the energy pattern of rage. There is no consciousness because the Awareness level is missing. Once he becomes aware of the rage, then two of our basic conditions for consciousness have been met: he is experiencing his rage, and, on another level, his Awareness is dispassionately informing him of this fact. What remains is the requirement that the Ego utilize these two levels and become more aware.

Let us look at a different kind of experience. A woman experiences powerful energies during a meditation. She identifies these energies as spiritual. However great the impact, this is simply one of the myriad of energies. In this instance, the energies are spiritual rather than rageful. Again, if there is an Awareness level that witnesses this spiritual experience, then we have met two conditons of consciousness and we would say that here, too, there is a consciousness process.

Let us take yet a third example. Susan is at a party with her husband. She is feeling very jealous because he is showing a great deal of attention to one of the women there. She has had strong spiritual training, however, and has been taught that feelings such as anger and jealousy can and *should* be transmuted. She has learned how to do this by meditating. She meditates briefly until she feels separated from the situation. Soon, she is no longer feeling jealousy; she is feeling love.

From our perspective, she has actually controlled her

emotional reaction with the help of her Protector/Controller, and then, through her meditative capabilities, has tapped into a love energy on the spiritual side. She, however, believes that she has transmuted the jealousy, that she has changed her feelings of jealousy into feelings of love. To us, in this situation, there is no transmutation and no consciousness. There is simply the burial of the energy pattern of jealousy. Consciousness would require her to feel the jealousy that exists within her and to become aware that she is feeling this.

It is important to remember that perfection is, thank God, beyond the grasp of most of us. Therefore, we do not expect Awareness and experience to occur simultaneously. Life must be lived fully, with Awareness eventually entering into the picture.

So far in our system we have described Awareness and the experiencing of the energy patterns. As we have stated before, we view the experiencing of the energy patterns from a holistic perspective. This means simply that it is all-inclusive. It incorporates experiences deriving from physical, emotional, mental and spiritual dimensions. Our perception of, and experience of, the world in which we live is through this holistic spectrum of energies. We must yet incorporate the third level to complete our definition of the consciousness process, and that level is Ego.

In its traditional definition, the Ego has been referred to as the *executive function* of the psyche, or the choice maker. Someone has to run the operation and it is the Ego that does the job. Our current definition of Ego is exactly the same as the traditional one. We see the Ego as the executive function of the psyche. It is the one who, hopefully, makes the choices. The Ego receives its information both from the Awareness level and from the experience of the different energy patterns. As one moves forward in the consciousness process, the Ego becomes a more Aware Ego. As a more Aware Ego, it is in a better position to make real choices. However, what we discover very early in this work, is that the Ego has succumbed to a combination of different sub-personalities which have taken over its executive function. Thus, what in fact is functioning as the Ego, may be a combination of one's Protector/Controller, Pusher, Pleaser, Perfectionist and Inner Critic. It is this unique combination of sub-personalities, or energy systems, that is perceiving the world in which we live, processing this information, and then directing our lives. Therefore, we say that the Ego is *identified* with these particular patterns. Most people believe that they have free will because ''they'' choose to do a particular thing and they think that this is really choosing. What we have discovered, however, is that there is remarkably little choice in the world. Unless we awaken to the consciousness process, as we have described earlier, the vast majority of us are run by the energy patterns with which we are identified or by those which we have disowned.

Let us contrast an Ego identified with a particular set of sub-personalities with an Aware Ego. A physician, John, wishes to go to Mexico to practice medicine in order to help the poor people there. He considers himself very altruisitc, very spiritual, and he wishes to do some kind of planetary service. He has a dream shortly after he has made his decision.

Dream of Mexican Peasants

I am sitting on a throne chair somewhere in southern Mexico. Peasants are coming to me and bowing and bringing me gifts as though I were some kind of god or king.

From our perspective, we would say that John's Ego has been identified with a spiritual, self-sacrificing energy pattern. He has always been a very responsible man and service is a part of the way the Responsible Father within him acts in the world. The dream brings up a different energy pattern, one of which he is unaware. It is the power side of him, that part in him which seeks selfishly for his own aggrandizement. This does not make his choice wrong. It simply means that when the choice was made, there was no Aware Ego present. The spiritual, service-oriented, Responsible Father made the choice.

John now has the possibility of stepping back from this part and witnessing, from the level of Awareness, the spiritually oriented, self-sacrificing part with which he has been identified. Furthermore, he can witness the other side, his need for self-aggrandizement. His Ego receives the information made available by the Awareness level *and* by the experience of his two sides. His Ego is now more aware. He is now in a position to make a *real* choice about going to Mexico. He now holds the tension of these opposites with his newly Aware Ego. He may choose to go, not to go, or to defer the decision for the time being. The decision is inconsequential. What matters is what part makes the decision. It can readily be seen that when one is in the consciousness process, decison making becomes somewhat more complex!

Thus far, we have described the three aspects of the consciousness process and we have seen how they are interrelated. The consequences of this definition are far reaching. If it is accepted, then there is no reason to feel bad or guilty about the way we are. Each part of us is fully honored. The Awareness level simply witnesses what is.

However, most of us have a surgeon's mentality when it comes to the parts of us that we dislike. We try so hard to get rid of our tempers, our rage, our jealousy, our pettiness, our shyness, our feelings of inadequacy. The list is endless. In the attempt to eradicate these rejected parts, we do exactly the opposite—we make them much stronger by driving them into the unconscious, from which they are free to operate beyond our control. If, instead, we step back and allow the Awareness level to come into operation, we not only become aware of the activities of these parts, but we also become aware that our wish to surgically eradicate these patterns is another part too. We have within us a sub-personality that labels these unwanted selves as detestable, making us feel absolutely dreadful for having them in the first place. It is amazing what one begins to see when the Awareness level is allowed to operate and when one is able to separate from this surgical mentality. It is also wonderful to feel the sense of freedom this brings to us.

The rejection of unacceptable energy patterns brings up the question of transmutation and how it fits into this scheme of consciousness. This is an important concept today because so many people are trying to transmute instinctual energies as they adhere to spiritual traditions. The idea of *transmutation* is quite different from *transformation*, or transformational process, a term which we use interchangeably with consciousness process. We have described consciousness as a continually changing, fluctuating evolutionary process which we must live out. In precisely the same way, the transformational process is a process of ever-increasing expansion of the Awareness level, of ever-increasing awareness

of the Ego, and of ever-increasing experience of the vast
multitude of energy patterns that are available to be experienced. Transformation, a change in composition
and character, can occur at any of these three levels. In
contrast, we have defined *transmutation* as changing
energies from one form to another as in the alchemical
sense. Let us now examine the issue of transmutation
through an example.

George is strongly identified with a spriritual, loving
part of himself. He believes that he has no reason to express negative feelings when he can just as well express
positive ones. Difficulties in business lead him to seek
therapy. He has become involved with dishonest people
and thereby has endangered his business. Since he rejects his own dishonesty, power and negativity, he is
blind to these qualities in other people. (The man who
will not see darkness may soon find himself bathing in a
sea of darkness.) His philosophy has always been that he
is successfully transmuting these negative energies in
him by learning to control them and to act in a loving
and kind way, instead of experiencing them. He truly
believes that experiencing them will add to the negative
energies in the world around him. He is committed to
transmuting the negative energies into gold, much as
the alchemists of old. During this period he has the
following dream.

Dream of Killing the Snake

I am walking on a path and I come to a tree. There is a
snake in the tree and it is angry at me. It jumps to bite
me and I have a sword and I cut it in half. Then the
part with the head jumps again and I cut it in half
again. I keep doing this until there is only a small piece
of the head left. This small piece leaps at me and I feel
the fangs sink deeply into my hand.

What is transmutation to George, is the repression of his instinctual life to us. The snake is angry with him —and for good reason. George was raised in a family setting where control was the keyword. There is no awareness level operating, hence there is no Aware Ego. His Ego is identified with a system of spiritual values. Thus, his natural Protector/Controller has simply taken on these spiritual values because they serve his purpose. Instead of transmuting his rage, dishonesty and negativity, Geroge is, in fact, *empowering* them in his own unconscious through the act of repression. Thus he makes himself much more vulnerable in the world to people who carry these same energies. The snake, the basic instinctual life, will not go away and it will have its revenge. Of that we may be sure.

Sam, on the other hand, is a man who was identified with power. He had always rejected his vulnerability. He became aware in the course of therapy of his power side and the degree to which he had been identified with it. He also became aware of the vulnerable child within him. His older brother, Jack, had also been a power person and a lot of Sam's need for power came from this relationship. He had the following dream shortly after the discovery of his Inner Child.

Dream of Transformation of Power Energy

I'm at a party and my brother Jack is there. He goes someplace in the room and when he returns to me, he is crying. I hold him in my arms and he tells me that someone hurt his feelings and he wonders why anyone would hurt him like that.

Sam has developed an Awareness level in his actual life. He is aware now of the opposite energy patterns in him of vulnerability and power. That is transformation;

the awareness of the opposites and the ability of the Aware Ego to honor both patterns and to tolerate the tension that exists between them. Out of this separation from the power (the part with which he has been identified) and the honoring of the child (the part that he has repressed), an organic transformation of the energy patterns themselves occurs. Jack, the brother who symbolizes the power side, becomes more vulnerable and Sam is now holding him. This is a symbolic portrayal of the transformational process as it occurs in a specific energy pattern.

You may have already noticed in your reading of this chapter that there is a dictum in all of this, a basic premise for our work. It is a simple one. We must learn to honor all the parts. Honoring all the parts means that we must have an Awareness level and an Aware Ego that can separate from certain patterns with which we are identified and claim other patterns from which we flee. Honoring all the parts in this way means that we have a much greater degree of choice in our actions. We shall have many examples of how this process works in the course of this book. The parts that we do not honor grow inside of us in unconscious ways and gain in power and authority. The snake that George tries so hard to kill is not dead. It lives inside him, growing in power, waiting to have its revenge. We see, therfore, that it is absolutely crucial to honor all the parts.

But who, you may ask are "we?" We have seen from our discussion of consciousness thus far that who "we" are can be rather problematical. In our context, the word "we" refers to the Ego which is involved in the consciousness process. It is an Ego that is becoming more and more aware as it processes the information received from the Awareness level and the experience of the different energy patterns.

THE ARCHETYPES

The term *energy pattern* encompasses parts that are personally conditioned (sub-personalities) as well as parts that are based on a genetic predisposition (archetypes). Jung used the word *archetypes* to refer to basic psychological instincts, and it is to these that we now turn our attention.

The early Greeks seemed to have a fairly well defined philosophy so far as honoring all the parts is concerned. It was clearly necessary for the heroes of Greek mythology to honor all the gods and goddesses. The god or goddess that you disowned was the one that turned against you. That is usually the basis of mythology.

For example, Hippolytus, the son of Theseus, worships Artemis, the chaste forest goddess and rejects Aphrodite, the goddess of love. Nautrally, Aphrodite is inflamed at this rejection and so she seeks to punish him. She inflames Phaedra, the wife of Theseus, with a mad passion for Hippolytus, her stepson. What better way to punish him? Phaedra attempts to seduce him and he rejects her in that special way that one does when rejecting the love goddess. Phaedra is furious, and filled with a desire for revenge at this rejection and so she informs Theseus that his son tried to seduce her. Theseus, in a rage, banishes Hippolytus from the kingdom and, in this proccss, Hippolytus is killed. Only then does Theseus discover that his son was innocent. The lesson for us is a simple one: what we deny becomes our enemy.

The Greeks did not require that all the gods and goddesses be worshipped equally. If Apollo, the god of light and order and structure was your favorite god, that was perfectly permissible. It was simply necessary that Dionysius, the complementary, or opposite, energy also be worshipped. If one visits the ruins of Epidauros, the ancient site of healing in Greece, one is struck by the fact that there are shrines built to all the gods and goddesses. In this way, we assume that those in need of healing could pray to their favorite gods and goddesses and make amends to the ones they had neglected.

When we visited Delphi, we had the opportunity to drive to a cave high above the ruins where the Dionysian rites were celebrated. Delphi, itself, was the center for the worship of Apollo for only nine months of the year. For three months a year, the priests of Apollo vacated the shrine and the priests of Dionysius took over. Everyone, it seems, was satisfied with this balancing of energies.

Listen to the following dream of a forty-year-old man, highly educated, very much of an Apollonian type, and strongly rejecting of the more expressive, experiential Dionysian energy patterns in himself.

Dream of the British Army and the Music Man

I am standing at one end of a large room. I am in charge of a group of soldiers dressed in British uniforms. We have guns and we are about to charge and destroy a group at the other end. They are music people. Their leader is a drummer and he is wearing shorts and is very hairy. He reminds me of a baboon. They are playing their music wildly. We start to march to destroy them when suddenly, within seconds, all of my men have been killed and the battle is over. I wake up in a sweat.

Our dreamer, Charles, is a worshipper of Apollo. He has lived in form and structure. His Protector/Controller dominates his life and requires him to keep his Dionysian tendencies at bay. These tendencies, however, have become too strong. They begin to break through in his life and he is driven to leave his home at night and seek excitement that could greatly endanger him. The dream comes shortly before the start of therapy, and in his own words, it is a precipitating factor. As a worshipper of Apollo, for whom he has built many shrines (multiple academic degrees), Charles has disowned Dionysius. He has disowned the part of himself that has the capability of expression, of ecstasy, of letting go, of releasing. From the control place, he keeps trying to destroy Dionysius, but these energies are too powerful. They now control him. No one demands that he give up his primary allegiance to a way of life that is fundamentally Apollonian. He simply is required, if he be true to the Greek way, to learn to dance the minor dance of Dionysius, to build a small shrine to him and to honor this way of being in the world as well.

Apollo and Dionysius are the names of gods in Greek mythology. In fact, they are simply energy patterns in projected form. Apollo represents that energy in each of us that predisposes us to act or think or feel in a rational, controlled, clearly defined fashion. Dionysius has to do with that energy within us that predisposes us to act or think or feel along the lines of release, experience or ecstasy. The Greeks projected these innate energy patterns and made gods of them. Jung took these innate energy patterns and called them archetypes. The archetype is an energy pattern that is built into the structure of the psyche, one that predisposes us to act, feel or think along primordial lines. Archetypes are, in effect, psychological instincts.

We would now say of our dreamer, Charles, that he has been identified with the Apollonian archetype and that he has disowned the Dionysian archetype. As was

the case with Hippolytus, the disowned archetype will
have its revenge. His life already has started to be controlled by these disowned elements as he is literally forced out of his home against his "better judgment" to
seek the excitement that his Apollonian nature would
never allow.

The archetypes are amazingly varied. We saw a beautiful example of the Mother archetype in the dream of
Marilyn. It is as though someone had turned on a tape
cassette inside her, playing the music of "Mother." One
can become a total prisoner of the archetype in that it
lives out its energy through us, taking over the executive
function that belongs to the Ego, and making most of
the choices that we think *we* are making. The other side
of the archetype of the Mother in Marilyn might have to
do with her selfishness, power, rage and warrior energy.
All of these energies were essentially unknown to her.
Some time after the discovery of the Great Mother within, and after she began to dis-identify from this archetype, she had the following two dreams.

Dream of the Beast Man and Dream of
Imprisonment of Feelings

I perceive a strange being, half man and half beast. The
creature wears bands of steel on his feet, arms and
chest, to which are fastened chains that hold him fast.
On seeing me he begins to strain at his bonds and
seems certain to burst them.

In a second dream, I dream that there is a man who
has imprisoned the "ability to express." This imprisonment has finally reached great proportions and is doing
great harm. He has imprisoned many people and there
is a real danger to these prisoners. Through my work
(therapy) I am finally given a chance to expose him as

the evil person he is. I have managed to free the prisoners he has confined and now I need to nourish the people who were starved during their imprisonment.

If a woman is identified with the archetype of the Good Mother, or if a man is identified with the archetype of the Good Father, then we may be sure that on the other side there is the Beast; that there are a multitude of parts that have been starved into submission. Being locked into these archetypes without an Awareness level operating, means that our essence level feelings are not available to us. We generally do not know how we feel. We feel what the archetype feels because that is who "we" are.

The dis-engagement from the Mother archetype, and then from her rational, Apollonian, archetype, cleared the way for Marilyn to come into contact with the Beast, with her daemonic nature. What is our daemonic nature? It is our natural instinctual energies that have gone underground. Our Protector/Controller learns from family and society that it is dangerous to express these instinctual energies and to express real feelings, and so these energies go underground, where they become increasingly more powerful and more negative. The beast that wishes to kill us is the result, the inevitable consequence of, this process of repression.

Through her transformational work, Marilyn has discovered the man (Protector/Controller) who has required her to bury these feelings. Her Protector/Controller came into operation initially to protect her painfully sensitive essence level. It soon took over totally and developed a life of its own that required her to kill all instinctual feelings. Living out a Mother archetype is one remarkably effective way of doing this.

Donna, a young woman in her twenties, has the following dream a few nights after her baby is born, as she
begins to identify with this Mother archetype.

Dream of the Hanging

I am on a platform. I'm wearing the milk-smeared
nightgown that I wore when my baby was born. Across
from me is a hangman's gallows. A motorcyclist who is
me, dressed in my motorcycle gear, is standing there
and they hang him.

Here, with the birth of her first child, Donna suc-
cumbs to the Mother archetype. This is certainly a
necessary event if one is going to take care of a child
properly. Unfortunately, her "Adventurer" side is lost
to her completely. He is hung, wearing the motorcycle
outfit that Donna will not be permitted to wear again.
She is taken over by the Mother archetype without
Awareness operating. It is in this situation that she loses
the balancing energy of her adventurous, non-motherly
side. This energy was not to be regained for many years.

The Hero is another powerful archetypal energy. It
simply describes the fact that we each have within us
the capacity to behave in heroic ways. Archetypes, it is
to be noted, are not inherently good or bad. The question is always whether or not there is an Aware Ego
operating which is separated from the archetype and is,
therefore, able to make independent decisions.

For example, the American president is inaugurated
on January 4th in Washington, D.C. The weather is
quite cold but the president always wears a suit with no
coat or hat. Why is this? Why can't a president wear a
coat on a cold day like any other human being? The
answer is that he must live the archetype of the Hero.

He must not appear to be cold! We discovered a secret during the inauguration of President Carter—namely, that there was a heater inside the lectern. There was a short in the wiring and so the great secret was out.

Kennedy's ill-fated visit to Dallas is another example, in our view, of the hero archetype in action. This does not allow a man to be in touch with his vulnerability. It is not all right to be afraid. It is not acceptable to be cautious and to ride in a bullet proof car! Vulnerability is a feeling that is not even available to the Hero. If it is available, it is not honored; it is to be ignored.

The Hero archetype grabs someone by the scruff of the neck and can lift that person to heroic heights. It can then drop him or her at any moment, and what is left is an empty shell. We had the opportunity of hearing about one of the many leaders of the student movement of the mid-sixties. He had been grasped by the archetype and had performed amazing tasks in leading the student movement. He had truly behaved heroically. Some years afterwards this same man was a psychological cripple, a shell of a man, dropped from heroic heights, just as he had been lifted to heroic heights years earlier. What we are trying to learn how to do with all archetypal energy is to use it with an Aware Ego. In this way, we use *it* rather than *it* using us.

What are some of the other archetypes? We have in us a capacity for great wisdom, far beyond anything our ordinary Egos could possibly imagine. There is the Child. There is the Mother, Father, Son and Daughter. There is the Incest Archetype, that which bonds us to the familiar. There is the archetypal energy that requires us to unbond, to move to the unfamiliar. There is the Judas principle, that which betrays the Hero. There is the archetype of Power and of Vulnerability. There is

the Aphrodite energy and the Mars energy, our Sensuality and Warrior natures. In the course of this book, we
shall be seeing over and over again, in a multitude of
different ways, how these archetypes operate. We shall
see how they balance each other and how they dance in
relation to the other people in our lives. We shall see
what happens when we identify with them and when
we try to ignore them.

CHAPTER II

VOICE DIALOGUE

Exploring the Selves

BACKGROUND

There are many ways in which we awaken to the consciousness process, as we have seen. Once this process has started, however, it is usually impossible to go back.

A 35-year-old woman, Sylvia, who has been identified with her rational mind all her life, is introduced to the process of guided imagery, a procedure which directly taps into symbolic energies. This begins to activate all of her non-rational sub-personalities, both feeling and spiritual, and she has the following dream.

Dream of the Closed Door

I am in a round building. It is perfectly planned and beautifully maintained, but I find myself walking out of it. As I leave, I turn to look behind me and while I am looking, the sliding exit door closes noiselessly and disappears. The building is perfectly round and completely smooth and I know that I'll never be able to re-enter it. I turn and look around me. I am in a freshly

35

tilled garden. The soil is black and moist and nothing
has been planted yet but a row of magnificent rose
bushes around its borders.

Sylvia has lived a well-ordered, rational life. In her
dream she is leaving the perfection, predictability and
safety of this life. She finds herself in a new setting, a
garden where things grow organically. How does one
care for this garden, this garden which is oneself? This is
really a beautiful image because, as we awaken to the
consciousness process, we each become gardeners of the
soul.

Just as there are many ways of awakening, many
doors through which one can leave one's initial state of
consciousness, there are many ways to proceed further.
We would like to introduce you now to an approach
that is very special to us, both for initially igniting the
consciousness process, and for facilitating its expansion.

This method is called Voice Dialogue, which we, the
authors, developed as a means of working with one
another psychologically when we first met in the early
1970's. We felt that we needed some new tool to help
us in our own transformational processes, one that
would be inclusive and flexible and fun. We needed a
technique that would help us to move beyond our own
rational, intuitive, and psychologically sophisticated Pro-
tector/Controllers, and would encourage an ever-wid-
ening expansion of consciousness.

BASIC COMPONENTS OF VOICE DIALOGUE

Over the intervening years, Voice Dialogue has proven
itself to be a dramatically effective and frequently

humorous tool for igniting and expanding the consciousness process by helping us to explore our sub-personalities, expand our awareness and clarify our Egos.

1. Exploration of Sub-personalities or Energy Systems

First, Voice Dialogue provides direct access to the
sub-personalities and archetypes that were discussed in
Chapter 1. It offers the opportunity to separate these
out and to deal with them as independent interacting
psychic units or energy systems. When we speak of using Voice Dialogue, we mean that we directly engage
these sub-personalities or Voices in a dialogue without
the interference of a critical, embarrassed, or repressive
Protector/Controller. Each sub-personality is addressed
directly, with full recognition of both its individual importance and its role as only a part of the total personality. Each of these sub-personalities experiences life
differently. Each concentrates on its own portion of the
energy system.

Each sub-personality is a distinct energy pattern.
Each animates our physical body with its own particular
energies. We can feel them from the inside—think of
those queasy feelings that belong to your Frightened
Child. It is, however, from the outside that they can be
viewed with awe. The changes that these energy patterns bring about in the body are remarkable.

A man with a taut jaw, dull eyes, and furrowed brow,
whose energy is that of a captain of industry, can transform before our eyes until we feel as though we are
with a young child. His eyes will widen and sparkle, his
furrowed brow will smooth miraculously (without a face-
lift). His jaw will relax and his smile will turn from a
grimace to an infectious grin. His shoulders will relax

and the persistent headache that is like background music in his daily life will disappear. All this will happen as a different energy takes over the same body.

2. Clarification of Ego

Secondly, Voice Dialogue definitively separates the Ego from the Protector/Controller and the dominant sub-personalities that work alongside it. The Ego is given its own central physical space, and the sub-personalities play out their conflicts around it. When a sub-personality begins to take over the Ego, the alert Voice Dialogue facilitator will point out this takeover, will ask the subject to move to another space, and will engage the sub-personality directly. In this way the Ego becomes more and more clearly differentiated. That is to say, it becomes a more Aware Ego.

3. Enhancement of Awareness

Last of all, Voice Dialogue introduces Awareness into the system. There is a physical space for each sub-personality that does the experiencing. There is a physical space for the Ego who coordinates and executes, and there is a physical space, separate from all the others, for Awareness. From this still point, in a non-judgmental way, with no decisions to make, the Awareness can witness and review all that is going on. From this still point, everything is noted and accepted. Nothing need be changed. From this still point, the drama played out by the sub-personalities about the Ego is clearly visible.

DERIVATIONS OF DIALOGUE WORK

Before we go on to show Voice Dialogue in action, we would like to review the contributions made to our thinking by other therapeutic systems. Voice Dialogue is really a blending of a number of other systems— Gestalt, Jungian, Transactional Analysis, Psychosynthesis and Psychodrama. The Awareness level used in Voice Dialogue comes from esoteric teachings about the Witness state and is not unlike a number of meditational systems.

Gestalt therapists have always recognized the reality of the sub-personalities and have used the "hot seat" method to work directly with them, as well as shifting the subject to different places in the room. The Gestalt therapist often encourages the client's Ego to relate to the sub-personality early in therapy. The various sub-personalities are frequently encouraged to speak directly to one another.

Gestalt therapists have developed rich and complex techniques for tapping into the sub-personality work. However, traditionally there are no attempts made to develop an Awareness level—that is, a viewpoint that is separate from emotions and values and can provide an unbiased and fully objective view of the interactions of the sub-personalities and the Ego. Furthermore, one's Protector/Controller frequently masquerades as an Ego, and when this Controller-as-Ego is pitted against a sub-personality that it finds unacceptable, it will try to establish immediate supremacy. The unacceptable sub-personality (such as Guilt or the Critic) may seem to disappear but, in reality, it just goes underground and operates unconsciously.

With Voice Dialogue, we try to keep an Awareness of

all the conflicting Voices so that the unpleasant surprises that can be cooked up by the unconscious sub-personalities will be diminished. The move is toward an inclusive and expanded consciousness, rather than a solution of conflicts and ridding oneself of "undesirable" Voices.

We would like to point out that Voice Dialogue can be used in conjunction with any therapeutic modality and, in our view, is not antithetical to any system. For instance, a wide range of Gestalt methods can be used while the subject is in different Voices in order to intensify the subject's experience of the Voice. Conversely, Voice Dialogue can be used adjunctively with other therapeutic systems in order to deepen the subject's understanding of his own intrapsychic processes.

Assagioli and the Psychosynthesis movement have worked at great depth with sub-personalities for years. They are deeply committed to the spiritual evolution of man and stress movement toward the higher self. They see the evolution of consciousness as a dis-identification from, and a learning about, sub-personalities, much as we do. As one becomes conscious of the sub-personalities, one develops an "Observing Self" as "Awareness," a most important still point and witness state that exists outside of the sub-personalities and the Ego. We do not, however, see this either as consciousness or as the essential self. We see it as one level of the three levels needed for the evolution of the consciousness process.

Jungian psychology provides another major contribution to Voice Dialogue through its concept of splinter psyches and its techniques of active imagination. This latter process evolved in 1913 when Jung was writing the book that marked his break with Freud, *The Psychology of the Unconscious*. While he was writing this book, he heard a voice that he associated with a female patient of his and the voice said to him, "This is art!" Jung responded to this by getting angry and saying to the voice, "No, this is not art; this is science!" This was the beginning of a serious dialogue between Jung and the voice. It was the beginning of the method now known as "active imagination" in Jungian therapy. One sits with a paper and records upon it the interaction between the Ego and the unconscious.

One can easily see how the Gestalt and Jungian systems are shadows of one another. The Jungian approach is the more introverted and the Gestalt, the more extroverted, in relating to sub-personalities. What occurs in active imagination, as in Gestalt work, is that the Ego is often taken over by the Protector/Controller. Without the Awareness level of an independent outside observer, the system is a closed system and the sub-personalities may well remain under the domination of the Protector/Controller. Once an Awareness level is established, and the Ego is clearly differentiated from the Protector/Controller, the method of active imagination greatly enriches and extends Dialogue work. Again, as with Gestalt work, Voice Dialogue can only enrich the Jungian and Psychosynthesis methodologies.

Psychodrama is another system that has fed into Voice Dialogue, because there is definitely an acting component in the use of this method. Voice, posture and mannerisms change, and these changes are encouraged because they give the Ego a better opportunity to experience the reality of the sub-personality. This can be done either individually or in a group.

Transactional analysis is the last system that contributed to the development of Voice Dialogue. TA is very effective with people who are new to therapy or new to the ideas of psychological growth or transformation. It provides a simplified conceptual framework of sub-personalities, so that people have an opportunity to arrive at important insights early in their work. The problem here is that the sub-personalities tend to be labeled too quickly and thus lose a dynamic quality.

For example, let us say that someone goes to a party and reports feeling terrible there. In Dialogue work, the facilitator simply asks to talk to the part that felt terrible at the party. We are not asking for the child or the adult or any specific part. We keep the process fluid by keeping labeling to a minimum. We wait and see which part appears. It is not that we do not label parts. It is, rather, that we try to let the sub-personalities emerge organically. When they do, we will know what to call them. Or, better yet, they will know what to call themselves. This is one of the reasons why Voice Dialogue remains ever fresh and alive for the therapist. One never knows what will come forth next!

GUIDELINES FOR THE USE OF VOICE DIALOGUE

Sub-personalities or Voices are constantly operating within everyone. As we have stated earlier, they are the energy systems that experience life. Voice Dialogue gives us a chance to objectify them, to recognize them, to name them, to understand them and to work with them creatively. When we use Voice Dialogue, we are sensitizing ourselves and others to the dramas played out by these sub-personalities or voices.

1. Identification of Sub-personalities

The first step in facilitating Voice Dialogue is the identification of the sub-personalities. The facilitator observes the subtle psychological and physiological changes that signal the activation of a sub-personality. As the facilitator alerts the subject to these subtle changes, the subject's Awareness level begins to get its first training in recognizing shifts in the energy patterns. As one's Awareness expands, one is able to make these distinctions independently of the facilitator through an Aware Ego. In addition, the more an individual acts as a Voice Dialogue facilitator, the more highly developed this sensitivity to changing energy patterns becomes, because the facilitator's Awareness is in a constant state of expansion as well.

Voice Dialogue is a joint venture. The facilitator and the subject cooperate in the search for the sub-personalities and in the attempt to understand their functions (both positive and negative.) Since this is a joint exploration, it is not necessarily limited to a therapeutic setting, but can be used in a variety of interpersonal or healing interactions. The facilitation process activates sub-personalities in the facilitator. He or she must be willing to become subject at any time. There may be therapeutic situations that occur where this is not clinically appropriate. The principle, however, is clear, for we are all accountable to each other at the personality level.

2. Physical Separation of Sub-personalities

When the facilitator decides (with the consent of the subject) to talk to a sub-personality, the subject should be asked to move to a different space in the room. This

can mean changing seats or simply moving the chair.
The subject should, whenever possible, choose this new
position. Different sub-personalities like different
places. A Vulnerable Child invariably chooses a corner
of a couch (often with a pillow clutched in front). The
position an Inner Critic wants is usually an imposing
space or chair. A Judgmental Voice might want to stand
or to sit on a window seat higher than the others. An
Angry Voice might want to pace about. As work continues and the sub-personalities stake out their territo-
ries, one may find the extroverted power Voices on one
side and the sensitive Voices on the other, or perhaps
the Vulnerable Child will be surrounded by protecting,
defensive sub-personalities. Some sub-personalities like
to sit close to the therapist and some prefer distance.
For some, the placement of sub-personalities is like a
map of the psyche. For others, it is of little importance
and will change from session to session.

If the subject is too uncomfortable to choose a new
placement for the Voice, then the facilitator could unobtrusively suggest a move to a particular spot. Especially in the beginning, the task of choosing "the proper
position" can be very threatening to someone who is
self-conscious. Thus, to allay anxiety, and to start the
process off, the facilitator can lend a gentle hand. If
the facilitator is feeling frisky and it looks as though the
subject is ready for an adventure, the facilitator might
suggest (with humor) "Instead of talking to the Voice
we were planning to talk to, let's talk to the part of you
that has to make the 'right' decision on where to sit."

3. Facilitating the Sub-personalities

From this point on, one just talks to the sub-personality as one would to a real person. This becomes easier

with time, since it is a real person. Draw it out empathetically and non-judgmentally. Ask questions when appropriate, or just sit back and listen if it happens to be a particularly garrulous sort. A basic principle of Dialogue work is that we are not trying to solve problems in any one session, so do not try to encourage the sub-personality to solve a specific problem. Problem solving is the responsibility of the Aware Ego of the subject.

Voice Dialogue, when done properly, is a relaxed but alert exploration. It does not require great effort. If the facilitator is feeling pressured or tense, we might assume that there is a Pusher at work, a Psychological Pusher that has some specific agenda and that the subject's Protector/Controller is resisting this agenda. Then the Voice Dialogue becomes a power struggle between two sub-personalities.

If, as facilitator, one's Awareness is alerted to this situation it is often possible to step back and conduct a quick interior dialogue that might sound like this:

Ego: There's something wrong. I'm pushing too hard. What's the matter?

Inner Therapist: (taking advantage of Awareness Level) You're trying too hard. You're trying to do an "important" piece of work and to do it quickly because you want to make a good impression. Just relax.

Ego: It's hard to do that with the Pusher operating.

Inner Therapist: Just let go. The subject's Anger Voice can't come out right now because the Protector/Controller is stopping it. How about dropping it and checking with the Protector/Controller to find out what he's worried about and what his rules are.

At this point, the facilitator might say out loud something like: "There's some part of you that isn't happy about our talking to the Anger Voice. Let's move over and see what it has to say." The focus then switches to the new Voice, and the facilitator (with the help of the Awareness level) drops the need to do a brilliant piece of work uncovering the Anger Voice, and starts to move in a different direction.

As we have said before, Voice Dialogue is a transformational process for everyone involved. Ideally, one does not invest too much energy in bringing forth a particular Voice. During the natal process one should not grab at the head of the baby in an attempt to deliver it from the mother. One should be a good midwife and just assist gently as needed.

But ideals are ideals. And, as humans, we *do* occasionally fall a bit short of perfection! So, if you identify with a particular pattern, if your Pusher starts pushing too hard, just treat it as part of your own process. Step back and consult your own Awareness, as suggested above. If that does not free you from the need to get the Voice out perfectly and immediately, you might return the subject to the Ego position and discuss the interchanges. This, too, requires a certain amount of Awareness and objectivity.

If you remain stuck in the power struggle, just know that you *are* stuck. No blame. End the work as quickly as possible and use the experience to learn about yourself. If you are a therapist working in this modality, you might have someone else work with the Voices in yourself that got hooked into the interchange.

If you are working with a spouse or a close friend, you might explain what happened to you and reverse roles. Let the other person be the facilitator and work with the Voice that has been activated in you. We would suggest that this kind of role reversal be done when it is safe and appropriate—when both people are feeling pretty good about one another and are engaged in a mutual exploration. If there is a power struggle as a core issue, get a third person to help break the deadlock.

The exciting aspect of all this is that there are no mistakes! Every hook-in, every difficult facilitation, every wrong turn is a possible source of growth. Each one has something to teach us—each one can add to our own Awareness of how we function in this world.

4. Separating the Sub-personality from the Aware Ego

In order to separate the sub-personality from the Aware Ego, encourage each Voice to speak of the subject as a separate entity. This is particularly important in the early stages of Dialogue work when the Voice will invariably say "I" when speaking of an event in the subject's life. For example, the Voice might say, "I went to a party last night and I met an interesting woman and I suddenly felt very inadequate." The facilitator then separates out the subject's actions from the Voice's reaction. "You mean, *he* went to a party and *he* met an interesting woman. . . and *you* started to feel inadequate."

Sometimes this is not possible, even after many such interventions. If all else is going well and the subject seems to be making the differentiation between the sub-personalities and the Aware Ego, do not persist, just relax and continue the process. When you, as the facilitator, talk, you continue to differentiate between the sub-personality and the Aware Ego. This distinction can be strengthened by pointing to the differing positions occupied by the various parts when one talks about them (including the Aware Ego).

The Aware Ego has its own position, clearly differentiated from the sub-personalities. After each session, we
return to the Aware Ego in its own particular position,
and the facilitator and subject discuss the session in
whatever fashion they choose. This differentiates between the Aware Ego and Voices and ensures that the
subject has been returned to ordinary Ego functioning.

5. Remaining Non-judgmental

It is important to remain non-judgmental when doing Voice Dialogue. The Voices are like people. If the
facilitator is truly open and interested, they will blos-
som. If they sense a lack of acceptance or a disapproval,
they will withdraw or even attack. The Voices may be
more sensitive to our judgments than we are ourselves!
Again, since you are human, it is not unlikely that at
some time or another, you will find yourself judging a
Voice. Just be aware of this and explore your own judgment later. If your judgment is strong and you cannot
separate from it, stop the work and go back to the Ego
position. If at all possible, do not criticize a Voice. This
may well put an end to any communication and cause
the subject to terminate the work.

It is helpful, when talking to a Voice that does real
damage, to discuss this damage objectively and to see
how the Voice feels about it. This can bring about some
surprising insights. This kind of discussion is delicate,
so be sure that there is no judgment—just curiosity.

Let us see how this can work when questioning a
Critic:

Therapist: I was wondering about how you feel toward
Janet. You criticize her all the time about her looks

and her lack of accomplishment, and every time you say something, she freezes up and can't get anything done.

Critic: I don't care (with real venom) She's better off dead than living in that half-assed fashion. I despise her and, frankly, I don't care if I kill her. She deserves to die, the creep!

Here, the facilitator has given the Critic a chance to show the depth of its hatred and the extent of its destructive potential. That is an important piece of information for the Awareness level to have. If the facilitator were judgmental, the Critic would have seen the question as an attack and would most probably have withheld the information.

Sometimes we can be surprised at the motivations and feelings of a Voice if we just withhold judgments and keep questioning. A similarly virulent Critic was asked pretty much the same question:

Therapist: Tell me how you feel about Frances. You've been pretty irritated with her over just about everything and it looks as though you paralyze her so that she can't get anything done.

Critic: Well, she deserves everything I say. (Pause—long silence—bursts into tears). I just don't want anybody to pick on her. I figure that if I criticize her first, I'll keep her from making mistakes and nobody else will pick on her. I really don't hate her. I didn't know that I hurt her so much. When I criticize her, I never think of how it might hurt her.

Here we have one of those great surprises that occur so often in this work. When we are open to all possibilities, there is no predicting what will happen.

One of the most difficult areas to be non-judgmental about is the conflict between the energy of the Protector/Controller on the one side, and the Freedom/Expressive energies on the other. For people in the human potential movement in particular, there is a tendency to identify with the Voices that want freedom, emotional and creative expressiveness, and new frontiers. The energy of the Protector/Controller is seen as resistance, as negative, as not supporting the development of consciousness. The fact is that the Protector/Controller energy in many people in the consciousness movement has become practically a disowned self. Increasing numbers of people try mightily to grow and expand and change, and in this process they deny the controller energy and lose the balance that this energy can provide for them.

In Voice Dialogue, it is important to honor both sides. If the facilitator is identified with Freedom and Expression, then this part will be supported and the Protector/Controller axis will be denied, or at least not honored. This causes the Protector/Controller to contract against the change in the other side and to begin to operate unconsciously. In this way a split takes place between Control and Freedom, with the Control side feeling maligned and rejected and quite angry. If the Protector/Controller feels honored, then it trusts the facilitator and the process and it will gradually open, quite like a flower, and transform in a natural and organic way.

6. Relax and Take Your Time

Sub-personalities, as we have said over and over again, are like people. They like to feel that they have our undivided attention and that they have plenty of time to express themselves. So, whenever possible, give them lots of time to emerge. One may have to sit in silence for quite some time before a Vulnerable Child will even speak. It is often the Voice that takes 40 minutes to be fully uncovered that is a most important part of the personality. So, put the Pusher aside and be patient.

But be observant. There are some Voices that really do not want to stay around too long. They will probably tell you that they are finished and they will go away. A Vulnerable Child may say, "It hurts too much to stay here any longer. I want to go now." A Pusher may say briskly, "That's it. I've said what I had to say. Now go talk to someone else."

7. Observing Changes in Energy Patterns

Each Sub-personality is a distinct energy pattern. Each has a distinct facial expression, posture, tone of voice, and each creates a different set of energetic vibrations in its surroundings. When we participate in Voice Dialogue either as a facilitator or a subject, we become increasingly aware of the nature of these energy patterns. We become experts in the detection of shifts in the energy patterns even when the words remain the same.

We are fond of saying, "It's not what is said, it's who says it." This was illustrated dramatically in the following incident. A 19-year-old friend was visiting from New York. We took her out to dinner and we all ordered drinks. The waiter asked our young friend for I.D. and she said, with great assurance, "I don't have any I.D. with me, but I'm 19 so you can give me a drink." When he left, we laughingly told her that the drinking age in California was 21, not 18 as in New York, and we assumed that she would not get her drink. Amazingly enough, he brought her the drink—the energy pattern had such authority that it was stronger than the actual words that had been spoken.

When acting as facilitators in Voice Dialogue, we become aware of these changing patterns. We alert the subject to changes as other sub-personalities take over. We ask the subject to change position, and address ourselves to each new Voice. In this way, one's Awareness can learn to recognize the different Voices. It can also learn about the flow of sub-personalities. It sees how Anger is replaced by the Hurt Child, which is replaced by the Withdrawn Father, and so on.

Oftentimes there is a group of sub-personalities with similar energy patterns that present themselves as one Voice—for example, as Critic-Pusher-Perfectionist. For the sake of simplicity, we might choose not to separate them. This is a personal choice that varies from one situation to the next. The second time we encounter this grouping, we might move toward separation of the individual energies.

Thus, both the facilitator and the subject experience a marked expansion of their Awareness levels as they become more and more sensitive to the shadowplay of sub-personalities in a person. And it *is* like the play of shadows—like the changes we see in a landscape as the clouds pass overhead and the land beneath changes with the changing illumination.

8. *Voice Dialogue as an Altered State of Consciousness*

Voice Dialogue puts the subject into an altered, or non-ordinary, state of consciousness. The Aware Ego and the Protector/Controller are set aside temporarily as other energy patterns are given the opportunity to express themselves fully. The subject's condition when in a sub-personality, is very similar to someone under hypnosis. Therefore, the facilitator must remain alert and not let his or her attention wander.

With this in mind, the facilitator will automatically be careful when dealing with a Voice. Interruptions should be avoided whenever possible. The subject is in a vulnerable state and intrusions—such as phone calls or other people entering and talking—are jarring and quite unpleasant.

The facilitator should take care not to leave a subject alone while in a Voice. It is like leaving someone in a hypnotic trance. If an emergency arises, take a few minutes and return the subject to the Aware Ego. Explain the circumstances in as much detail as is appropriate, in order to ensure the grounding in the Ego space before you leave. Tell the subject how long you will be gone and make arrangements to continue your exploration at that time.

If the session must be ended and will not be resumed, try to take enough time to go to the Awareness level and then back to the Aware Ego before leaving. A few minutes spent in the Aware Ego discussing the Voices that have been worked with should ground the subject and provide the necessary re-entry into an ordinary state of consciousness.

There are times when a subject may experience a deeply impactful altered state of consciousness. You will be aware of this when it happens. You will also be ready for this when it happens because our Protector/Controllers serve to protect us from these experiences until we are appropriately prepared and the situation is a safe one. Just leave a little extra time at the end of the session for wrapping it up. As facilitator, you might suggest that the subject should not re-enter immediately into the daily routine. If possible, an experience of this depth should be followed by a period of quiet, even if there is only time for a cup of coffee alone or a walk around the block. It is really best at a time like this to be able to take a few hours to let the experience sink in and to savor it.

9. Voice Dialogue Is not to Be Used as a Substitute for Personal Reactions

Voice Dialogue is a technique for the exploration of sub-personalities and the expansion of consciousness. Although we encourage its use in primary relationships and among friends, it is not intended as a substitute for interpersonal interactions. If there are strong feelings between the subject and facilitator—particularly negative or judgmental ones—do not try to "solve" them by doing Voice Dialogue. Talk directly with one another about them to "clear" these negative feelings or work with a third person if the negative interaction cannot be worked through.

It is important that Voice Dialogue be carried on in an atmosphere of mutual trust and respect. That is why the above-mentioned clearing is necessary. One needs the assurance that the process will be objective and free of agendas or manipulations. It is not a good idea to do Voice Dialogue to prove a point. The different parts are very sensitive to being manipulated.

10. Taping Sessions

Many people who work in Voice Dialogue like to tape their sessions. This can be quite valuable because there is often not much recollection of specifics after a dialogue session. We are not specifically recommending this. We are simply reporting that it is frequently done and with good results.

Video taping is also effective because it gives the subject a picture of the major shifts that can take place in the different parts. It is a very powerful process to see, as well as to experience, the differences between major energy systems as they come into operation.

THE AWARENESS LEVEL OF
CONCIOUSNESS IN THE DIALOGUE

We talked earlier of the Awareness level of consciousness and of its importance. How can we expand this level? One way is through meditation. When one steps back in meditation, and witnesses the thoughts and feelings as they flow through, an Awareness develops. It is important, as we mentioned elsewhere, to make a clear differentiation between Awareness and the Protector/Controller who simply loves to masquerade as an objective Awareness. The Awareness level, whether expanded through meditation or Voice Dialogue, is a pure witness state. It is non-judgmental and is therefore capable of looking at all aspects of ourselves with equanimity. It is separate from our thoughts, feelings and values. It is separate from our sub-personalities and the energies that they represent.

Voice Dialogue presents us with a tangible way of expanding the Awareness level and clearly differentiating it from the other components of consciousness. We give it space all its own. After the facilitator has finished working with whichever Voices have been facilitated during a session, the subject moves the chair back to the original Ego place and is asked to *stand* behind the chair. This is the position of the Awareness level. From here, the subject can literally get an overview, as a witness, of the different Voices as well as the Ego. The facilitator reviews the session objectively and briefly for this Awareness level, while the subject remains silent. (Any interchange regarding the Voices is left for the final wrap-up of the session with the Aware Ego.)

After this, the subject is invited to sit down and resume the position of the Aware Ego. Reactions to the work and possible differences of perception between the facilitator and the subject are then discussed. The session is reviewed briefly again and is then ended with the subject in the Aware Ego.

There are no hard-and-fast rules about the direct work with the Awareness level. For subjects who have done a fair amount of meditation or Voice Dialogue, it may not be necessary to stand up for this review. They may be able to sit in the space of the Aware Ego, close their eyes, and review the Voices this way. Still others do not need to close their eyes to be able to sense the Awareness level.

The important issue is that the Awareness be treated as distinct from the Aware Ego; that we develop a witness or Awareness level that is free of judgment and separate from the parts—a vantage point from which to view them, all of them. When this ''vantage point'' starts to exclude parts or judge them, we know that we have been tricked by the Protector/Controller.

Each bit of work done as subject or facilitator adds some bit of information to this Awareness level and thereby expands our consciousness. Each ''wrong turn,'' each power struggle, each dream that we work on also adds to it. It is an exciting ever-expanding process.

In our everyday life we become more and more adept at calling up this Awareness level. We learn to put ourselves into this Awareness level when we feel a Voice is too strong or too weak. In this way, we can step back and consider a Voice objectively. What are its valid points and what are the ways in which we need to detach from it? Our Pusher may be nagging us to get to work on a project. It may be right. We may need to motivate ourselves, but we need not identify with it. We need not become tense and not enjoy ourselves if we are already out to dinner!

We can also use this concept of stepping back into the Awareness level to help us in the search for an energy that is currently too weak. Are we spending too little time with Aphrodite, with our Spiritual selves, with our Introversion, with our Businessman, with Apollo? The Awareness level can help us to assess these issues as well.

Each foray into Awareness strengthens and expands it. It is pleasant, too. Stepping into Awareness is like putting a cool hand on a fevered brow. It is soothing, calming, and refreshing. If it is not, if there is blame and tension, then we have the wily Protector/Controller again.

BUILT-IN PROTECTION IN VOICE DIALOGUE

It has been suggested that Voice Dialogue is almost tamper-proof. Sub-personalities automatically protect themselves. If they feel judged, manipulated, seduced, or in any way mistreated, they react. They will withdraw or they might verbally attack the facilitator. Voices are extremely sensitive—they will sense issues of which the facilitator may be totally unconscious.

At one beginning workshop, a man who was strongly identified with the Pleasing Son was trying to facilitate the Anger Voice in another participant. His Pleasing Son was activated, or "out," as we say. His job was to please the workshop leader and facilitate Anger, but his Pleasing Son did not approve of Anger and was a little afraid of it. The Anger Voice in the subject reacted as follows:

> *Anger*: I don't like you and I won't talk to you. I'll talk to her (pointing at a group member who was clearly comfortable with anger). You just make me mad. I feel like hurting you. That's all I have to say. I'm leaving now.

The facilitator in this interaction had no idea that he was identified with the Pleaser. His judgments of the Anger Voice were totally unconscious. But the Anger Voice knew all about it and protected itself accordingly.

This interaction, incidentally, resulted in much growth for both facilitator and subject because the next piece of work was with the Pleaser and the Judge of the facilitator. The facilitator learned about the way his Judge operated almost constantly and unconsciously when he was in the Pleasing Son energy.

Sub-personalities protect themselves, but the Protector/Controller, who often stands in the way of exploration, is there to protect the subject as well. If the subject's vulnerability is threatened, or if the work is proceeding too quickly, or in an unbalanced way, the Protector/Controller will automatically take over and stop the process. (For the facilitator this can feel like hitting a brick wall.)

A Frightened Child might be talking and getting very

upset. If this is not too threatening, the dialogue will continue. If it is problematical, the Protector/Controller intervenes as follows:

Protector/Controller: That's enough! She's spent her entire life being frightened and it's taken us all a long time to learn to take risks. Now she needs to know how to speak up for herself. She needs to tell her husband about how she feels and she can't go around at work like a scared rabbit.

I don't think it's a good idea to give too much time to that kid (referring to the Frightened Child). It's been too long and hard a fight to balance its Voice. We need to look at her extroverted fun-loving Voices; the ones that are sure of themselves.

In this way, the Protector/Controller helps the facilitator to keep the session in balance. Continued work with the disempowered fear side would slow down the process of empowerment of this woman. Her need is to balance her fear while being aware of its power. She does not need to spend more time exploring it.

RESPONSIBILITY OF SUBJECT

Voice Dialogue is a method that encourages empowerment of both the facilitator and the subject. It is a *joint* exploration. The ultimate expert is not the facilitator, it is the subject's Awareness. This most definitely discourages child-parent bondings and the subject is discouraged from giving up power to the facilitator. As one becomes more expert, one becomes a more sensitive subject. With an expanded Awareness, the subject is able to detect the shift in energies as one Voice moves in to replace another. Experienced subjects will often say, "I feel as though this Voice is leaving and a new one is coming in." Then the facilitator can decide whether to begin to explore the new Voice or to try to continue to clarify the current one.

Since this is a joint exploration, it is the subject's responsibility to react to the facilitator. This work has as its aim the expansion of consciousness, not the validation of the facilitator's view of life. Thus, if anything feels wrong or uncomfortable, the subject is responsible for stopping the facilitation, returning to the Ego space and discussing the interaction.

It is not always possible to do this. Sometimes one must finish the piece of work first. But then, when back in the Ego state, by all means react! The facilitator is becoming more conscious, too, and your reactions will only help matters.

For example, one subject complained after a very intense piece of work, "I didn't like it when you handed me the tissues, it broke my flow." Another might be angry: "I felt that you were judging that Voice that just spoke. It felt unfair and I don't feel as though I can trust you." Another reaction might be: "I sensed that you were afraid of that Voice." Sometimes the subject says, "You ask too many questions. You keep interrupting me when I stop to think."

All of the reactions give the facilitator the opportunity to study his or her own Voices. In the first instance, a "Hovering Mother" may have been activated; in the second, a "Judge;" in the third, a "Frightened Child;" and, in the fourth, a "Pusher." There is always something new to learn and to experience.

So, when you are a facilitator in this work, remember to relax—you are only half the team. You will come up against your own areas of unconsciousness, your own disowned selves, your own projections, and the subjects with whom you are working will become your teachers.

As facilitator, you must be willing to become the subject (or at least to have your actions closely scrutinized) and as subject, you are to accept some responsibility for what goes on.

This, last, is one of the most important safeguards of the system. The subject is encouraged to remain in a state of empowerment at all times and to accept a major share of the responsibility for what happens. As we mentioned before, the more expanded the subject's Awareness, the more the subject will be familiar with the subtleties of his or her own Voices and the more responsibility he or she will take. Sooner or later, the subject takes almost full responsibility, knowing which Voices need facilitation at what time and essentially using the facilitator as a helper.

CONTRA-INDICATIONS FOR THE USE OF VOICE DIALOGUE

The study of multiple personalities is becoming increasingly popular in the field of psychiatry. By and large, these parts are still viewed as representing a pathological condition. The practice of Voice Dialogue teaches us very quickly that multiple personalities are perfectly natural and belong to all of us. What is it then that determines pathology? If there is no Ego capable of reflecting on the Voices that are elicited, then we have a condition of pathology. There must be a reflecting Ego. There must be an Ego that can say—"This is a Voice." One cannot do Voice Dialogue without such an Ego.

Other than this basic limitation, the use of the method is really a function of the degree of comfort of the facilitator. The greater the skill and experience, and the more highly evolved the personal process of the facilitator, the wider is the range of people with whom he or she can work.

IN SUMMARY

Voice Dialogue is a tool for transformation. It is one among a multitude of approaches that can be used in the evolution of consciousness. It can be used in relation to any approach to growth, healing and transformation. It lends itself beautifully to being used with visual imagery, and combines with a multitude of Gestalt, Psychosynthesis and Dramatic techniques. It can dramatically enhance the analytic therapies.

To practice Voice Dialogue, a subject needs to be ready to acknowledge the fact that there are parts. This is not acceptable to many people, so do not force the method. There is a rich array of approaches, and different people need very different things at different times in their process.

As a general rule, we would say to facilitators: do only what is comfortable. Remember that Voice Dialogue is basically a communication tool. It certainly has therapeutic implications, but fundamentally it is a way of gradually learning to experience, to live, and to communicate much more of our totality. In this framework it is significant to note that learning to facilitate Voice Dialogue is as important as experiencing it.

CHAPTER III

DISOWNED SELVES

DEFINITION

We humans are a most delightful mélange of energy patterns or selves. Some of these energies are familiar and comfortable to experience. Some are curious or unfamiliar, and some are downright distasteful. It is this last set of patterns that we will now consider. We call them the disowned selves.

The disowned self is an energy pattern that has been partially or totally excluded from one's life. The concept of the disowned self was introduced by Nathaniel Brandon, and we have not found a more apt word for describing this special kind of self. Nathaniel was particularly interested in the disowning of emotionality and passion in our culture and the concomitant over-valuing of the intellect. We have noted disowned selves of *all* kinds—and a most interesting group of sub-personalities they are.

First, let us give you, the reader, an experience of a disowned self. Pause for a moment and think of someone whom you dislike intensely, someone who deserves this dislike because of totally reprehensible character

63

traits. Think about this person's unsavory aspects. What
is it that makes this individual so worthy of contempt?
Be specific about the characterological and moral de-
fects that repel you. If you are feeling righteous and
glad that you are in no way similar to this despicable
person, you have discovered your first disowned self.
You have discovered an energy pattern that you do not
wish to integrate into your life under any circumstances.
Most probably, as a matter of fact, you have discovered
a wonderful new source of energy. But more about that
later.

It is always fun to think about disowned selves. There
is such a rush of enthusiasm as we judge them. One can
feel one's adrenalin level increasing, one's heart beat-
ing faster, one's perceptions sharpened. When group
members discuss their disowned selves with one another,
the air is invariably charged with excitement.

A hard-working newly remarried mother of four, who
goes to work all day and then comes home to household
chores, can be heard describing her new husband's
ex-wife as "unbelievably lazy and self-indulgent. She
doesn't do anything. She just collects her spousal support and goes to the beautician. Would you believe she
watches soap operas all afternoon?"

A man who has been an honest, sincere, and faithful
husband for 30 years is outraged by a woman who "has
no sense of loyalty or commitment, whose idea of a relationship is a two-day sexual involvement with someone
whom she'll never see again."

A dreamy, spiritually oriented young man sees his
financially successful older brother as "almost Satanic
in his pursuit of money, power, and women." A
thoughtful, gentle and kind woman "can't bear" her
boss, who is "cruel, selfish and only interested in

results. He doesn't care how anyone feels. He doesn't care whom he hurts! He only does what is good for him and will further his career." Conversely, a tough, self-made and self-sufficient man "can't stand wimps or victims. They make me want to puke!"

By now you have a feeling of the affect attached to the disowned self. There is much energy in the disowned energy pattern itself and much energy utilized in keeping it disowned. It is no wonder that intense feelings come into play as we confront one!

There is one important distinction that needs to be made. The generic term for a self that is not conscious is an *unconscious* self. Not all unconscious selves are necessarily disowned. For example, there is a part of us that is concerned about issues of death and dying. At the age of 21 this might simply be an unconscious self. At the age of 80 it might well be a disowned self. An unconscious self is simply unconscious. There is no energy that is holding it down, that is maintaining its unconscious status.

Every disowned self has an opposite energy with which the ego and the Protector/Controller are identified. This opposite energy, in conjunction with the Protector/Controller, is constantly holding it at bay. We have no way of knowing that a self is disowned until the Awareness level is separate from it and can witness it.

THE DEVELOPMENT OF THE DISOWNED SELVES

The disowned self is an energy pattern that has been punished every time it has emerged. These punishments might have been subtle—a raised eyebrow, the withdrawal of attention, a "that's rather unattractive, wouldn't you agree?'' or they may have been powerful, like beatings or public humiliation. Whatever the nature of these repressive environmental forces, the result is the same—a set of energy patterns is deemed totally unacceptable and is, therefore, repressed, but not totally destroyed. These energy patterns are alive in our unconscious.

In Jungian terms, they are a part of our shadow and, when we see them on the outside, when we see someone unashamedly living out a disowned energy pattern, we feel the corresponding pattern ourselves. The energies vibrate together, sympathetically. Since this pattern has been associated with pain and punishment in the past, we want it to go away as soon as possible. In order to quiet the internal energy pattern (which we experience as only a feeling of discomfort), we must rid ourselves of the corresponding external stimulus. We must kill off the person who lives out our disowned self, whether this be done literally as in a Jack the Ripper type of murder, or symbolically as when we sit in judgment of someone. Hester Prynne in *The Scarlet Letter* is a wonderful example of the price paid for living out the adulterous disowned self of the Puritan community.

Let us take for an example a woman, Jane, who has been raised to disown her sexuality. From an early age, she has been punished for any evidence of flirtatiousness or sexuality. The energy pattern of sexuality is soon buried, thereby becoming a disowned self. She dresses soberly, values her objectivity, rationality and independence, and sees sexuality as an incidental part of life. But the particular energy pattern of her sexuality exists someplace where she can no longer see it, someplace in her unconscious. She then goes to a party and there in a corner, flirting outrageously, dressed in a very revealing decolletage and surrounded by men, is a woman who matches Jane's disowned self.

Now an interesting thing happens. Jane's disowned self starts to vibrate sympathetically with this woman's. In the past Jane has been punished for behaving like this woman, so she becomes acutely uncomfortable as their two energy patterns vibrate with one another—the one unashamed and flamboyant, the other a hidden and an unrecognized echo of what it might have been.

Jane must remove the source of her discomfort and she does so by judging "the other woman." "I've never seen such a disgusting, vulgar exhibition in my entire life! Isn't she ashamed to walk around like that? I'd think that her husband would be embarrassed to death!" And on and on with great vehemence and self-righteousness. Our judgments and our angers are the way most of us elminate the vibrating energy of our disowned selves.

Anger and irritability are other major energy patterns that are usually disowned fairly early in life. There are very few parents who can resist the temptation to do away with these "negative" energies in their offspring. Therefore, most of us were taught not to express these directly. People often will remember that, as children, they had "terrible tempers," but this rarely persists into adult life. When talking to Joan's Anger Voice we hear the story of its disowning:

Anger: I can't ever come out because if I do, nobody is ever going to like her. I get irritated by everything. I can't stand seeing people who are happy or smiling. I just want to make them feel as miserable as Joan feels. I would go around complaining all the time. I'm furious with her boyfriend—every time she needs him, he

abandons her. I'm fed up with her, she never learns and
never grows. I'm irritated by her mother and by her
therapist. They don't understand how desperate she is
and how angry I am.

She doesn't dare let me out. She thinks I'll alienate
everybody around her. And I think I would. But I really
don't care.

I had to go underground when she was very young
because whenever I came out, her mother got upset and
her father withdrew. He'd just walk out of the room if
Joan said anything negative. So she learned to hide me.
She learned how to please everyone and to make everyone happy, but she never let me out. She never said
anything negative or angry or selfish.

A self that is disowned accumulates energy around it.
It is as though a dam has been built that blocks energy
from flowing through us, a different dam for each disowned self. Behind the dam accumulate all kinds of
debris and dirty water. Dialogue work is a way of becoming aware of these dams and the powerful energies
that accumulate behind them. It is also a way of gradually allowing these energies to come through to us in a
safe environment.

These disowned selves are constantly coming through
to us in our dreams. Our buried instinctual energies are
reflected in the following dreams:

• Someone is trying to break into my house.

• I'm being chased by wild animals.

• I'm driving my car and there are Mexican teen-
agers in the car next to me and they are leering at
me.

• I'm with some bad teenage boys and I'm very
perturbed with them. They are trying to molest me

sexually. I'm trying to lecture to them. One of the boys touches me on the vagina and I am inflamed sexually.

Each of these dreams reflects instinctual energy that has been repressed and that is returning in the dream to make itself known to us. One of our greatest allies in the consciousness process is our dream process. In observing our dreams we are able, over and over again, to catch hold of energy patterns that are disowned and energy patterns with which we are identified. Our disowned selves constantly call out to us in our dreams to come and pay attention to them.

CULTURAL ASPECTS OF THE DISOWNING PROCESS

There are certain energy patterns which are culturally disowned. In Western civilization, for example, we have the Seven Deadly Sins. Who amongst us has not been encouraged at one time or another to disown pride, covetousness, lust, anger, gluttony, envy, and sloth?

We have tended, since the Age of Enlightenment to disown all the "darker" energies. We admire, almost worship, rationality, detachment, scientific objectivity, and clarity, while we disown the passionate, the irrational, the mystical, the unclear and the paradoxical. In this way, we have learned to negate much of the information that is available to us as human beings. We have also learned to negate our anger, our irritability, our insecurities, and our confusions, in favor of balance, good humor, certainty, and self-confidence.

The disowning of these seven deadly sins results in a particular buildup of instinctual energies in the unconscious which we call daemonic energies. We will be spending time with these energies in Chapter Eleven. They are among the major disowned energy patterns and, as a society, we pay a particularly heavy price for their negation.

THE FASCINATION AND REPULSION
EXERCISED BY DISOWNED SELVES

The parts with which we identify usually determine our choice of relationships. For instance, if we are identified with a Rational Self, that self will want us to relate to rational people. If we are identified with a Spiritual Self that self will want us to relate to spiritual people. Although, as we have said, our basic tendency is to be repelled by our disowned selves, they *do* hold a certain fascination for us. The highly indignant sober citizen who wants to do away with pornography and spends months at a time evaluating pornographic material is a fine example of this type of behavior.

A recent movie, "Terms of Endearment," shows this combination of fascination and repugnance beautifully. A sexually repressed, very controlled, perfectionistic widow lives next door to a man who is totally identified with his Dionysian impulses, and is impulsive, sexual, and self-indulgent. The two have much to teach each other and they move back and forth between attraction and repulsion until, finally, each is able to help the other to integrate the self that has been disowned. He introduces her to her sexual self and she introduces him to his nurturing and conservative self.

In the movie classics, we have "The African Queen." Where could one find a better juxtaposition of disowned selves than in Humphrey Bogart and Katharine Hepburn? Here, again, we have the repulsion, the fascination, and the eventual integration of the disowned selves, with each character transformed by the addition of the energies represented by the other.

Unfortunately, in our daily lives, we are more likely to see individuals lock into a destructive relationship with someone who represents a disowned self. Thus, a woman who negates her sexuality and her physical being will be fascinated by a "he-man" and marry him. She will then do all that she can to tame his sexuality and get him to "calm down and take fewer physical risks." She will object to his sexual demands and complain of his needs for an outdoor life. He, in turn, may have been attracted to her timid, non-physical, way of life and intrigued by her sexual inaccessibility. Once married, he is likely to object to these behaviors. Instead of learning from one another, instead of incorporating disowned selves, they live with these selves expressed in their mates, judging them and being angered by them.

We pull in our disowned selves with an intensity that matches that with which we disown them. Generous men fall in love with selfish women, strict parents have rebellious children, "victim" employees have unreasonably demanding employers, perfectionistic women have sloppy daughters, nurturing women fall in love with withholding men, loving mothers have daughters who are selfish and impersonal. It is as though there is a divine mathematician in the universe who wants the balanced development of consciousness. If we disown AX^2B^4, we will receive in kind from the universe AX^2B^4. Whatever energy we disown, life brings to us, exactly as we have disowned it.

We can be helpless victims to the multitude of relationships in our lives that are a function of our disowned selves. In contrast, we can accept the challenge of these

relationships and ask—"How is this person my teacher?
How is this situation my teacher?" Asking this question,
in itself, represents a major shift in consciousness. A
great deal of the stress in our lives comes from our disowned selves and the requirement that we keep attracting them in our relationships, and we continue to suffer
as the same patterns repeat themselves. The moment we
step back from relationships in which we are angry and
judgmental, and we ask the questions: "What is the
teaching? How is this person my teacher?", we begin to
minimize this stress. At this moment we begin to find
our way out of the jungle. Of one thing we may be sure:
energy does not disappear. It returns, over and over
again, to plague us until we finally claim what is our
own, until we embrace our selves. Let us now see how
this is done.

EMBRACING OUR DISOWNED SELVES

First, you will notice that a disowned self is operating.
You become aware of your irritation with some person.
It feels good. You feel self-righteous. The other person
is really so dreadful! Unfortunately, you have read
about disowned selves so you cannot bask in the sunshine of moral superiority too long. Rather than trying
to reform the other person, it is now time to look at the
qualities in yourself with which you are over-identified
(you know, the ones that make you proud) and see how
they might be limiting your own journey.

You might be excessively neat, relentlessly hardworking, compulsively kind and thoughtful, always caring
and giving, always right, never complaining or angry.

There are numerous qualities that we feel make us special, that we really do not want to give up. Think a bit,
if you will, about how these qualities can limit you, can
make you intolerant, inflexible, unable to relax and to
accept yourself and others as full, complex human beings. For example, it is nice to try to live a perfect life,
but what if that means never trying anything new so
that you will never have to take the chance of making
an error?

Now comes the fun. Start to talk to the disowned self
directly. At first this may seem awkward. See what it
thinks, how it would run things if it were in control.
Feel its new energy, see the world through a new perspective. It is bound to be a source of new ideas, new
inspirations, new solutions to previously unsolvable
problems. After all, its views have never been available
before. You will be surprised at the new energy that
will become available.

It is extremely important to note, at this moment,
that we are not suggesting that you *become* the disowned self. Just allow its energy to speak. Keep Awareness operating and use the new energies wisely.

In the past couple of decades, we have seen some cas-
ualties when people were given permission to identify
with previously disowned selves. We know of a high-
ranking, well-mannered business executive who learned
to express anger and to assert himself in an encounter
group. When he returned to work, his formerly disowned anger dominating his behavior, he started an
argument with his formerly feared boss, told him to
"fuck off" and was fired. He had a great deal of trouble getting another job once the circumstances of his
dismissal became known. This is a perfect example of

over-identifying with first one extreme (the Obedient
Son) and then with the other (the Angry Father) without benefit of an intervening Aware Ego. When anger is
first released, there may be an increase in overall irritability and reactivity but one should try not to over-
identify with these, as our executive did.

The release of primitive earth energies, which include
sex and aggression, is followed by extremely favorable
consequences when this is monitored by an Aware Ego.
When it is not, watch out!

For instance, a highly spiritual man who had spent
years in self-discipline and self-denial was involved in a
legal action with some rather unscrupulous characters.
He was quite concerned about this since a substantial
sum of money was involved. His disowned primitive energies emerged during Voice Dialogue in the form of
a howling wolf who had been caged for years. The wolf,
itself, was afraid to be released because it felt so destructive. The wolf explained that whenever he had previously threatened to break out of his cage, Alex would
meditate or do yoga for a couple of hours and would
weaken his power so that he was no longer a threat. The
wolf, after some opportunity for expression, gradually
stopped howling and became a most attractive masculine energy of amazing power. Alex was able to use this
energy, without any verbalization whatsoever, and the
legal action was settled in his favor. His new power was
recognized and honored in a most dramatic fashion.
And, we might add as a post script, his love life im-
proved dramatically as well.

It is amusing how persistent a disowned self can be.
Mary's business partner, Jack, represented a disowned
self but Mary did not use him as a teacher. They broke
their relationship bitterly. For many years thereafter,

Mary dreamt disturbing dreams of him. He was ''a self-centered man whose primary concern was his own well-being both financial and emotional.'' In the dreams he invariably appeared irritated with her lack of self-assertion and he was always trying to tell her how to run her life. She, in turn, would become defensive and angry and try to argue with him and make him go away. She would wake up angry and frustrated, thinking of how manipulative, controlling, and selfish he was and how angry she was that she had dreamt about him again.

This is a perfect example of how a self, disowned by day, might try to get through to us at night. Night after night this sub-personality came to Mary, trying to talk to her, and night after night he was sent away. (It almost has the quality of a fairy tale.) He was trying to balance her, to show her that she need not be a helpless victim to the world around her; but such was the strength of the combined cultural and personal history of disowning, that she could not listen to him. She found his suggestions odious and she drove him away.

One day when a hopeless little girl sub-personality was talking, this power side, Jack, slipped in for a moment:

Jack: (with irritation) Mary needs to get her life organized.

Therapist: You sound like a totally different voice from that little girl. How about moving here and telling us what you have to say about Mary's situation?

Mary changes chairs but looks uncomfortable. She doesn't really want to hear this voice.

Therapist: I can see that she doesn't want you to talk, but let's give it a try. I hear that you've been trying to give her advice for some time.

Jack: Yes, I have. She doesn't like me though, and I don't like her at all. She's a wimp. I know what she has to do to make money. I'm very good at making money. And I'm not ashamed of it either. She's ashamed of wanting to make money.

Therapist: And you're not?

Jack: You bet I'm not. I need money to enjoy life. I like nice things. I like comfort and I like power. You need money for all of that. She's too worried about whether or not people are going to like her.

Therapist: Don't you worry about that?

Jack: Not at all. People like me. I'm happy with myself. I like being the center of attention and people love to be with me. I think they're lucky to get a chance to be with me. I give them a chance to bask in my warmth and they love it. You know, like in the sun. As I said before, I think *they're* lucky to get to be with me, not vice versa. (Smiling, very self-satisfied.) People don't like it when you try to please them. Besides, if I don't go out of my way for them, I don't resent them. So I don't get angry with them.

Therapist: But what about people not liking you? Mary worries about that.

Jack: As I said, I just don't care. She thinks I'm selfish but I don't care. And because I don't really care, I can be very persuasive and charming, too. I'm not worried about being genuine, you see. She is. And as far as I'm concerned, that kind of worry doesn't work. I like to figure out what works and then I go ahead and do it. I don't waste time worrying about other things.

Therapist: Speaking of figuring out what works, what would you suggest to Mary in terms of her business?

"Jack" then proceeded to give detailed suggestions, some of which he had already given in dreams. Mary and the therapist were able to listen to these. When Mary returned to the position of her Aware Ego, she had a great deal more color in her face and strength in her voice than previously. She was excited about these ideas and eager to try them out. There was a totally new sense of self-containment and self-sufficiency.

However, when a disowned self breaks through like this, there are other selves who object and try to push it back down. In Mary's case, it was a witch-like sub-personality who emerged briefly two days later, just long enough to do away with the sense of self-sufficiency that "Jack" had provided for Mary. Mary was aware of the loss of the "Jack" energies and the re-emergence of the despondent child, but the "witch" was so fast in her attack on the previously disowned "Jack" energies that she had remained almost invisible. It is very important, when uncovering disowned sub-personalities, to talk to the sub-personalities like this witch, or the Protector/Controller, that want them to stay disowned.

Witch: (with venom) I have to teach her the Awful Truth. I had to put her (Mary) back in her place. She was taking too much attention for herself. She needed to be punished for that! To be pushed back there and over there (gesturing to a corner)

Therapist: Why?

Witch: Because that's where she belongs! In the background not in the front. I get very irritated when she pushes her way out in front like that!!

This is a fascinating introject! We can imagine (with the help of our feminist writers) how Mary's mother felt when she had to teach Mary to disown her power and her desire for attention. We can surmise that when Mary's "Jack" sub-personality came through in Mary as a child, it resonated with the mother's own disowned "Jack" voice which craved attention, and that the mother punished this voice with all the bitterness and judgment that one feels when the disowned self is seen in another. Thus, the sub-personality in Mary that echoes the mother's teachings to be a second-class citizen, is like a destructive witch who carries with her many generations of hatred.

With this hypothesis in mind, the therapist continued the questioning:

Therapist: Why does she belong in the background like that?

Witch: I don't know. Just because she does.

Therapist: Tell me, do you feel the same way about Mary's brother?

Witch: No.

Therapist: Would you feel the say way if Mary were a man?

Witch: (hesitating) I'm not sure. (Gaining power again) I don't care. All I know is I have to remind her about the Awful Truth, to slap her down and keep her back there (pointing) out of the way. And I don't like it when she doesn't stay there!

Therapist: But why do you have to slap her down and keep her there?

Witch: Because if I don't, her father will kill her! It's better that I push her out of the way.

The last was such a surprise, that the witch sub-personality disappeared and Mary's Aware Ego took over again. As we have said repeatedly, there has usually been a very good reason to disown a sub-personality. The discovery of this reason, through working with the sub-personality that enforces the disowning, gives the Aware Ego a chance to deal with the disowned sub-personality in a conscious and constructive fashion. We might expect that this "Witch" will no longer have unquestioned authority and will no longer be able to push the "Jack" sub-personality down automatically without any resistance from Mary. The Aware Ego will know what is happening and, we hope, will intervene.

We have seen in the last section how critical an issue it is to understand the concept of disowned selves and to actively accept the challenge of the multitude of life situations that bring our disowned selves to us. The challenge to embrace these selves in a creative fashion is, perhaps, the most difficult task in the consciousness process.

CHAPTER IV

THE PROTECTOR/CONTROLLER

Meeting "The Boss"

INTRODUCTION

We would like now to move into a deeper understanding of the full range of energy patterns, to help
make them come to life for the reader. We wish to demonstrate their amazing diversity, their depth, and how
they interact with one another. We would like you
to hear their voices, their complaints, their desires—to
have a sense of how real they are. In Chapter Eight, on
the Consciousness Model, we will explore the issue of
how our different parts interact with related energy patterns in other people.

To discuss these energy patterns with you, we have to
give them names. Once we have named a part, we will
illustrate how it works, using Voice Dialogue transcripts.
Listing sub-personalities by name is a mixed blessing
because the adventure of the work is in learning how to

tune into an unfamiliar energy pattern and to pursue it without preconceptions. Just remember that the names we have chosen are simply convenient labels to help you recognize the patterns we are describing. Please do not marry yourselves to the names we use. See them only as ''temporary relationships.''

In the interest of clarity and simplicity, we will be listing these different parts as separate entities. We will try to give you a sense of the psychodynamics of these entities, how they are constantly interacting with each other inside of us, and to some extent how they behave in relationships with other people. However, the fact that we have to list them in some kind of order or sequence can be misleading. Please understand that each energy pattern is always interacting at some level with a wide range of other patterns. Also, the sequence that we are using is not related to the value of the part. They are all important, though certain ones may be more meaningful in the work or our lives at certain times.

THE DEVELOPMENT OF PERSONALITY

We are born into this world in a condition of extreme vulnerability. We have discussed this to some extent in Chapter One. In this condition of vulnerability there is no armor; there are no defenses. There is, in fact, no such thing as personality. We live in a condition that might be described as *essence level*. We have a special vibration, a uniqueness of being. We are without guilt, without the need to build a wall of protection around ourselves.

This situation soon changes, for we discover fairly early in the game of life that there are rules of conduct. We discover that certain behavior pleases and certain behavior displeases people in our environment. So it is that there develops a part of us that begins to pay attention to these environmental cues. The birth of personality is, first of all, the birth of what we call the Protector/Controller energy pattern.*

The Protector/Controller begins to watch and see and make determinations about what works and what does not work, what pleases and what does not please. At first these perceptions are rather simple. We learn to smile and coo appropriately. Even though these may have been genuine reactions at first, the Protector/Controller soon begins to override their natural functions. We become "less natural" because this Protector/Controller energy begins to evaluate planetary dangers.

The Protector/Controller functions increasingly as a master computer network and it utilizes other mechanisms to accomplish its ends. Pleasing may be a significant requirement in our environment, and so this develops as an early energy pattern. It gets desired results —that is, the approbation of parents and other figures in the environment. Becoming successful in psychomotor activities or in school can be the beginning of a well-endowed Pusher. If we try hard and succeed, we get rewards. There well may be something in us that wants to do these things under any circumstances, but the Pusher, like the Pleaser, becomes an overriding energy under the overall domination of the Protector/Controller which is always in the background.

There are large numbers of patterns that develop

---

*We are grateful to our friend and colleague, Mackie Ramsey of Carmel, California, for her use of the term *Protector* to describe this vital energy pattern.

and begin to coalesce into what ultimately becomes known as one's personality. Some of these factors may be related to genetic predispositions, others to purely environmental factors. One child, for example, may be more predisposed to introverted behavior patterns. As this child meets blockages in the environment, the tendency may be to go into himself or herself in a fantasy process. Another child may develop a pattern that is more extraverted out of a combination of many factors that might include genetic considerations, sibling placement, and the particular kind of relationship existing between the child and the parents.

As Maurice Nicoll aptly points out in his *Psychological Commentaries*, if we are going to develop a personality, we might as well have a good one. Otherwise life on the planet is not pleasant. What we begin to see is that the personality is fundamentally a system of energy patterns that helps to protect our vulnerability. We become powerful and strong.

Vulnerability, as we have said, is generally not rewarded in our planetary sojourn. Power and strength are rewarded. So we go to good schools and get a good education and we become more powerful. We learn how to study. We learn how to work. We learn how to get what we want. We learn to please. We learn to drive ourselves unmercifully in our quest for success. And we become even more powerful.

Our Pushers learn their lessons well from our parents and our culture, and so they make their demands upon us and tell us what we should be doing. We accept these demands as coming from ourselves, and since the requirements of the Pusher energy can never be met, we become subject to the increasingly vehement denunciations of our Inner Critics. After all, if the Pusher says we

have to read all of Jung, Freud, Adler, Horney, Esoteric
Psychology and much more besides, and if we accept
these requirements as being the gospel, then the Critic
has a plethora of possibilities available to it. We can
never satisfy the endless needs of the Pusher nor can we
ever satisfy the endless and unique criticisms of the Inner Critic.

One day we awaken full grown. We have a personality. We have learned how to be successful on the planet
and we are powerful. This is not meant judgmentally. It
is an absolute requirement for survival. If we have not
learned these skills already, we must learn to develop
them in some way after we are adults. Many therapeutic
approaches in the consciousness movement help people
to learn how to move from helplessness and vulnerability to power. It is a most significant step. The tragedy of
personality development, of this move to power, is that
we lose our connection to our vulnerability. We lose our
connection to that unique vibration that constituted
our essence level as a child.

There is a wonderful fairy tale called *The Snow
Queen*. The story begins with two small and loving children, Hans and Gerda. They love each other very much
and they spend hours listening to Gerda's grandmother
spin stories about life and about the mysterious and
magical things of the world. They love the flowers and
the sunshine and together live beautifully the essence
level that is so much a part of childhood.

At the same time, there is another drama going on.
A goblin has built a special mirror that has a very pecu-
liar property. Whenever someone looks into this mirror, everything that had looked beautiful begins to look
ugly.

He flies up to heaven, holding the mirror so that

when he reaches God, God will look into it. As he reaches higher and higher levels, the mirror starts to vibrate and soon it shatters into millions and millions of pieces. These fly all over the world and one of them flies into the eye and another into the heart of Hans. He suddenly sees his love Gerda as a big bore. The grandmother is perceived as an old fool. The roses that grow on the ledge are covered with worms. In short, Hans becomes a fully rational young man. When the Snow Queen comes to visit that evening, as she has on many previous evenings, he suddenly finds her irresistible. He goes with her and she kisses him on the mouth, thus sealing the bargain. His heart freezes totally. He is taken to the far north, to her home, where he spends his days working on puzzles and formulae. He sees the frozen world around him as a place of great beauty and he no longer remembers anything about warmth, love, and feelings. It is now the task of Gerda to find him and to redeem him from the power of the Snow Queen. It is Gerda's consciousness process and her ability to remain in contact with her own essence level of being that ultimately redeem Hans.

Sad as it may seem, the fate of Hans is really the fate of all of us to some extent. The development of personality generally requires the death of our more sensitive feeling sides. Their redemption is part of the task of the consciousness process.

One of the first tasks of redemption, then, is to begin to discover which parts have developed in us that are in charge of our personality. Who and what is it that is *really* in charge of this entity that we call the Ego? So we shall start our journey of redemption by examining the phenomenology of the Protector/Controller. We shall see how it operates in the scheme of things and how the

Protector/Controller and its many friends determine which parts of us are rejected in our growing-up years.

THE PROTECTOR/CONTROLLER

The Protector/Controller is somewhat related to the Freudian "superego" or the TA "parent." It is this Protector/Controller who makes sure that the disowned selves remain disowned. It arises early in life and, after checking around to see what is socially acceptable, starts to create a person who can face the world. It acts protectively. It protects our vulnerability and can save our lives by being sure we act appropriately. It is basically rational in its orientation—it figures out what is acceptable in a situation and makes sure we behave accordingly. The Protector/Controller is both cultural and familial. Each person's Protector/Controller has its own basic inviolable principles and each usually has a few totally unacceptable disowned selves hidden away.

In the Voice Dialogue process the work with the Protector/Controller is very significant because it is the basic energy protecting the human vehicle. This energy pattern is generally afraid of psychological work. It does not necessarily want expansion and is not usually interested in growth. It is related to our inner conservative nature.

With any person who does Dialogue work, in any part of the world, one of the first steps is to discover the wishes and desires of the Protector/Controller pattern. The Protector/Controller must feel safe with the work and with the facilitator. It must have the right to control the work to a considerable extent. If it becomes too fearful, if the work feels too threatening to it, it must have the right to stop the work or slow it down. This, more than anything else, creates a condition of safety that is so essential for real trust in the process.

It is fascinating to look at typical Protector/Controllers. There is an overall similarity. They are all basically rational, all want to maintain an appearance of appropriate behavior (which may vary greatly from Los Angeles to New York to London, for example), and they all want to maintain control in interpersonal situations, and to protect the individual—however this may be done— at any price! Let us listen to a typical California Controller:

Therapist: Since you seem to be the one who runs Fred's life, I'd like to find out some more about you.

Controller: (Stretching his arms across the back of the couch and adopting an expansive pose) Fine, ask me anything, fire away!

Therapist: OK. Let's get down to basics. How do you want Fred to appear to others?

Controller: Oh, that's an easy one. (with a charming and comfortable smile). I want everyone to like him. He should be at ease with people, very empathetic, helpful, understanding and enthusiastic. You know—a fine person. I want everyone to be able to say, "Now, there's a *really* good person."

Therapist: You seem to do a great job. Everyone *does* like him.

Controller: You bet! His family likes him, his friends like him, his ex-wife and ex-girlfriends like him. I'm great in groups. Groups like him, his therapists like him. I've studied a lot of psychology and I know just what to say and do to charm everybody. I do a good job with you, don't I?

Therapist: (Smiling) You certainly do.

Controller: I'm really pleased with myself. I've got things just the way I want them and I don't want them disturbed. Not at all!

Therapist: Tell me, what is it that you really wouldn't want Fred to do?

Controller: That's simple. I don't want him to be selfish or inconsiderate. I never want him to disregard others or hurt their feelings. I also want to be very sure that nobody dislikes him or can say a bad word about him. I don't want him to lose his reputation as a real nice guy. No matter what!

Therapist: Even if it makes him unhappy?

Controller: I really don't care about his happiness. *I just want everyone else to be happy with him.* And everyone *is* happy with him.

Therapist: But he came to see me because he's not very happy with his life. He feels alienated and unfulfilled.

Controller: As I said, that's none of my concern.

This particular Protector/Controller had a familial background as well as a cultural one. It chose to keep Fred the "good boy" in contrast to his brother who was more self-involved and had been quite successful in everything he tried. Here the Protector/Controller is combined with Pleaser, Good Son, and Good Father. In later work, these other Voices would be separated out.

No attempt is made to change the Protector/Constroller. Our aim is to help Fred's Awareness level witness this pattern so that his Ego will become more aware and not be identified with it. A weakening of the Protector/Controller would erode Fred's image and threaten his particular niche in the family. Many families divide up personality attributes and help Protector/Controllers to develop along specific lines that give an individual a particular role in the family.

A Protector/Controller from New York presents another picture. This Protector/Controller is very interested in achievement, although Judy, herself, is more concerned about her social life:

Therapist: Judy has talked about her inability to be as spontaneous as some of her friends in California, so I thought I'd like to ask you how you feel about spontaneity—about trying new things.

Protector/Controller: It looks pretty immature to me. I don't want her doing anything that she hasn't really thought through . . . nothing that she'll have to repudiate later . . . these Californians and their spontaneity . . . just give them something new and they'll go after it with a passion. Then, two years later, there they are . . . another fad and they've made fools of themselves by giving in to it. I don't want her to look foolish! That's my biggest fear—looking foolish or, worse yet, acting immature. You have to maintain a certain maturity, a dignity, even a little cynicism in this life or people won't respect you. I mean—you know—one year they're all eating vegetables and another year they're all doing TM and another year it's aerobics. As far as I'm concerned, they all look like a bunch of children running after some magical prescription for the good life. There *is* none. And knowing that fact is maturity. *I* know.

My job is to keep Judy mature, wise and to never, never let her look foolish. That includes falling in love.

If she misses a little fun, that's fine. Fun is for children anyway. Life is serious and Judy should stay serious and responsible.

I make sure that Judy is a person that people will respect and trust. They can depend upon her to be rational, like I am, and careful in all her decisions and actions. I've done wonders for her professional life.

An Israeli Protector/Controller has grave concerns for safety, both physical and psychological:

Protector/Controller: As far as I'm concerned the most important thing is to keep his vulnerability covered. He must never show his fears . . . and never show his needs or his feelings . . . someone might use them against him. He should always look as though he's in charge of the situation. That's why I don't like him talking to you. He is—actually—I am—not always in charge. And if he isn't in charge, it could be dangerous for him. He needs me to protect him so that he doesn't react impulsively. He's got to think things through or he could get into trouble. That would be the worst thing as far as I'm concerned—acting impulsively and not being in control of things.

Many Protector/Controllers in Israel have this concern. Confusion, vulnerability, lack of direction, "uncontrollable" anger, sexuality, fear—any of these are seen as potentially dangerous by the Protector/Controllers who view the need for rationality and absolute control as a matter of life and death.

As you may have noticed, Protector/Controllers have a tendency to support a national or regional stereotype. They usually are eager to keep people as close to the local or familial norm as possible in order to prevent the difficulties that can arise from behaving in too individualistic a fashion. It is important to know the rules of these Protector/Controllers when doing Voice Dialogue. This was particularly brought to our attention in London.

The British Protector/Controllers, as a group, objected to the uncovering of unpleasant, earthy, or foolish sub-personalities. However, the British Protector/Controllers would never allow anyone to be impolite or to refuse to cooperate. Thus, there was superficial "cooperation" with the work until we began to talk with the Protector/Controllers and ask them about their rules for disowning sub-personalities:

Therapist: Norma's adventurous sub-personality has talked about her desire to travel and to create an exciting new kind of job for her. She's feeling very constricted here in London. What do you have to say about that?

Protector/Controller: That's all very well for her to say, but Norma is getting along in years and it's most embarrassing for me to hear her talking with such enthusiasm and lack of sense. I'm just happy that none of her friends could hear her. As far as I'm concerned, it's all rubbish. I will *not* have her going off chasing rainbows. I don't find enthusiasm and excitement attractive and I do my best to keep them subdued. If she comes up with a good solid plan, presented soberly, I might listen to her, but basically I agree with that other voice you talked to, the one that says she should face the fact that nothing much will ever happen in her life. And the sooner she faces that fact the better off she'll be.

I might also mention that I don't like the way you stir her up. I don't like her excitement and hope. She'll only be disappointed. I'll save her that trouble. By the way, I don't want her to start dressing colorfully like she used to, I prefer sober unobtrusive colors.

And, speaking of colors, (as she gets even more emphatic), I *don't* want her showing off, flirting, wearing makeup and making a sexual spectacle of herself. I want her to be sensible and sober as is appropriate for someone who'll be 34 next year! She's too old to act like 20, even though people often think she is. She should act her age.

Therapist: But you see how unhappy she is and how that other sober voice that you like just wants to die. Do you have any room to negotiate? We won't encourage her to do anything without your approval.

Protector/Controller: Well, it *is* true that the sober voice makes Norma want to die. Perhaps if we can work out a way that she won't look too foolish, I might, I just *might*, be willing to compromise a little. At least in terms of how she dresses. She *has* been looking a little drab lately.

The therapist is now able to enter into an alliance with the Protector/Controller, to respect its cultural demands for being sensible, tasteful, appropriate, and reserved. The British Protector/Controller must be assured of respect and cooperation in order to permit any real investigation into disowned selves. If not, it will reappear, undermine, and finally negate the subpersonalities that it has been keeping disowned or controlled in the past. In addition, it may well try to block further forays into these forbidden areas.

Whenever one is working with an energy pattern and one feels a contraction in the person, it is generally the case that the Protector/Controller is reacting to the work. In the following example, the facilitator was talking to a voice that the subject identified as a Freedom Voice. It wanted Calvin to be more adventurous, to take more risks, not to be so bound by form. In the midst of this Dialogue, the facilitator felt a contraction in Calvin and it appeared that there was a different presence.

Facilitator: It seems like a different part is here now. Could you move over so we could talk to this new part? (Calvin moves over) Well, hello—who are you?

Protector / Controller: I don't know who I am, but I don't like what's going on. I don't like what this other voice is saying. I've worked hard and long to stabilize Calvin's life, and I'm not about to see it go down the drain.

Facilitator: What worries you the most?

Protector / Controller: He's going to end up taking risks and giving up his job and losing all of his financial security. I've seen too many people do that. It frightens me. I need stability. He's not a millionaire. He needs that weekly check.

Facilitator: You do understand that I'm not encouraging Calvin to give up his job or to follow the advice of the Freedom Voice. My job is to help him to hear all the parts. It certainly sounds like you would help him not to do things too rashly or precipitously.

Protector / Controller: You bet your ass I would—and I'm glad you have some sense of how important I am.

The facilitator now has the option of going back to the Freedom Voice, or staying with the Protector / Controller. The direction is not important. What matters is that Calvin's Awareness level now witnesses the conflict

of opposites. It will be difficult now for Calvin to identify with either the Freedom or the Protector/Controller
Voice. The purpose of the process is to learn how to
drive one's own car, psychologically speaking. Then we
can receive advice from different energy patterns, while
we drive—we make the choices and decisions with
greater awareness.

Conservative and *liberal* are not simply words that
describe outer forms and the way people are in politics.
They are energy patterns that exist within each of us.
We each have our conservative and liberal natures. The
conservative is connected to traditional values. It is fearful of change and it contracts against possibilities of
greater freedom.

The liberal in us moves us towards greater risk taking. It is an energy that moves us to break form, take
chances, move toward alternative forms of behavior,
and it gives us more choices. The Protector/Controller
energy is our inner conservative nature. It tends to be
more cautious, whereas the liberal side encourages more
risk taking. If we honor both, we do not have to project
either our liberal or conservative nature onto our environment, and our decisions in life will be more balanced.

From our general consideration of the Protector/Con-
troller energy pattern, we get some feeling of what a
significant place it occupies in our lives. This energy is
also important in the consciousness process itself. In
many individuals today who have been involved in the
consciousness process, we have a new phenomenon. In
their pursuit of freedom they have disowned their
Protector/Controllers. They have struggled for years to
become free emotionally and sexually. They meditate,
visualize and expand in all kinds of directions. Very

commonly, in this process, they literally negate the Protector/Controller. They see no reason for its existence. In the following Dialogue the facilitator has picked up on the fact that the Protector/Controller has been rejected by the subject's Freedom Voice.

Facilitator: I have the real sense that Drew hasn't been listening to you for many years.

Protector/Controller: It's true. She always tries so hard to be free, to act free. She does so many things that I hate.

Facilitator: Like what, for example?

Protector/Controller: (Quite distressed) I don't like it when she sleeps with so many men. I hate a lot of them. They're not nice. Some of them are downright creepy! And she's always ready to ''grow''—always ready for another workshop. And she never has any money. That other voice says spend it—the universe will take care of you—it's worth it. Well, it's *not* worth it to me. If she would listen to me she wouldn't be anxious all the time. She wouldn't need all the workshops to reduce her anxiety!

This rejection of the Protector/Controller energy is amazingly common in parts of the world where people have been involved in consciousness work for extended periods of time. Conversely, in those parts of the world where psychological work is relatively new, the Protector/Controllers are very strong.

As we have already mentioned, when we do training in different cities around the world, it is the Protector/Controller that is the first order of business. It is the energy that first comes into operation and saves the persons' life. It has been functioning as though it were an Ego for many years. It is not about to be displaced by any upstart therapist or any form of consciousness work. It must be honored. The job it has done must be honored. Its viewpoint must be considered when other kinds of work are being done.

The basic key to working with individuals of any unfamiliar country, religion, race or psychological predisposition is to immediately contact the Protector/Controller and discover the ground rules that are operating. If these requirements of the Protector/Controller are honored, the work can proceed quite organically.

CHAPTER V

THE HEAVYWEIGHTS

The Powerful Selves

In the last two chapters we entered into a general discussion of disowned selves, and then we explored the Protector/Controller energy pattern. In this chapter we will continue our exploration of energy patterns, those with which we tend to identify as well as those which we tend to disown. The first grouping that we shall be dealing with is the combination of Pusher, Critic, Perfectionist, Power Brokers and Pleaser. Any of these subpersonalities might be part of a general Protector/Controller pattern. Each can exist separately. This will vary from one person to another.

THE PUSHER

A strong Pusher will certainly help us to achieve success in the world. It might also give us migraines, backaches, heart attacks, and a generally bilious attitude toward life. The Pusher is one of the easiest voices to hear. Most of us are able to tune in at almost any time of the day or night to this sub-personality who, whip in one hand, a list of unfinished business in the other, urges us on. "Your journals are unread, the beds are unmade, the dissertation unwritten, your exercise schedule awaits you, the garden needs weeding, the faucet is leaking"—its list is endless. Our hours of work go unappreciated. We can count on one thing in this world. As soon as we cross an item off the top of the list, the Pusher will add one to the bottom.

The Pusher acts on us all. It may seem that the successful "Type A" professional who is well organized and constantly on the go has the strongest Pusher, but we've spoken with even stronger Pushers in housewives who sit around all day in their bathrobes, the dishes undone and the beds unmade. These Pushers have lists so long and unattainable that the women have just given up and fallen into a depressive sub-personality who sees that any attempt to get anything done is futile.

How to Experience Your Pusher

Before any further theoretical discussion, we would like to give you the opportunity to experience your very own Pusher. In order to move into this particular system, start to think about all the things that you have to get done. Keep compiling mental lists until you experience a change of mood. A few leading questions might help. For example: What needs to be done around the house, for your spouse, for your children, for your parents, at work, about savings, career planning, investment planning, keeping abreast of inflation, retirement planning? What reading material have you left unread? What projects are unfinished? What needs repair? Whom haven't you phoned? What needs cleaning or organizing? What growth potential—physical, psychological or spiritual—is as yet unrealized?

Hopefully, by this time we have helped you to activate this specific sub-personality. See how you feel as your list of "things to do" grows. Until now, you have been focused on your reading; now a sub-personality has taken over. You, yourself, are no longer in control. Feel the physical sensations that belong to this sub-personality. They are different from those you experience when you are peaceful and relaxed. See where the tension focuses. Is it in your jaws, face, hands, head, stomach? Is this a feeling that is with you most of the time, or is it intermittent? If you lose this feeling, you can get back into this sub-personality by thinking of additional things to do. Is the sub-personality so strong that you feel you had better drop this book and get something else done? Are there any feelings that have become stronger, like "I don't have enough time," "There's so much to do," "It never ends," "Better just get going and get some of this done . . . ?"

This is your particular Pusher, an energy which seems universal in our society. It does not like us to rest, relax, or waste time. It is particularly fond of interrupting our moments of relaxation with reminders of what must get done. It will try to keep us from enjoying a second cup of coffee before starting work, and it may totally disrupt any attempts to lie out in the yard and enjoy the sunshine on a Sunday afternoon. It can be a rather harsh taskmaster, but it gets its job done.

Success in the Western world is usually dependent upon the Pusher. The Pusher develops early in life, encouraged by parents, teachers and employers. In some very ambitious families, this sub-personality is so valued that it clearly overshadows all the rest. We all know at least one man who brags of not having taken a vacation in years—there you have a man who has no Aware Ego, and whose life is completely run by this particular sub-personality, his "Pusher." Our Pushers are generally rewarded by everyone around us. It is great to have somebody else who is willing to work constantly.

When the Pusher takes over, we can feel it. We tense up. Our jaws may become set, our teeth may clench, our neck or shoulder muscles may tighten, we may feel a sick panicky feeling in our stomachs. We can see it in the mirror, as well. Our faces do not look relaxed and glowing and we tend to look tight and, perhaps, a bit haggard. A dominating Pusher is the major characteristic of the "Type A" personality that is particularly vulnerable to heart attacks.

Please keep in mind that we do not view the Pusher as a negative energy. There is no energy pattern that is inherently positive or negative. Everything depends on our Awareness and our ability to direct energy through an Aware Ego so that we may make real choices about what we do. When the Pusher is in charge, we are being driven down the freeway of life at very high speeds. This Pusher may be mildly amusing or an active demon whose demands can easily destroy us. It certainly destroys the joy of living for many people.

Sylvester, a man in his early forties, has dreamt repeatedly for ten years that he is driving to work on the freeway at high speeds and each time his car crashes into something. This image of driving at high speeds on the freeway is a perfect image for the Pusher energy. The unconscious is delivering clear warnings to Sylvester. At the end of ten years, he has a heart attack. Our physical bodies often pay the price of an overly endowed Pusher, and it is the breakdown of the physical body that often-times gives us our first real opportunity to develop an Awareness level so that we can begin to realize that our car has, in fact, been driven by the Pusher rather than ourselves.

The Pusher, the Critic and the Perfectionist make an awesome trio when they run our lives, as they often do. We would like to take this opportunity to introduce you to some of our favorite Pushers.

Reading Lists for Professionals (and Non-professionals)

One of the cooperative ventures of the Critic and the Pusher has to do with making people feel bad because they do not know enough (Critic) and then providing them with reading lists to help them to improve (Push-er). The following dialogue will help illustrate this re-markable partnership. The therapist is conversing with the client, a therapist himself.

Therapist: From what you're saying, you're not sure of yourself when you're doing therapy.

John: That's right. I always feel that I don't know enough. I think of therapists I know and they all seem so well read—like they know what they're doing all the time.

Therapist: Could we talk to the part of you that feels like you don't know enough?

John: That would be easy. It's our old friend again. (John has done Dialogue work before and he moves over.)

Critic: Hello again. I'm glad to be back—not that I'm ever really gone.

Therapist: Are you there most of the time?

Critic: Well, to tell you the truth, the real issue is whether he is ever there. Me, I'm always here.

Therapist: You're pretty sure of yourself.

Critic: I love working with therapists, especially younger ones. It's so easy to make them feel bad about themselves.

Therapist: How do you do that with John?

Critic: Just the way he said—I make him feel bad about how little he knows. Once I've got that going it's just a question of suggesting things to read.

Therapist: Do *you* make these suggestions?

Critic: I think so—I never thought about it. I guess someone else does that.

Therapist: Could I talk to the part that suggests the readings?

(John shifts chairs again)

Therapist: Are you the part of John that suggests his readings?

Voice: (Hereafter referred to as Pusher) Yes, that's me. I work with the Critic. Once John starts listening to the Critic, he's ripe for me.

Therapist: What is the reading list you have for him?

Pusher: Well, first of all there are the journals.

Therapist: Could you list some that you require?

Pusher: Well, let's start with the basic psychoanalytic journals. Since this is a main interest of his, I expect him to read the basic journals concerned with psychoanalysis. He needs to keep up with current trends in psychology, so I expect him to read the *American Psychologist*. I also expect him to read some of the basic Jungian journals. I also like him to keep on top of what is happening in medicine, so I like him to read one good medical journal.

Therapist: That's a good list already. How about books?

Pusher: Books I have a plenty. The whole basic series on psychoanalysis is an absolute must. The complete Jungian series is a must.

Therapist: Does that include the Alchemy and Mysterium?

Pusher: Absolutely. Everything. It's all a must.

Therapist: Is there anything else?

Pusher: Of course. I like the image of knowing something about everything, so I'm asking him to read the Fritz Perls and Polster books for Gestalt, the basic Reichian literature, and then there is the philosophy.

Therapist: Hold it. Do you mean that he listens to this and actually plans to read all these books?

Pusher: He has the journals and books piled up in his bedroom. They're always there for him to see. When he goes into a bookstore I remind him of all the other things he needs to know about. It's really fun.

Therapist: It sounds like a real gas. Doesn't he ever wise up and know what you're doing?

Pusher: What do you mean, wise up? These books are all important. Would you deny that?

Therapist: Well, let's say that many are interesting but I haven't found reading all of them essential for the work I do.

Pusher: Well, don't tell him that. He might start balking.

Therapist: What if he did?

Pusher: I don't know. It's never happened . . . I couldn't even imagine it.

After doing Dialogue work with a large number of Pushers, one wonders what percentage of books in the world are purchased by Pushers, rather than by the choice of an Aware Ego. One can only admire the supreme confidence of the Pusher at a time when so many of us doubt ourselves. Listen to this dialogue between a therapist and the Pusher of her female client:

How the Pusher Helps Plan Our Leisure Hours

Therapist: (speaking to Pusher) Sally tells me that she has one day a week free when she can do absolutely anything she wants to do, and that you really don't have any power over her on that day.

Pusher: (innocently) That's true. Anything she wants to do.

Therapist: (suspiciously) How could she have a whole day free when she has her child to take care of? What time does this free day start?

Pusher: Oh, well it doesn't start until she drops her daughter off at school at 9:00 and she has to be home in time to pick her up at 2:30 PM.

Therapist: Oh, I see. It's not *quite* a full day, is it? I bet you have lots of plans for her between 9 and 2:30.

Pusher: No, she just does what she likes to do. She gets her nails done and goes to the hairdresser. Then she gets her shopping done. Then she has lunch with her girlfriends so she's sure to see them once a week because that's the only day she can see them. You realize these all are things for her own good—things just for her. She's just spending the day taking care of herself.

Therapist: I see that you've learned that Sally has to take care of herself and it seems to me that you've set up a pretty busy schedule for her to do this. But, tell me, even though you sound so accepting of her need to take care of herself, what if she decided she needed to spend the day in her bathrobe reading a novel or doing nothing?

Pusher: (totally incredulous) Never, *absolutely* never!

How much of our lives do we live under the domination of such voices, thinking all the time that we are doing exactly what we choose to do? How little we understand the lack of freedom that characterizes most of our lives.

Pusher as Killer

Adele has disowned Power all her life. Her mother was dominating and bossy and her father was passive. She grew up never wanting to be like her mother. She saw her mother as being dominated by a compulsive, driving voice that was always wanting to control everyone and everything around her. Adele became very passive and submissive in her life and marriage and eventually developed breast cancer at the age of 36, requiring a mastectomy. A year later she had a second mastectomy and a lung involvement. It was at this time that she sought psychological help in addition to her medical regimen.

After some preliminary work, it became clear to the therapist that Adele was very disempowered. She could not react emotionally. She felt encased in passivity. Yet her head was filled with activity, with injunctions about what she should and shouldn't do.

Therapist: I have the sense that you have a lot of voices going on in your head all the time.

Adele: I do. They drive me crazy. They're always telling me what to do.

Therapist: Could I speak to the "should" voice in you —the one who is always telling you what to do?

Adele: (As Adele moves over, she says, "That's my mother.")

Therapist: Good morning . . . how are you?

Pusher: How am I? I'm frustrated. I talk constantly and she pays no attention. There's a million things to do and she does nothing. She sits. She does nothing.

Therapist: What would you like her to do?

Pusher: She could start by keeping the house clean. There's a lot to do in the house. She's married. She has a daughter. She could take better care of her daughter. She's lazy.

Therapist: Let's be real specific. What do you want her to do?

Pusher: I want her to keep busy—all the time. I want her to keep a clean house.

Therapist: What does "a clean house" mean to you? Do you want her to mop the floors every day?

Pusher: It wouldn't be such a bad thing. She has a maid twice a week. How hard can she work? She's a real lady. She could mop the floor every day. She could drive her daughter to school every morning. She doesn't have to take a bus. She could cook a meal for her husband.

It is obvious that the inner Mother is a combination Pusher and Critic and a very strong one at that. With no father image to balance this shrewish voice, Adele has become increasingly passive. The louder the demands on her to do things, the more passive she becomes.

The discovery of the Pusher energy was a total revelation to Adele. Her Awareness separated immediately and she began to differentiate between this Pusher and her real feelings. She started feeling better, had much more energy, and within a three-month period was functioning in a way she had never functioned before. She was working part-time and going to school part-time. Her real power and authority in the world were emerging as she separated from, and had some control over, this amazing Pusher energy. She did extensive psychological work during this period, but this work with her Pusher was pivotal.

The time was now October. The transformation in Adele appeared to be total. Her friends couldn't recognize her as the same person. She had more energy than she had ever had in her life. The lung cancer was clear, for the time, according to her doctors. In late October, Adele and her husband planned a trip to Europe to celebrate her recovery. She spoke to her therapist about the trip, asking her if she thought it was a good idea.

The therapist was very caught up in the recovery and quite excited by everything that had happened. It was natural that she would be excited by the idea of the trip. Her self-esteem was somewhat involved, and this no doubt diminished her therapeutic objectivity.

The issue here was, who was planning this trip? Everyone assumed that Adele was planning it. What no one realized until it was too late, was that Adele's Pusher had taken over again. In the cold of a December winter, the Pusher had planned a three-week trip to at least eleven cities. When Adele returned to the United States, her lung cancer had reappeared, she had pneumonia, and within six weeks time, she died. Her killer Pusher had done its job, too well.

The New Age Pusher

Nothing in recent history has been more exciting for the Pushers (of the West Coast, at least) than this current period of New Age expansionism. The possibilities are limitless and the Pushers delight in the unfolding of a myriad of "shoulds." Up until now, Marilyn's Pusher had been satisfied with a career, a home, a husband, children, travel and a few extra frills. After Marilyn read a few books on consciousness expansion in the New Age, she began to experience a tightness in her shoulders:

Therapist: Let's talk to the Voice that's making your shoulders tight—do you know which one that is?

(Marilyn moves over to the Pusher's chair. The Pusher has been talked with before.)

Pusher: You bet we do; it's me again.

Therapist: I'll be darned! I thought you'd decided to take a vacation. You sure had me fooled.

Pusher: Well, I did let her go to Hawaii, but I brought a couple of books for her to read. I let her take it easy for a couple of days and then I got her again.

Therapist: Amazing. How did you do it?

Pusher: I got her to read *The Aquarian Conspiracy* and now there's so much to do.

Therapist: Hold it—what do you mean, there's so much to do?

Pusher: Well, first of all, we got a chance to visit a Kahuna while we were in Hawaii. I think she should study about Kahunas and psychic surgery too. To back up to the beginning: this New Age consciousness is fascinating, just fascinating. First, we have to get her diet under control. Then she has to join a health club and start working out regularly. And I want her to do yoga. We need to refine her energies. There's a lot to read —dozens of books. Next, she needs to study about energies. Energy fields, balancing, clearing—you know, all that.

The Pusher gets more and more excited. One idea leads to the next. No encouragement is necessary. There is a seductive enthusiasm to the gleam in its eyes as it goes on:

Pusher: Of course, she'll have to start some form of meditation and I'd also like her to study with someone who will sharpen her psychic powers and teach her to read auras. She should do some reading—it's OK with me if it's in popularized form—on the new discoveries in quantum physics that are paralleling mystical beliefs and also in brain research that supports the existence of ESP and other levels of awareness.

Therapist: And she's supposed to do all this while she works and runs a household? You're kidding me.

Pusher: (with great enthusiasm and urgency) No, I'm not. She'll be left behind if she doesn't.

Therapist: (laughing) No wonder she came back from
Hawaii with tense shoulders!

This Pusher is a sly one. It is excited and positive
most of the time. If Marilyn were to get carried away
by the excitement, she would be an exhausted woman
pretty quickly. But here, too, we have a hint of the Vulnerable Child underneath—the one who is afraid of
getting left behind when everybody else is out greeting
the New Age. A further exploration of the Child's fears
gave Marilyn's Aware Ego more of a perspective on the
situation and allowed her to make conscious choices
about what to do and what not to do.

The Pusher's Opponent: the Do-nothing

In order to balance the Pusher, who, as you may have
already noticed, has a rather major role in our lives, it is
fun to talk to its opposite. The opposite sub-personality
might be a Beach Bum, a Hippy, a Bag Lady, a Sloth, or
a Spoiled Princess. This voice is a repository of wonderful relaxing self-indulgent suggestions, much to the
Pusher's dismay.

The sub-personality that will permit, even encourage,
us to do nothing provides an important balancing energy to the Pusher and our generally Pusher-oriented
society. It is the voice that permits us to slow down, take
care of ourselves, and enjoy life. If this energy is not in-
corporated into our own lives, we will most definitely
draw someone into our orbit (a husband, a child, an
employer) who will carry this energy for us. Remember
Sally? Her Pusher ran her life totally. Sally had a husband who carried her disowned self—a Hippy. As long
as Sally stayed identified with her Pusher—worrying,

working and full of responsibility, 24, no 38, hours a day—her husband was locked into his Hippy subpersonality. He chided her about worrying too much, he refused to take any serious responsibility for their finances, and he talked about selling everything and going off somewhere where life would be simple and undemanding. The more Sally's Pusher heard this, the harder he pushed and the more judgmental Sally became of her husband's lack of responsibility. Then we talked to Sally's Hippy:

Hippy: You know (stetching back lazily and talking slowly) I just can't believe Sally.

Therapist: What do you mean, you can't believe her?

Hippy: (smiling) She's always worried, always has a 10-foot list of things to do, always busy. Do you really think that it gets her anywhere?

Therapist: She certainly thinks it does. What do you think would happen if she didn't work so hard?

Hippy: (Lazily grinning) Nothing! So things would take a little longer to do. Nobody's going to die from that.

Therapist: What will happen to the business?

Hippy: Somebody else will take care of things if she doesn't jump up and do everything immediately. You know, she's so efficient she doesn't even give anyone else a chance.

This last obvservation is so true. Well developed Pushers have a tendency to rush in and do things before ordinary mortals even see that there is something to be done. To continue:

Hippy: I'd like to show her that the world won't come to an end if she lets herself relax a little.

Therapist: What would you suggest?

Hippy: First, I'd have her leave all her bookkeeping at the store. What she doesn't do one day, she'll do the next. When she brings it home, she gets tense. I'd suggest she relax at night, watch TV, make love, ignore anything that isn't done by dinner time. Just leave it until the next day. And don't worry. Just don't worry. Especially about money. She should just relax. It'll all be OK. It always has been. She's forgotten how to trust. (smiling easily) The important thing is that she loves her husband and he loves her and they should enjoy one another.

It was amazing to see how Sally's physical appearance changed as this Hippy voice talked. Her face relaxed and the worry lines disappeared, her shoulders which were always tense, relaxed, and she smiled easily. She twinkled.

As Sally listened to her Hippy voice, her consciousness separated from the Pusher. She decided to try to relax and to follow some of these new suggestions. The change was nothing short of miraculous. As her Pusher pulled out of the relationship with her husband, his Hippy pulled out of his relationship with Sally—it happened in perfect balance. Sally's husband began to worry and to accept responsibility for finances and the burden was suddenly an equally shared set of concerns. Together, they handled everything beautifully and, together, they were able to relax, feel mutually supported and to move ahead in ways neither felt was possible before. Their relationship was deeper, stronger, and solidly balanced. They also had much more fun.

In another example of balancing the Pusher energy, we have a forty-year-old man who dreams that he sees a naked hippy type man walking in the forest with a gigantic erection. The unconscious here clearly underlines for him the truism of disowned selves—they carry enormous quantities of energy. The unconscious clearly shows our dreamer that his hippy side is not without redemption. His drive, his busyness is only one side of the coin. Much of his masculine power is carried by this disowned hippy energy pattern.

The Transformation of Sub-personalities

The power of this Pusher archetype to keep us moving horizontally usually prevents us from experiencing our vulnerability and our innner reality. There is no possibility of our thought patterns being connected to any level of soul reality. To recognize soul, one has to stop long enough to discover that there is one.

As we have said earlier, we are born into the world in a condition of vulnerability. We share this with our animal brothers and sisters. Fairly early in life, we discover that being vulnerable is not the best way to be. We develop a personality that is, in effect, a defense against being vulnerable. The Pusher is one of the *cornerstones* of that personality for most people. Working hand in hand with the Protector/Controller, it incorporates all the parental and societal injunctions, all the things we should and should not do. These injunctions become what we think is our consciousness. We live our lives in certain forms, at certain speeds, and we never realize that our life is being lived *for* us by an energy pattern that has dominated us.

The answer to this dilemma is consciousness. Consciousness is the awareness of an experience of these energy patterns. It does not attempt to eradicate or remove anything. As we saw with Sally, consciousness is simply an awareness and an experience, and, with these, she develops the possibility of choice. She heard her Pusher and she heard her Hippy. When we did Voice Dialogue, we were helping her Awareness separate from the system of ideas and attitudes and feelings that had dominated her way of being in the world. She began to "drive her own car" for the first time. She listened to the voice of the Pusher, but it was no longer a dominating agent, she no longer automatically believed what it told her. She was developing a more Aware Ego.

There is no way to demonstrate the total societal effect of the Critic and the Pusher. Our personal estimate would be that if we suddenly neutralized the negative energies of the Critic and Pusher in our country, 75% of the hospital beds would be emptied and 90% of the clients in psychotherapy would be finished. Surprisingly enough, the ability to say no to these energies changes them. Listen to this dialogue occurring at the time of such a change. The client is a hard-driven businessman who has just begun to discover his vulnerability.

> *Therapist*: How do you feel now that Don is saying no to you (Pusher)?
>
> *Pusher*: I'll tell you the truth—I don't mind. I'm tired.
>
> *Therapist*: I never thought I'd hear you say that.
>
> *Pusher*: I've been at it for a long time.
>
> *Therapist*: Aren't you afraid he'll stop doing things?

Pusher: I don't know; he seems able to handle things.
I don't know; my steam is gone.

The awareness of, and the experience of an energy pattern (Pusher, Critic or any other one) changes the nature of the pattern. In Don's case, as the Pusher lost weight, the Vulnerable and Playful Child gained weight. Consciousness was now available as a vessel for both systems. Don's new consciousness made it possible for him to carry the tension between these two opposites.

The Positives and Negatives of the Pusher and the Possibility of Conscious Choice

As we have seen in this chapter, a great deal that we do in the world is not done out of free choice, but rather, in response to the demands of this powerful sub-personality that we call the Pusher. What it does is coerce us to live our lives on a psychological freeway. We are always under pressure, always *having to do* something. Poor John lives his life in misery, always feeling that he must read more and know more, never recognizing that no matter how many books and journals he reads, the Pusher will always have more to put on his list. Sally thinks that she is free one day a week. In fact, her jailor has permitted her to walk in two rooms, instead of one room. Thus, there is no peace until there is a recognition that these sub-personalities are present and that they do, in fact, control much of our lives.

We do not mean to make the drive of the Pusher totally negative. Few of us would have gotten through school without this pressure. This book would never have been written without its help. A great deal of activity in the world is based on the power of this system, as it teams up with the Critic and the Perfectionist.

There comes a time, however, when we wish to live our lives with more choice. Choice means first of all, the awareness of who is driving our psychological car. The thought patterns of the Pusher and Critic (whom we shall meet in the next section) are deeply ingrained in the personality structures of our society as well as of ourselves. We often think of them as speaking "the truth." Unless we become aware of their presence and develop an Awareness that is separate from them, they continue to dominate our lives and to convince us that they are wise and benevolent.

It is only when our Aware Ego separates from them and considers objectively what it is they are telling us, that we realize they have malevolent qualities as well. They *always* sound as though they want to improve us, as though they have our best interests at heart. It is important, therefore, to listen carefully to what they say and then, from the vantage point of an Aware Ego, to ascertain the validity of their comments. Then, and only then, can we make conscious choices.

These choices are invariably more pleasurable, more creative, and more rewarding than those dictated by the Critic and the Pusher. They move us in the direction of self-actualization, and therefore feel effortless rather than burdensome.

Life was not meant to be lived on a freeway full time. Nor was it meant to be lived in constant pain over our errors and imperfections. Although we as psychotherapists, on behalf of the health care professions in general, thank the Critics, Perfectionists and Pushers of the world, we do feel that it is time for a new management team—a team headed by an Aware Ego.

CRITICS WE HAVE KNOWN AND LOVED

It is with a real sense of delight that we share in this next section, with deep admiration and unbounded respect, Critics we have known and loved. These Critics are particularly powerful sub-personalities that exert an untoward influence on our lives. We are sure that you will recognize many of them, both in yourselves and in the people close, and not so close, to you. There is a basic idea that we wish to bring through to you, our readers. This basic idea is that even Critics need loving. We wish you to see how helpful these often difficult sub-personalities can be. We are sure that you will all agree that the Critics of the world, and underworld, deserve a special section devoted to them.

So it is that we dedicate this section to the Inner Critic, that remarkable sub-personality that stops so many people from experiencing life as pleasurable. After all, too much pleasure could be dangerous. As therapists, we are particularly grateful to it for its services to us and our colleagues in providing us with the financial security so necessary in these times of stress.

The Critic's Modus Operandi

Where does one start to write about this highly versatile voice? First, we might note that it has a great talent for teamwork. It collaborates beautifully with the Protector/Controller (mentioned earlier) by pointing out areas of potential danger for the Protector/Controller to control. For example:

Critic: Tom is doing it again! I keep telling him that if he doesn't ignore his wife when she hurts his feelings and if he doesn't get that temper of his under control, she's going to leave him. She doesn't like it when he blows up at her for no reason. He's being stupid again. So what if she didn't say hello when he came in. He's too sensitive, too needy. And now the poor dear's feelings are hurt (sarcastically) and he's going to have a temper tantrum because she forgot to close the garage door.

Now the Protector/Controller can take over the job. Tom's hurt feelings are to be ignored and his anger is to be squelched. He is to behave rationally and manfully. (He will probably take the newspaper, ignore everyone, and go into the next room to watch TV.)

Another great partner to the Critic, as we saw in the last section, is the Pusher. The Pusher sets up enormous tasks and unreasonable deadlines and then the Critic will criticize when these are not met. Similarly, the Perfectionist will set up ideal standards of behavior or of achievement and the Critic will criticize when these standards are not met.

Let us see how the Critic works with the Perfectionist. The following is an excerpt from a woman who has, with great persistence, become aware of her sub-personalities and how they interact. The Perfectionist, needless to say, expects her to be perfectly aware and to act consciously all the time. Carol, since she is human, has her moments of unconsciousness. One of her biggest challenges has been to control the power of her Critic. Her Critic is delighted to criticize, among other things, her inability to limit its power.

Critic: I can't believe her (with total disgust). After all these years, you'd think she'd know how to handle her own Critic! She did a wonderful job over Christmas—even *I* have to admit that—but then she let me get her. I started in gradually, reminding her that she'd gained a little weight and had stopped exercising during the holidays and next thing you know she really let me in. She listened to me when I told her that she's always dealing with the same stupid problems and that she's never made any headway. Then I told her that she'll never be perfect at work, she's bound to make mistakes, and then I told her that her marriage isn't as perfect as it should be. By the time I was finished with her, she was in full depression. You'd think she would have learned not to listen to me by now. She even let me wake her up at night and pick on her. (mockingly) And then I criticized her for letting me wake her up and worry her.

The Unusual Abilities of the Critic

We never fail to be amazed at the intelligence of the Critic. It must have an I.Q. somewhere between 395–470. If you understand I.Q. scores, you will recognize that this is at the top of the scale and we ordinary mortals will have difficulty in dealing with it. The Critic is absolutely brilliant in its ability to make us feel rotten about ourselves.

In addition to intelligence of a logical kind, as represented by the high I.Q., the Critic seems to have a deep sense of intuition. Somehow, the Critic always knows where we have soft spots and how to dig the knife sharply into them. If we are worried about our physical appearance, if we are worried about being unlovable, if we are worried about being stupid, about being undereducated, about being disempowered, sexless, selfish, not as good as the next person, too aggressive—

all of these are acceptable to the Critic. It is holistic in its orientation. It uses its keen clinical intuition to find out what we most fear to be, and then it attacks.

Its powers of perception are remarkable as well. Nothing is too small or too large to escape its notice. From something as small as a spouse failing to comment appreciatively on one's new haircut (the Critic will point out how unattractive one has become) to something as large as the threat of worldwide destruction (the Critic will criticize our inadequate involvement), the Critic is always ready to point out our inadequacies and our failures. It monitors our actions thoroughly and will wake us in the early morning hours to review, with distaste, our behavior at a party the night before or an interaction with a loved one, a colleague, or family member. It will remember every negative detail and, unless we are very alert, it will convince us that we have behaved abominably and have done irreparable damage.

Another quality in the Critic to be admired is its capacity for total candor. It has no desire to hide its power and, when spoken to directly, it seems to revel in the possibility of sharing its philosophy and methodology with any reasonable listener. Critics have been known to brag of their ability to snare an individual no matter which way he turns. In fact, they often get so carried away by the sheer delight of their power, that they give away valuable information. Let us see how this arrogant honesty helped Alice to learn of the impossibility of pleasing her Critic.

> *Critic*: Basically, I just don't think that she measures up. That's all.
>
> *Therapist*: Can you be more specific? For instance, we were just talking about her weight. How do you feel about that?

Critic: She's too fat. You know that.

Therapist: But when she'd lost weight, remember what you said?

Critic: Sure. She was too thin. Boney in the shoulders. She wasn't sexy enough. I think she should look sexier.

Therapist: (teasing) And what would you say if she looked sexier?

Critic: I'd tell her she looks like a tramp. I agree with her father. A woman shouldn't be provocative.

Therapist: But you just said she should be sexier.

Critic: I know. I don't like it when she's too sweet— too much the girl next door.

Therapist: It seems to me that you've got her coming and going.

Critic: (triumphantly) That's right. I'm like her father. Nothing ever pleased him either. I just think that everything she does is wrong. Besides that, she's stupid.

Therapist: But she does well in all her courses.

Critic: That's because she's a perfectionist and compulsive and she studies too much.

Therapist: What if she relaxed more?

Critic: (very self-satisfied) Then I'd tell her she's lazy. She can't win with me. She might as well give up.

How to Recognize the Critic at Work

And so it goes. A really top-notch Critic can get us from any angle. Only constant vigilance and a keen awareness of that sense of sinking that one gets in the pit of one's stomach can keep us alert in the face of its brilliant and well-aimed attacks.

There is a way to become aware of the Critic. When carefully attended to we realize that however we are, it is not okay with the Critic. Whatever it is that we plan to become will also not be okay. And, our means of reaching this unacceptable goal is not okay either.

The Critic knows just the right area in which to insert the blade of the knife. It is always, as we have said before, some sensitive spot and, once the knife blade is in, we tend to focus on the content that is being brought through rather than on the knife that is being shoved into us. The Critic is an outstanding knife-wielder. To become aware of the knife-wielding capa-bilities of the Critic, to be able to look beyond the content of its comments, and to recognize the destruc-tive capacity of the Critic, itself, beyond all the details, requires a powerful Awareness and an impressive devel-opment of consciousness. Before this Awareness, we are victims of the Critic. We feel insecure and inadequate. There is a sick feeling in the pit of our stomachs that we're always doing wrong and that someone is watching and taking note of that fact. We may even get to feel depressed and hopeless, because there is no place to hide—the Critic is within and sees all and knows all.

The Incomparable Comparer

The Comparer is a potent aspect of the Critic and has great versatility. It is totally holistic in its approach to comparison. With equal ease and delight it will remind you that your friend is brighter or has accomplished more. Possibly he has written a book. Someone else is a better mother and spends inordinate time with her children and seems to love them no matter what the conditions or circumstances. A business associate has a

better marriage and a friend dresses with more imagination. Someone has a penis that is larger, and someone
else's figure is the way yours should be. Whatever the
comparison, there is always a particular watchword with
the Comparer—however it is that you are, someone is
better at it. Whatever it is you plan to become, has
already been surpassed.

The following dialogue with the Comparer of an in-
telligent and successful middle-aged man gives us an
idea of how the Comparer works:

> *Comparer*: I say, "Why bother? Why bother?" It's too
> late in life and he's just not going to do as well as his
> friends.

The Comparer, by the way, does not necessarily burden
itself with facts.

> *Comparer*: As I said, he's not going to do as well as his
> friends. His work isn't as meaningful as E's, his rela-
> tionships aren't as deep as L's, his sex life isn't ade-
> quate. I don't think that people like him as much as
> they like other people. I look around at everybody else,
> then I look at him and I say again . . . "Don't
> bother."

The Comparer is incomparable when it comes to making us feel miserable. There always is somebody more
evolved, richer, sexier, more brilliant, more attractive,
younger, older, wiser, more relaxed, more accomplished, more efficient; etcetera, etcetera. Once the
Comparer starts its refrain, we feel diminished, reduced
to second class status, hopelessly outdistanced by those
carefully selected others held up to us as examples.

The Critic Looks at One's Physical Appearance

The Critic often combines with the Perfectionist, especially in women, when it comes to looks. Let us see how they look at our personal appearance. Their appraisal, as in the following example, often has no relationship to reality whatsoever. The client, Elaine, is a very beautiful woman and a talented actress. (It is to the credit of the Inner Critics that they are singularly unimpressed by the way people actually look. The Critic criticizes equally, no matter what the objective state of attractiveness or non-attractiveness may be. It is important to appreciate this egalitarian attitude.)

In the following dialogue, Elaine speaks about her competition for acting roles:

Elaine: I just feel unsure of myself whenever I go for an interview. I feel awkward and unattractive.

Therapist: Could we talk to that part of you that makes you feel unattractive?

(Client shifts into a different seat. Therapist continues.)

Therapist: You're the part of Elaine that makes her feel she's unattractive.

Critic: I don't have to make her feel that way—she *is* unattractive.

Therapist: Well, I have to tell you, friend, she looks pretty good to me. What do you see that you don't like?

Critic: Well, that's a rather open-ended question. I could go on for a long time.

Therapist: Well, just start somewhere. What's the main thing you want changed or don't like?

Critic: Well, obviously, her breasts. They're much too small. That's why I want her to have surgery. (It was not obvious to the therapist).

Therapist: What kind of surgery are you referring to . . .breast enlargement?

Critic: I want her breasts enlarged . . . of course. How can she pursue a career as an actress if her breasts are too small? You've seen actresses. You know what they look like.

There is another member of the healing arts community that owes a great debt of gratitude to the Critic, and that is the plastic surgeon. Here, again, is a whole segment of our professional population whose income is absolutely guaranteed by the Critic. Incidentally, the Critic has three surgical specialities: breast, nose and wrinkles. Let us continue our dialogue with Elaine's Critic.

Therapist: How do you manage to make Elaine feel so terrible about her breasts? I really have to tell you that they look pretty good to me.

Critic: I remind her of different women . . . especially different actresses who have very large breasts. I say to her . . . how did you feel at the party when you saw Lisa with that low cut gown. Now *those* were breasts.

Therapist: You sound like a man.

Critic: I am. That's why I'm such an expert on the subject of women and what's wrong with them.

Therapist: And apparently, if I understand you, comparing them to other women is a favorite method.

Critic: Not just women—men too. If I can compare Elaine to a man, that can work just as well.

Therapist: Not with breasts.

Critic: Oh, you know better than that. The issue isn't breasts. The issue is how to make Elaine feel bad about herself. I love telling her how dumb she is. Otherwise, she wouldn't want to be an actress. And when she does act, I maker sure to look at her films and tell her she looks dumb.

The Critic is quite remarkable in its ability to change its point of view once a woman has followed its suggestions for surgery. An equally disgusted Critic gave an opposing point of view after breast surgery:

Critic: She was really stupid to let them talk her into breast enlargement. Her breasts were perfectly good before and now they're too big and they're heavy and they ache. Do you see how she sometimes rests them on the table? She tries to be discreet about it but I point it out to her every time she does it. I just can't believe how stupid women can be about their looks.

There is no satisfying a Critic when it is out of control. First it attacks from the right and, as we swing round, it gets us with an uppercut. We listen to its criticisms, try to make things better, and it criticizes us for our new looks or our new behavior. That is why it is so important to go beyond the details of content to experience the energy that is operating. If someone is sticking a knife into us and, at the same time, talking to us very reasonably about our shortcomings, it might be more advisable to focus on the knife rather than the words. That is what we mean by experiencing the energy that is operating.

The Critic Transformed

As we think back over the many Critics we have known, we realize that they do provide some valuable services. First, it is frequently the Critic, and the discomfort caused by its complaints, that launches us on our journey of transformation. The Critic points out, in no uncertain terms, that there is something wrong and we had better act to correct it. Secondly, there are frequently gold nuggets buried in the trash. The Critic forces us to look at the distasteful sides of ourselves and, if we can avoid being incapacitated (or decapitated) by its judgments, we can begin to deal with these aspects through an Aware Ego. It can be very difficult to sort through the barrage of negativity in the beginning of this process, however.

Last and best, the energy of the Critic when transformed, i.e., after it has been made conscious, introduced into Awareness and clearly differentiated from the Aware Ego, can serve as a true ally. It can evaluate our actions objectively and can help us in improving our performance in any field of endeavor. It can also alert us to areas of unconsciousness, point out disowned selves, and let us know when we are caught in a bonding. As its judgments lose their bite, it can become a very effective, discerning, rational friend.

Its tendency to destroy remains a possibility, however, and a Critic is able to become deadly again after a period of benign cooperation. Never turn your back on a sleeping Critic! Accept its gifts, love it, but remember: you never know when it will revert to its original untamed state—and attack.

There is a team of players that works very closely with the Pusher/Critic combo. They are the Perfectionist, the Pleaser and the Ambition patterns. Let us see how these patterns work in people.

THE PERFECTIONIST

We have seen how the Pusher energy drives people to do things. Together with the Perfectionist, it sets standards which can be used creatively, if we are aware of these energies. Or, conversely, it sets requirements that make life an intolerable burden.

When the Perfectionist works with the Pusher, we are required to do things perfectly. This combination is very powerful. The Perfectionist can, however, exist by itself. It is rare that the Inner Critic is not part of the bargain.

Hank is a professional man who has wanted to write a book for a long time. He has a writing block, however. In the course of our conversation with him, it becomes clear that Hank has a very demanding taskmaster in him. This internal Pharaoh doesn't like shoddy work. He only appreciates "class" writing and "class" anything, for that matter. This provides a natural lead-in to Voice Dialogue.

Facilitator: I hear a voice, when you talk about life, that seems quite strong in you—someone who demands that things be done in a certain way. Could I talk to that part of you? (Hank moves over.) Good Morning.

Perfectionist: Good morning. What can I do for you?

Facilitator: I heard your voice while Hank was talking

so I thought I would like to talk to you directly. What is your job in Hank's life?

Perfectionist: Well, if you're going to do a thing, do it right. That's what my father used to say.

Facilitator: So, Hank's father was one of your teachers.

Perfectionist: He sure was. He was perfect in everything he did.

Facilitator: Well, how about you and Hank? What's your function in him now?

Perfectionist: I keep him clear. His book is going to be a real work of art. I hate shoddy writing. I hate shoddy workmanship. I hate shoddy people.

Facilitator: What's a shoddy person?

Perfectionist: Someone who does shoddy work.

Facilitator: Do you know many such people?

Perfectionist: (somewhat embarrassed—an indication that other parts are somewhat ashamed of what the Perfectionist is about to say.) Well, I'm surrounded by them. My wife is just the opposite. She doesn't care about whether the house is neat or not. I'm always picking up. And my son is the biggest slob you ever saw. I'm always after him. My daughter is like me.

From our discussion of energy patterns with which we identify and energy patterns that we disown, it is clear that Hank is identified with a strong natural Pusher and Perfectionist and that he disowns his own more relaxed selves, as well as his vulnerability. By the laws of energetics, Hank will always pull people into his orbit who carry his disowned self. So long as his Awareness level is identified with his Perfectionist and his Pusher, he will polarize his environment and his already easygoing wife will be driven into a "Sloppy Daughter" reaction to his Father/Perfectionist.

Keep in mind again that there is no energy pattern that is inherently good or bad. At issue is whether Hank's Awareness is separated from the Perfectionist energy. So far, from our dialogue, it is clear that it is not. Until Hank has an Awareness that is separate from the Perfectionist Father, his relationship to his son is doomed to perpetual conflict as the Father pattern drives his son, "the slob," into deeper and deeper withdrawal and fantasy, or active rebellion. Thus, the son lives out more and more of Hank's unconscious self. Let us go back to the Dialogue:

> *Facilitator*: So you have a hard time with all these slobs around.
>
> *Perfectionist*: Well—other parts of Hank are coming in now. They feel I'm too dogmatic. I don't think I am.
>
> *Facilitator*: Are there other areas in Hank's life in which you operate?
>
> *Perfectionist*: I don't like the way he reads documents at work. He needs to be more careful. He needs to study them more carefully. A mistake can be very costly.

The Dialogue proceeds to explore the many areas in which the Perfectionist operates. The facilitator at a certain point decides to explore the team that keeps being alluded to by the Perfectionist.

> *Facilitator*: I have the feeling when you speak that you're very afraid—as though if Hank doesn't listen to you, something terrible is going to happen. Could I talk to that part of Hank that feels that fear?
>
> (Hank moves over to a different place.)

Scared Voice: (sits very quietly, doesn't speak. Hank looks totally different physically from the way he looked in the Perfectionist Voice. A few minutes pass during which time the facilitator simply remains energetically connected to what turns out to be the Frightened Child. After three or four minutes of silence, the facilitator speaks.)

Facilitator: Hello—you seem rather scared.

Child: I am. I'm always scared. He always wants to get rid of me. He hates me.

Facilitator: You mean our friend over here (Perfectionist) hates you.

Child: I don't know who hates me. They all hate me. He never lets me be around.

Facilitator: How does he get rid of you?

Child: He just never lets me out. I hate his work. I hate law. I hate documents. I'm always scared at work. I'm always afraid something terrible is going to happen.

It is clear that Hank has developed an elaborate system of energy patterns to strengthen himself against a very vulnerable and very frightened little boy inside him. The more perfectionistic he becomes, the more he drives himself, the deeper the *angst* of the Inner Child. This *angst* may translate itself into anxiety, depression, physical symptoms and, quite sadly, confused and disturbed family relations.

For the Inner Child, it is the first time he has even been allowed to be present in Hank's life. Hank's Awareness now has the opportunity to separate from the Perfectionist and the Pusher and to witness the feelings on the other side that have been negated for such a long time.

The following Dialogue gives us the Perfectionist of a woman who would be considerd eminently successful by all who knew her:

Therapist: Would you be willing to tell us your expectations of Barbara?

Perfectionist: I'd be delighted! (With extreme self-righteousness). My basic philosophy is quite simple. I expect her to be perfect. There are to be no mistakes. None whatever. I don't compare her to anyone else, my standards are absolute. She must never say or do anything that could be reasonably questioned by anyone else.

Therapist: That could be a bit limiting, couldn't it?

Perfectionist: I'm *quite* clear. I'd rather have her say and do nothing than let someone else find a flaw in her. My aim is to be sure that she's perfect.

Therapist: In what areas?

Perfectionist: In all areas. When she speaks, it should be clear, well thought out, rational, in complete sentences and concise but it should not be pedantic. She should be spontaneous, entertaining and perceptive. When she writes, there should be no errors anywhere in grammar or spelling. Each paragraph should flow beautifully into the next. There should be a perfect marriage of meaningful content and elegant style. And, again, nothing that anyone could possibly criticize. I do want her to be sure that nobody can find fault with anything she says or writes.

Therapist: That sounds a bit difficult to achieve. What about other areas of her life?

Perfectionist: Whatever bookkeeping she does must be faultless. I can't tolerate a checkbook that doesn't balance with a bank statement. She should always do everything on time, have reports and repairs done immediately, return phone calls within hours, remember people's birthdays, be thoughtful.

Therapist: I'm getting exhausted. You're not kidding, are you?

Perfectionist: I most certainly am not! The world tolerates entirely too much imperfection these days. I'm here to uphold standards. Now, I also expect her to maintain herself in peak physical condition. She should be in perfect health—poor health suggests an imbalance somewhere and I can't tolerate imbalances—and she should always look good. She should be rested, centered and conscious at all times. Her relationships should be conscious, clear and intimate and she should always be on the best possible terms with everyone. I don't like tension or unpleasantness any more than I like mistakes!

This Perfectionist went on and on, gaining momentum and self-satisfaction as its demands multiplied. As the Aware Ego listens to these demands, as they become conscious, we are able to make choices for ourselves. We can see the futility of trying to please a Perfectionist like this whose demands are totally unrealistic and can never be fully met no matter what we do.

Needless to say, there are areas in which perfection is necessary and mistakes are catastrophic. We *do* want Perfectionists supervising the designing and building of our planes and bridges, our buildings and our nuclear plants. But the same perfectionistic demands brought to bear on all aspects of daily living can be totally debilitating.

The psychiatric community owes a real debt of gratitude to Perfectionists such as these. The anxiety created by the Perfectionist requires a steady diet of tranquilizers and sleeping pills in order to dissipate tension. Perfectionists are also marvelous supporters of all kinds of growth. They are eager to expand their demands into higher consciousness realms, psychic abilities, the martial arts, new languages, computers. You name it; they can decide to incorporate it into their plans; and, whatever it is, it must be done with expertise.

THE POWER BROKERS

Power is a fact of psychic life that many people today would like to believe can be eradicated or transmuted. But power is a reality of psychic life and, like all energy patterns, the issue is whether or not it is used to control people and whether it can be used with Awareness.

The Power Brokers are a group of energy patterns that may include Power, Ambition, Pusher, Money, Selfishness and a variety of other voices. The following transcript is an example of how this Power group operates. If one makes a choice to talk to the Protector/Controller, one might easily tap into an individual's Power group. The Protector/Controller's interests often coincide with the interests of the Power group which is in charge of operations. Let us see how this works.

Sam is a 38-year-old man, very successful in business and not very interested in anything related to the consciousness process, until one day his wife decides to leave him. He is very upset by this, doesn't understand it, but feels forced to begin to look at himself—something his wife has been asking him to do for years.

In the course of his training he does the following piece of Dialogue work with his facilitator:

Facilitator: Well, Sam, it would appear that power is a major issue for you in your life.

Sam: Well yes—I've been very successful. You don't do that by being passive and retiring.

Facilitator: Could I talk to the voice of Power?

Sam: I'm not sure there is anyone else.

Facilitator: Well, why don't you move over and let's see?

(Sam moves over)

Good afternoon. The person I wanted in Sam was his Power Voice. Is that who you are?

Power: So, who else? Of course it's me. He hasn't become a multi-millionaire by twiddling his thumbs.

Facilitator: Making him rich is one of your jobs?

Power: It certainly *is* one of my jobs. And a good one it is. How much money do you have?

Facilitator: Well, I'm comfortable. But why is that important to you?

Power: Money is a measure to me as to whether someone has made it or not.

Facilitator: What are the criteria you use for how much money is enough for success?

Power: I always told Sam he had to be a millionaire by the age of 30. He made it.

Facilitator: Did that satisfy you?

Power: Not really. I looked around at all the other investors and realized that he was a little fish in a big sea. So I upped the ante, to ten million. I told him if his net worth was ten million dollars, it would be a different ball game. He would have the Power then.

Facilitator: Well, how has he done?

Power: He's worth more than that now, but a lot of it is in real estate. He's actually cash poor.

Facilitator: What does it mean to be cash poor?

Power: His income isn't more than half a million a year. You may think that's a lot, but he has friends who have incomes of over a million a year.

Facilitator: Well, tell me—what would ultimately satisfy you?

Power: A net worth of a hundred million and an income that could simply keep building accordingly.

The compulsive accumulation of wealth is to a great extent an attempt to allay the anxieties and fears of the Vulnerable Child. This and the need to control others is always inextricably interwoven with the fears and vulnerability of the child. Compulsive wealth building is one aspect of the Power side in action.

It is obvious that the Power and Pusher and Ambition voices are all inextricably interwoven. We know from the theoretical structure of such a situation that Sam's vulnerability is totally unconscious. He has to keep building wealth to maintain the dominion of Power and also to keep away his vulnerability. He becomes more and more isolated as he distances himself increasingly from his vulnerable core. His wife knows it and, because of her own process, is no longer seduced by the pure glamour of money.

At a later point in Sam's process the facilitator attempts to talk to the Vulnerable Child.

Facilitator: We've talked about the issue of vulnerability, Sam. I'd like to meet your child, if I could. Are you up to that?

Sam: It doesn't thrill me, but I'll try. It's what my wife keeps talking about.

(Sam moves over to child space.)

Facilitator: Hello—are you there?

Child: (There is no real feeling yet of the child being present. The facilitator can be silent and try and induct the child energetically or he can start talking even though the child energy isn't fully present. He chooses to start talking.)

Facilitator: Well, I'm glad to meet you finally. How are you doing?

Child: I don't know. I don't know who I am.

Facilitator: Well, you're the part of Sam that would carry his fears—the part whose feelings get hurt easily— the part who feels overwhelmed very easily.

Child: He never lets me out. I don't think he even listens to me.

Facilitator: Does he even know about you?

Child: I don't think so. He's too busy. He doesn't know about me at all.

Facilitator: Did he ever know about you?

Child: It was too long ago.

Facilitator: Would you like to come out?

Child: I don't know. I'm no good. I can't do anything.

Facilitator: Actually, those are other voices in Sam that say you're no good. You're so used to hearing them you think it's you who feels that way. Sam has a lot of parts in him who don't like you.

Child: Why not? Why am I so bad? I know I'm scared all the time. I always feel scared.

The facilitation proceeds a while longer and then shifts to other work. The Child is able to speak and identify itself in a very limited fashion, but the real energy is not present. The Controller/Power axis is still much too powerful. One cannot force a disowned self to be present if the weight on the other side is too great. One must be patient and allow the process to work its way through.

THE PLEASER

We have included the Pleaser in the Heavyweight section. Even though its energy is decidedly different from the others discussed here and it may look like weakness to some, it wields immense power and deserves to be considered a Heavyweight along with all the others. There is nothing wrong with pleasing. The only question is, as with all energy patterns, who is doing the pleasing? Is there a real choice made by an Aware Ego? Or is the pleasing an automatic, unconscious response to the world?

Nancy is a committed wife, mother and daughter. She always does the right thing to make people happy. She drives her children wherever they want to go. She is available to her parents and she is available to her husband. She always smiles and she is generally very gracious.

Over time, she begins to have difficulty sleeping at night. She is aware that she is having bad dreams, but she cannot recall what they are; she just remembers that things are after her. Bedtime becomes nightmarish and she starts using sleeping pills to get a good night's sleep. She is in a state of physical and psychological exhaustion by the time she seeks help. After the preliminary contact is over, the facilitator asks Nancy about her role in the household.

Facilitator: It sounds like making people happy is a very important part of your life.

Nancy: It always has been. My father was a "growler" and I was the one who could keep him happy. So I did. But aside from that, I really enjoy having happy people around me.

Facilitator: Why don't you move your chair over. I'd like to talk to the part of you that needs to keep everyone happy.

(Nancy moves over.)

Tell me, how do you function in Nancy? How do you keep all these people happy?

Pleaser: Well, I've learned to recognize when people want things. My job is to see that no one gets grouchy. I'm very sensitive to moods and I can tell when they're coming on. So, I do whatever I have to do to stop the moods.

Facilitator: Can you give me an example that actually happened recently—one where you actually were dealing with such a situation?

Pleaser: Well, Nancy's husband was going to work this morning and he asked Nancy to drop off his clothes at the cleaners, and then to pick up some supplies at the stationery store after her appointment with you. So, I told him that of course I'll take care of these things. I know he's nervous about my coming here this morning.

Facilitator: Did he say something to Nancy to indicate that he was scared?

Pleaser: People around me don't have to talk. I'm a kind of psychic pleaser. I know. This way he went off to work happy and I don't have to contend with any difficulty.

Nancy's Pleaser clearly works automatically. There is certainly no choice involved in Nancy's behavior. She must always please. After considerable exploration of this Pleaser energy, the facilitator decides to look into an opposite energy pattern. There are several ways to approach this in Dialogue work. The facilitator might say: "I'm curious as to what part of Nancy is the other side of you. If you weren't around, what would happen? Who would be present?" The Pleaser says there would be anarchy.

The facilitator knows that Nancy must have enormous rage. She also knows from the nightmarish quality of Nancy's sleep that she must disown her whole daemonic nature. The facilitator chooses to go after the Selfishness, a relatively non-threatening energy that contrasts sharply with the Pleaser. She could have Nancy move over to the "other side" and see what comes. Instead she follows the lead of the Pleaser.

Facilitator: Anarchy means what? (still talking to the Pleaser.)

Pleaser: Without me she would do exactly what she wants.

Facilitator: Could I talk to the part that would like to do exactly what she wants?

Pleaser: (not happy) If you say so. I warn you though—it's anarchy.

(Nancy shifts to a new chair.)

We will label the voice Selfish Nancy. Please keep in mind that we do not have to give it a name at all. Nancy might give a name to this part, or we might simply work without a name.

Facilitator: Good morning.

Selfish Nancy: If you're going to talk to me you can forget the niceties.

Facilitator: Well, who are you? What do you do?

Selfish: I DON'T DO ANYTHING. That's the trouble; I don't do anything.

Facilitator: What would happen if you did do something? What would happen if you were in charge of Nancy's life?

Selfish: One thing I can tell you—I wouldn't please anyone. Not ever again. Her husband could take in his own laundry and buy his own office supplies. He treats Nancy like a slave girl and she smiles and smiles and does and does. And those children! She's creating monsters. She does whatever they want. They're nice kids and she's turning them into monsters.

Facilitator: Could you give me an example that's more specific? What are some of the things you'd actually do if you were in charge?

Selfish: I would go to the gym every morning. It would
be the end of "breakfast by Nancy." I would go back to
school *now*. I wouldn't wait 'til the children are grown.
Nancy has a thing about waiting 'til the children are
grown. Now she's supposed to take care of everyone.
When she's 45 she's allowed to go out on her own. I'd
have her meet new and interesting people. I'd have her
dress differently. It would be a totally different scene.

The facilitator has gotten into a core disowned energy
pattern in Nancy. Many facilitators are seduced by the
anger that they sense is underneath Pleaser patterns. It
may certainly be necessary to tap into the Anger Voice.
From our perspective, too much time gets spent in
trying to elicit Anger when, instead, we are often able
to get beneath the anger, to the problems that are eliciting it.

The analogy would be a man who sits down on a
chair and in doing so, sits on a tack. He is in much
pain, so he goes to someone who has him emote and,
though this feels better, the tack is still there, firmly
embedded in him. Then he goes to meditation training. This helps some and he learns to rise above his
pain, but he still has the tack in his seat. He tries bio-
feedback, reflexology, hypnosis, but when all is said
and done, the tack remains.

What is the tack in our lives that creates so much
anger in us? It is the ability, or inability, to say yes and
no. If we live life on our terms, saying yes and no appropriately, then we tend to have less occasion to be angry.

Nancy has a deep rage. The negation of that rage is
exhausting her. Her rage is a function of living a life of
pleasing, a life where her needs come last. Moving into
the reciprocal relationship of the Pleaser/Selfishness
energy pattern gives Nancy an Awareness of two basic

opposites in her—one with which she has been identified, one that she has disowned. It is the start of a process of reclamation.

Do remember that every disowned self requires a certain amount of energy to be used in order to keep it unconscious. Too many or too powerful a system of disowned selves means that the psycho-physiological battery goes on drain and eventually the system goes into an exhaustion mode. This can lead ultimately to a serious breakdown on either a physical or a psychological level.

CHAPTER VI

THE INNER CHILD

The Vulnerable Selves

INTRODUCTION

Working with the Inner Child is one of the most significant and rewarding aspects of Voice Dialogue. It also requires some of the deepest sensitivity. There are three aspects of the Child that are of particular importance: the Vulnerable Child, the Playful Child and the Magical Child.

The Vulnerable Child carries the sensitivity and fear. Its feelings are easily hurt. It generally lives in fear of abandonment. It is almost always frightened of a multitude of things that the Protector/Controller and the Heavyweights know nothing about. Remember that the Protector/Controller develops to protect this Vulnerable Child and, in doing so, buries it so that it will not be hurt.

The Playful Child is just what the name implies—it is playful. It knows how to play as a child knows how to play. It is generally easier to reach than the Vulnerable

Child. The Protector/Controller is much more likely to permit play than it is to permit tears and pain.

The Magical Child is really a brother or sister to the Playful Child. It is the child of imagination and fantasy. It is the child of our right brain, of our intuition and creative imagination. It is, in part, the source of our vision. It, too, is lost very early in our lives as the Heavyweights take over. It often has to be coaxed out, and this requires great sensitivity on the part of the facilitator. The Magical Child needs the facilitator's magical-child energy to be present before it will show itself because it is usually quite shy.

The Inner Child never grows up. One hears over and over again great surprise in Dialogue work when the child discovers that the facilitator has no requirements that it grow up, act adult or, for that matter, even use words at all. Some of the most profound Voice Dialogue sessions with the Inner Child are held without words. This is less true of the Playful and Magical Child than it is of the Vulnerable Child.

The Children of our inner world know how to "be." Most of the rest of our personality knows how to "do" and how to "act." The gift to the facilitator in working with these patterns is that he must learn how to "be" with them; otherwise they cannot emerge. When dealing with the Inner Child, the dictum is: "There's nowhere to go and there's nothing to do."

The loss of the Inner Child is one of the most profound tragedies of the "growing up" process. We lose so much of the magic and mystery of living. We lose so much of the delight and intimacy of relationship. So much of the destructiveness that we bring to each other as human beings is a function of our lack of connection to our sensitivities, our fears, our own magic. How different the world would be if our political figures could say: "I feel very bad. You really hurt my feelings when you said that," or: "I want to apologize to my colleague for my remarks yesterday. My feelings were hurt and I was angry and I am sorry."

If the Inner Child is operating in our lives autonomously and without protection, we can be fairly sure that we will end up in some kind of victim status. The Child, however wonderful, cannot drive our car any more successfully than any other energy pattern. It, too, needs balancing. But so long as the Protector/Controller is in charge of the personality, the Child remains buried and therefore inaccessible.

As we separate from the Protector/Controller and as we become aware of the Inner Child, our Aware Ego gradually becomes the parent to the Inner Child. We then begin to take over the responsibility of using the energy of the Inner Child in our lives and providing it with appropriate protection when needed.

When the Aware Ego becomes more effective, the Protector/Controller, quite willingly, begins to surrender control. So long as the person is protected from being hurt too badly, so long as the Protector/Controller feels that the vulnerability is being protected, it can begin to relax, knowing that the fundamental integrity of the system is in good hands. Let us look now at how the Inner Child manifests in the Dialogue process.

VULNERABILITY— A PRIMARY DISOWNED SELF

Perhaps the most universally disowned self in our civilized world is the Vulnerable Child. Yet this Vulnerable Child may be our most precious sub-personality

—the closest to our essence—the one that enables us to become truly intimate, to fully experience others, and to love. Unfortunately, it usually disappears by the age of 5. This child cannot exist in our civilized societies without the protection of a very strong Protector/Controller structure. The only way a Protector/Controller knows how to handle the Vulnerable Child is to disown it. And disown it we do. It is usually so completely disowned that the Protector/Controller does not even worry about it.

What is this child like? The most striking quality is its ability to be deeply intimate with another person. One feels a warmth, a physical warmth, and a fullness between oneself and this child. It is as though the space between the two people is alive and vibrating. When the Vulnerable Child withdraws (as it does at the slightest provocation) this warmth and fullness disappear and one feels a slight chill. For someone who has not had this experience with another adult, it is somewhat similar to the special feelings that might occur with a small child or with a dog in a moment of deep affection and mutual trust. This ability to be fully "with" another human being is most precious.

However, this being in a full energy interchange with another person brings its share of discomfort as well as pleasure. The Vulnerable Child is tuned in energetically, which means that it is aware of *everything* that is happening. Words do not fool it for a moment. You can continue your conversation, but the Child will know if there is any change whatsoever in your energetic connection with it. An outside thought may have intruded; you may be wondering what time it is; you may suddenly decide you're hungry—the Child will know that you have withdrawn. It is exquisitely sensitive and reacts immediately to any abandonment that it perceives. It may not know why there has been a withdrawal, but it will know that one has occurred.

Getting in touch with this sub-personality opens one to the most embarrassing feelings of rejection, such as feeling abandoned when one's spouse leaves the bed in the morning to go to the bathroom. However, this sub-personality *does* know without question who is to be trusted and who is not. It *does* recognize without question the people who disown their own vulnerable children and who can, therefore, hurt others either accidentally or deliberately.

The first contact with a Vulnerable Child using the Voice Dialogue technique might just involve sitting very quietly and encouraging it to come forth. It is often pre-verbal and might just sit quietly or cry. In its initial emergence, it might curl up in a foetal positon, cover its head, and weep with great wrenching sobs. Another might be very tentative, checking out the facilitator's ability to sense its presence or absence. Above all, no Vulnerable Child will appear unless the facilitator can be trusted not to hurt it. It has invariably been hurt in the past and is fearful of being hurt again. A very dramatic example of this was the vulnerable child of a Jewish woman who had managed to stay alive in Europe through WW II.

Child: It hurts so to think of everything that she's been through. I had to go away when she was very, very young (crying). It's too painful to exist. It just feels like a skin full of tears.

Therapist: (with concern) Do you want to go away now?

Child: No, it feels good to have you here with me. I always go into hiding, but it hurts even worse when I'm alone. I need someone to be with me and let me be sad.

The pain of the Vulnerable Child is a deep pain that requires respect and empathy. The Child will know if you are feeling aloof or rational and it will not emerge. It sometimes requires that one actually search for it. With Natalie, a therapist herself, the vulnerable child emerged in a most surprising fashion. Natalie began the session by talking of her discomfort with hugging the therapist—actually it was Natalie's Rational Voice, as it turned out later, but it certainly sounded like an Aware Ego when we started:

Rational Natalie: I've been thinking a great deal about this business of hugging you at the end of our sessions and it's not comfortable for me. It seems to me that it's a way of discharging anxiety and that it works against the therapy. Also, I don't feel free choice in the situation.

Therapist: (equally rational to protect her own Vulnerable Child) Well, why don't we forget about hugging and see how that works. I can certainly see your point about the discharge of anxiety and tension and it's not comfortable for me if it feels compulsive.

At this point, the therapist noticed a change, a sense of sadness in Natalie.

Therapist: Wait a minute. Let me talk to the part of you that wants me to hug her.

Vulnerable Child: (bursts into tears) I was afraid you wouldn't know I was here. She's so sensible, I was afraid she'd hurt your feelings and you wouldn't think of looking for me. I *want* you to hug me. I like it. I *want* you to pay attention to me. (A fresh outburst of tears)

Therapist: I'd love to pay attention to you. Tell me about yourself.

Child: I'm very little, about 4 years old, and I'm cute. But I'm scared. And I'm hiding. I'm hiding in the closet. And I hope that someone will come looking for me but (more sobbing) nobody comes, nobody ever comes. I really want somebody to come and look for *me* and pay attention to *me*. She's acted grown up and sensible ever since she was little and nobody has ever even thought to look for me. Nobody ever misses me. I need people to notice I'm gone, and to care.

This gives us a most touching portrait of our Vulnerable Child. It wants to be missed, sought after, and valued although the Protector/Controller and other rational sub-personalities do not want it to exist at all. Men have even greater difficulty than women in agreeing to contact their vulnerable children because it is socially unacceptable for men to be vulnerable. Theirs, too, are often in hiding. They have been found hidden in closets, under the kitchen sink, in a cave, up in a tree house, in the woods, in a barn or in an attic. Sometimes one can make an initial contact by asking for the part that runs away from people or stays hidden:

Therapist: I know that Mike is very efficient and successful but I'd like to talk to the part of him that's a little more sensitive and needs to keep away from people, maybe it even needs to hide.

Child: I certainly do need to hide. When he was little, I used to go out into the woods when somebody hurt my feelings. I'd wait and wait for somebody to come looking for me. I was really scared that if they'd find Mike, they'd hurt my feelings again, but I really wanted them to notice he was gone and to come looking. And do you know what? They never did. And then I'd really feel bad.

Once Mike knows how his feelings have been hurt, he can speak to his wife about this issue. If he doesn't know, he withdraws into a cold parental sub-personality, her Vulnerable Child gets hurt and she becomes even more rejecting to protect herself.

The Vulnerable Child helps us to remove ourselves from painful situations if they cannot be changed. It is the Vulnerable Child who finally pulls us out of an unrewarding relationship or a thankless job. That is, when we listen to him. For instance, Frank was in a relationship with a younger woman who was fond enough of him, but let it be known quite clearly that she didn't love him enough to see their relationship move toward marriage as he hoped it would. Frank had disowned his Vulnerable Child so completely that at first we could only talk to it through the Protector/Controller. However, the Protector/Controller agreed to let us consult with the Child regarding the relationship.

Therapist: Would you please tell us how you feel about Frank's relationship with Claire?

Child: I don't like it at all. I get hurt all the time. He keeps thinking that she's going to learn to love him but I know she's not. She's just sticking around for what she can get. He's nice and he does things for her so she stays around. I know that she doesn't love him and it makes me feel bad. But he doesn't care how I feel.

Therapist: If you were running Frank's life, what would you do?

Child: I'd get away from her. It makes me feel too lonely when he's with her. It's much worse than being alone.

As we have said before, the Vulnerable Child often sees emotional matters clearly and can give good advice. Frank had to decide what to do with this information. There were other sub-personalities to consult. But, to his own great relief, he listened to the advice of his Vulnerable Child, confronted the situation and, with tact and diplomacy, ended the relationship.

In contrast with its ability to end an unrewarding relationship, the integration of the Vulnerable Child into a relationship encourages unparalleled intimacy and depth. Let us trace one such experience.

Suzanne had been raised by a very cold and rejecting mother. Her Vulnerable Child was disowned quite early in life and replaced with charm, sophistication and a whimsical, delightful wit. Suzanne was irresistible to men but very lonely. She was shocked to find out that she had any vulnerable feelings and the child, itself, felt worthless.

Child: But what good can I do her? I just get hurt and frightened.

Therapist: I know that it feels awfully good to be with you and that you have lots to tell both Suzanne and myself. You're delicious.

Child: I don't know about that (but she smiles because the energetic contact is good).

Therapist: Tell me, why did you have to hide?

Child: Her mother (she starts to cry)—her mother is very mean and she made her cry all the time. She always told Suzanne that she was ugly and stupid and that she didn't want Suzanne in the first place. Do you know that she still tells Suzanne that she never wanted her? (She cries for a while as the impact of this revelation is absorbed.)

Therapist: Well I can certainly see why you wanted to hide. Tell me more about yourself.

Child: I'm really sensitive and lots of things hurt my feelings. Suzanne keeps getting into these relationships where another part of her laughs and I feel bad. Like Eric. He has lots of girlfriends and he likes them all to think he's terrific but he never really loves them. He just collects them. It hurts my feelings every time she's with him but she just gets sophisticated and laughs.

Therapist: That sounds as though it must be difficult for you. Tell me, how do you like being here now?

Child: (shyly) I really like it. I trust you and it feels good.

Suzanne embraced her Vulnerable Child very quickly. She enjoyed the very special opening of the heart energy that it brought and she wanted to seek it elsewhere. She had a great deal of strength, above average looks and intelligence and unusually good social skills to protect the Vulnerable Child. She used everything she had quite consciously. She calmly and objectively confronted Eric with the Child's observations (over an expensive dinner) and she ended her romantic involvement with him, but not her friendship.

Her next relationship, begun shortly after the introduction to this Vulnerable Child, was like none she had

ever experienced. She found herself telling about feelings and reactions immediately. She actually talked of
her past and of her mother. She verbalized each "little"
hurt and fear as it arose. And the man did likewise. For
each, it was a depth of sharing never before experienced.
It took real courage, but Suzanne was a determined
woman who learned quickly and her bravery encouraged
equal intimacy in her partner. As each risk was rewarded
with deeper mutual understanding and love, they became less fearful and more daring in this mutual exploration of their own complex humanity. This was not
always easy or pleasant, but it was deeply satisfying to
each of them. With the information provided by their
Vulnerable Children, they were able to deal on a practical level with hurts in the relationship and were able to
protect the delicious energetic interchange, that warm
pulsating energy that vibrates between people when
they are truly open and trusting.

A warning—this is not to say that all is forever perfect. There are circumstances beyond the control of the
Aware Ego that sometimes cause the Vulnerable Child
to withdraw from a relationship. But once this warmth
has been experienced it is something to strive for, to return to, and most of us are willing to experience much
discomfort in order to do so.

We would like to give you one final example of an
excerpt from a Voice Dialogue session with the Vulnerable Child. In this instance, the facilitator is asking
questions that will allow the Awareness level of the subject, Peter, to witness the requirements of the Inner
Child.

Facilitator: We've been talking so far about how lonely
things are for you and how much you feel left out in

Peter's life. Is there anything that Peter could do that might be helpful to you?

Vulnerable Child: I don't know what he could do. He always runs away from me.

Facilitator: Well, I know that—but Peter is listening to our conversation and he might learn a thing or two about you. I can't guarantee that, but Peter could learn how to be a proper parent to you. I know that he's never done it before, but it could happen.

Vulnerable Child: I'd like that. I'd feel better if he took care of me. It's especially when I get scared that I need him, and I get scared a lot. I wish he would just learn to be with me and not run away all the time. If he would just talk to me I'd feel so much better.

Facilitator: So one of the things he could do for you is just learn to be with you.

Vulnerable Child: And maybe he could save more money. I get scared when there's no money. He likes to do things with money that are scary to me. I hate the stock market. I hate the feeling that he could lose it all. He likes to gamble.

Facilitator: So now we have another thing that would make you feel better. You need the feeling of financial security. Is there anything else?

Vulnerable Child: He could show me more. Nobody knows about me. Everyone thinks Peter is strong and tough. That's what everyone sees. No one ever sees me. That makes me feel lonely. Even Margaret (his wife) doesn't know about me. He never tells her about my feelings.

As a child grows up, it is common for parents to reject its vulnerable core because life demands strength.

Additionally, parents usually have no conscious relationships to their own vulnerability. So it is that we,
too, reject our own Inner Child, further perpetuating
this ancestral disowning process. Through Dialogue
work, one hears the voice of the Child and gradually
begins to be able to take over the responsibility of child
rearing from the Protector/Controller network.

We have seen individuals do very interesting things
as they begin tuning in to the the needs of this Inner
Child. Cynthia built a large doll house and furnished it
and made clear to her children (outer children) that this
was her doll house. John constructed in his imagination
a home for the Child where he would visit him regularly.
Ann took her special pillow to sleep on when she went
on business trips. Sam started reading spy novels rather
than purely redemptive literature. Lianne got a job to
help her Child become more secure about money.
There are a multitude of different activities that support
the needs of the Child.

Once the reality of the Child has been established,
Journal writing becomes an excellent tool for working
with it. The problem in Journal writing, before the
specific pattern has been defined, is the question of
who is doing the writing. If an Aware Ego has not
separated from the Protector/Controller, then it may be
the Protector/Controller who is doing the writing.

For an Aware Ego to be able to take care of the Child
properly, it must have the Power energy available to it.
Without the Heavyweights we talked about earlier, the
Child is not safe, and generally knows it. What we aim
at here is an Aware Ego that is related to the energies of
the Heavyweights on the one side and the Vulnerability,
Playfulness and Magic on the other. This is true empowerment. Learning to be powerful and knowing how to

use our Heavyweights consciously is generally an important step in this movement toward empowerment.

THE PARADOX OF OMNIPOTENCE

When we disown our vulnerability, we identify with
our omnipotence. It feels ever so good to identify with
an omnipotent sub-personality, one which knows its
superiority to the rest of humanity. This omnipotent
voice can feel superior because of a high I.Q. or great
spirituality; as a result of achievements in life (the more
varied the better), or of intensity of feeling; good looks
and youthful appearance, or good taste, social standing
or charisma; intuition, depth of wisdom, exquisite sensitivity, efficiency, etc.

Any quality that is admired by any segment of our
society can be used to build upon and to create a sub-
personality that feels it has mastered its environment. Of
course, the sub-personality must be used in the proper
setting. It probably won't do much good to try to impress a group of psychics with the announcement that
one graduated first in the class at Harvard Law School.
Conversely, the ability to see auras and to read energy
fields is not likely to carry much weight with the admis-
sions committee in most medical schools.

At any rate, each of us has our omnipotent or "top
dog" personality that we love dearly. This sub-personality is fun to share with "like-minded" people. All the
special voices get together in a little group and feel
superior to the ordinary people out there. We can see
this in social groupings like fraternities, sororities, and
country clubs. We can see it in our educational institu-
tions—the Ivy League is special. We can see it in our

spiritual communities, many of which feel they have exclusive access to knowledge of the secrets of the universe. In contrast, we can see this in groups that see themselves as the lowest, the most dangerous, the most dissipated or the worst. Any superlative will do.

When this omnipotent or special voice takes over, we feel terrific:

> *Laura*: I was feeling so great, I couldn't believe it. I suddenly realized how clearly my mind worked, how many rich experiences I had and how much more advanced I was than all the other people around me. I felt like I could do anything, and so I started to make contacts to sell my product.
>
> *Therapist*: Let's talk to the voice that was operating on that day. (Laura moves over.) Hello there.
>
> *Special Voice*: Hi! (looking very self-confident) I really did beautifully that day. You know, Laura *is* quite special. First of all she's unusually smart—I'd tell you her exact I.Q. but she doesn't want me to brag. Actually, I *love* bragging. Then, she has a great ability to see through to the essence of a problem and do away with all the trimmings that other people waste time thinking about. She abstracts well, verbalizes well and knows how to approach people so that she gets what she wants, but never looks pushy. I think she's terrific and I tell her so. It's important to me that other people realize that as well. When they do—when they compliment her—then I'm *really* happy.

Now we come to the paradoxical part of our Special Voice. If we let it take over, if we identify with it because it feels so good, the opposite energy is not far behind. As high as the Special Voice flies, that's how low the Frightened Voice will fall. An Aware Ego will enable us to assess our assets and use them wisely and will allow us to enjoy a feeling of mastery or accomplishment, but we must be wary, for there is a certain line that must not be crossed. There is a particular feeling of self-satisfaction that is a signal that we have gone beyond an appropriate level of self-appreciation, that our Awareness level has disappeared and we have begun to identify with the Special Voice.

It does not take long before the opposite energy takes over. If the Special Voice has confidently made promises about a product, an investment, or a workshop, then the Frightened Child wonders if we will be able to back up those promises. For instance, let us see what happened to Laura after she made her phone calls.

Laura: When I finished setting up all the appointments, I suddenly became frightened about what I had done. I started to worry about all kinds of details.

Therapist: It sounds as though your Special Voice made the appointments, and then your Frightened Child took over. Let's see what she has to say.

Frightened Child: I'm scared. Just plain scared. I don't feel ready to meet those people. What if they don't like her? What if they ask questions about her products?

Therapist: Her Special Voice feels pretty good about Laura, but you don't sound so sure about her.

Frightened Child: I'm not. I worry. I worry all the time. First of all, I don't think she's done her homework. She should know more about what it is that she's trying to sell. People are pretty sophisticated these days. If she's trying to sell tax shelters, there's a lot to learn.

You know, about tax law and investment credits and about the oil drilling itself. People ask questions and I'm scared because she doesn't have the answers.

Therapist: You also said something about being scared that they won't like her.

Frightened Child: I certainly am. What if they don't like her? . . . if they don't think she's smart? Worst of all, if they can see right through her brave front and see me? I'm most scared that they'll find out about me and how scared I am. I'm only about 9 or so, and I need to be sure about things, but I'm not sure about anything anymore. Other people look so sure of themselves. I want her to be like them. I don't like me. I feel awful. Just awful! I wish she could make me feel better. Or make me go away.

Therapist: So you're afraid they'll find out about you?

Frightened Child: Sure. Then how are they going to trust her and to buy anything from her? It's hopeless . . . just hopeless. The more I think about it, the more scared I get. The more she impresses everybody else with her cleverness, the more scared I get.

Therapist: What if she doesn't promise too much?

Frightened Child: You know, that sounds a teeny bit better. After all, if she promises less, I'd have less to worry about. There'd be fewer things she'd have to know. If she'd only be able tell people that she didn't know something—that she had to look up the answer. . .

Special Voice: (interrupts here) I don't like that. You're not giving me enough credit. I bring the customers in. They need to have faith in her, to know that she knows what she's doing; that she can answer all questions.

Therapist: Can she?

Special Voice: Listen—she can figure anything out. She can learn all the answers. I told you—she's terrific. She's more clever than those people she'll be talking to. She should be able to answer all the questions. Just watch her. She can do it.

Therapist: I appreciate your feelings and I do agree that Laura is smart and special, but I'd like to go back to the part of Laura that is scared.

Special Voice: I don't like that one. I don't really believe that she needs to exist. From my point of view Laura doesn't need her.

Therapist: But she has her and we need to find out more about her needs, so that Laura can function more efficiently.

Frightened Child: Do you see why I'm scared? She wants Laura to be perfect and to impress everybody. Then I get scared that they'll find out she's not perfect and they'll make fun of her. I don't want anyone talking about her.

We see here the war that rages between the Special Voice and the Frightened Voice. The more Laura identifies with her Special Voice and needs to impress everyone with her superiority, the more frightened the Child becomes and, we might point out, the more miserable Laura feels.

As Laura begins to dis-identify from her Special Voice —as she no longer allows it to seduce her with sweet words—she begins to pay attention to her Frightened Child and to take care of some of its concerns. She does her homework. She learns the basic facts she needs so that the frightened part of her no longer has to worry about her lack of preparation. She has integrated her vulnerability and fear into her life and her work.

Most important of all, she stops looking to her Special Voice to provide her with a sense of strength. She realizes that, although she feels absolutely terrific when her Special Voice can find support and validation, this is illusory. Her real strength emerges after the integration of her vulnerability. It comes from her Awareness level and from the consciousness process itself. Her ability to sell her product is now based upon a commitment to, and a belief in, her work, rather than a need to impress others and to get something from them. Others can feel this change and will respond with increased support and realistic encouragement. Laura has finally freed herself from her special extremes of self-importance and self-doubt.

Power by itself is illusory. It depends upon one's superiority and upon the disempowerment or the inferiority of others. This is beautifully illustrated by the following dream:

Dream of Power and Disempowerment

A very well-dressed man from some middle-Eastern country is driving a huge Rolls Royce. His totally disempowered wife sits in the back seat and he makes disparaging comments to her from time to time. He thinks he knows everything. She thinks she knows nothing. Actually, his experience is limited because he comes from a very small country and it is quite different from America, where he is now driving his car. He sees a small dirt driveway off to the right and because this looks like roads look back home, he veers off and drives down it quickly. He comes to a dead end almost immediately. His wife, incidentally, could see that this was the wrong turn.

Here is a perfect picture of an omnipotent or power sub-personality. The man's superiority depends upon superficial conditions—his beautiful clothes and his Rolls Royce. His superiority is also built upon the acknowledged inferiority of his wife, who sits in the back seat while he drives the car thinking that he knows everything. He is unconscious. He does not know that he does not know. He does not even have a clue. He drives right into a dead end.

And that is the way our power sub-personalities work. They are dependent upon the disowning of our vulnerability. Although they may have acquired the trappings of success, there is no consciousness, no empowerment from within. They can be toppled by someone more powerful or they can be ousted by the Critic.

The omnipotent parts of us provide the *most* delicious feeding-grounds for our Critics. Even if nobody else can tell when we have become identified with a Special Voice, the Critic can. And the Critic will be ever so happy to let us know about our inadequacies. Let us see how this works. Arnie's Power Voice has been outlining a financial plan which would make him quite wealthy in just a short time.

Power Voice: It's quite simple. With his background and his contacts in the business, he should have it all tied up in about 8 weeks. It will only take a few calls and a little razzle dazzle.

This Power Voice is quite convincing. It could sell anyone anything . . . anyone, that it, except Arnie's Critic who had this to say about these plans:

Critic: He'll never do it. He's really good about making an impression and starting something, but he can't follow through. He has no self-discipline, and besides that, he's a coward. You know those calls he's talking about?

Therapist: Sure, what about them?

Critic: He's never going to make them. He'll procrastinate until it's too late and the whole thing falls through. He's chicken.

The Critic was right. The plans have been made by the Power Voice, but there is no real empowerment to back them up and they fade into oblivion just as so many others had before this.

We see again in these examples the basic difference between being powerful and being empowered. Being and acting powerful means that we are identified with the energy patterns on the Power side. Empowerment means that we have an Aware Ego that can honor, and to some extent embrace, both Power and, ironically enough, Vulnerability. Empowerment is certainly one of the inevitable outcomes of this whole process we are describing.

THE PLAYFUL AND THE MAGICAL CHILD

The Vulnerable Child is important in matters of relationship and empowerment. The two other aspects of the Inner Child, the Playful Child and the Magical Child, bring joy and magic to our lives. Let us see how this operates in Jon. He has been introduced to Dialogue work but this is the first time that his playful child has been out. Jon is Dutch. He is serious and hard working and respects the authority of the father.

Facilitator: From what Jon has said, I've wondered whether you would be available or not.

Playful Child: (Hereafter, Child)—Oh I'm here, but just barely. He would rather suffer than have fun. (wistfully) I could really show him how to have a good time if he'd let me. Take this workshop for example. Everyone is so serious. Jon is so serious. (He makes a mock-serious face.)

Facilitator: What would you do if you were in charge of the operation? (This is a common question used when eliciting information about a particular pattern).

Child: I would have fun. I would make faces at people. I would play tricks on people.

Facilitator: Could you show me one of your faces? (Jon makes a face at the facilitator—then a second). Those are really funny faces. What kind of tricks would you play?

The facilitator gradually leads the Playful Child into an increasing amplification of its own energy, always keeping in mind the Protector/Controller on the other side that may be objecting to what is happening. From this place, one may enter into a variety of techniques of Gestalt work, creating experiments for the Child, but always willing to reduce the risk level as the occasion requires. The facilitation of the Playful Child requires tact and whimsy.

Sean is a serious man, long involved in the spiritual movement. He has done Dialogue work before, but the facilitator on this occasion asks him whether he would like to learn something about his Magical Child. He is still a fundamentally rational man but he has learned enough about energy patterns to be intrigued by the idea. Once Sean's Magical Child is fully present, the facilitator asks the following question:

Facilitator: It seems that Sean doesn't use you very much in his life.

Magical Child: He's afraid of me. I don't make sense.

Facilitator: What do you mean—don't make sense?

Magical Child: I make up things. He (Sean) always has to make sense. I would make up stories and say things that didn't make sense.

Facilitator: Can you give me some examples?

Magical Child: Sure—The moon is blue and cheese is blue and you're blue too.

Facilitator: Well, you're a poet—and you don't know it.

Magical Child: (Beginning to get warmed up) Onions and garlic are dear to my Harlick/Nunchies and Crunchies have bunches of lunches.

Facilitator: That's really amazing. Let's play a game—I'll say a word and you make up a poem. Do you sing?

Magical Child: (Contraction occurs) I would, but he won't let me.

Facilitator: Well that's okay. Remember all this is pretty new to him (pointing to the chair of the Protector/Controller) so we have to give him the right to stop whatever is going on when things feel too uncomfortable.

It is abundantly clear that in drawing out the Magical Child, the connection of the facilitator to his or her own Magical Child is quite significant. On the other hand, it is in the role of facilitator that certain energies in ourselves are activated and then we can do the necessary work to connect to them. Thus, in facilitating the Magical Child in someone else, we can strengthen our own.

In general, the Playful Child is easier to access than the Vulnerable Child. Many people who are spiritually identified have access to the Playful Child but not to the Vulnerable Child, and they tend to confuse the two. Marie is such a person. During a session the facilitator asks:

Facilitator: Marie, could I talk to your Child—the one who carries the sensitivity and hurt?

Playful Child: Oh I'm an important part of her. We have lots of fun and she takes me very seriously. I sing a lot and I love to dance.

Playful children generally love to talk. Vulnerable children do not. The facilitator senses this and comments as follows:

Facilitator: It isn't really you that I want to talk to. It's your sister, the quiet one. Could you move over again?

Vulnerable Child: (Marie has moved over and immediately starts talking.)

Facilitator: Let's just sit quietly for a few minutes. (Facilitator makes contact with her own Vulnerable Child and simply sits quietly with Marie in the new place. After a few minutes tears start to come, slowly at first, and then with more intensity. After about 10 minutes the facilitator responds:

Facilitator: I had a feeling you were in there somewhere—How does she get rid of you so easily?

Vulnerable Child: It's easy—she loves everyone and she takes care of everyone. She has time for everyone except me. When she begins to feel small and vulnerable, she gets chatty and acts cute and playful. She doesn't really know about me (looking very woebegone).

In this excerpt, the Awareness of the facilitator helped her to sense that the Playful Child was not the real issue. Marie was convinced that she had a real connection to the Inner Child. She did, but only to one part of it.

We hope that we have demonstrated to you the beauty and complexity of the Inner Child. Without a connection to these patterns within themselves, the facilitators in Voice Dialogue work would not be able to enter into some of the deepest and most profound feeling and pain places that exist in the subjects being facilitated. Without the Inner Child, we are committed to a course of destruction in our personal lives because we are thrown over and over again into an identification with the Heavyweight sub-personalities inside of us. Their function is to attack, erect defenses, and not to show feelings, pain or need. They keep us from our deepest selves.

The discovery of the Inner Child is really the discovery of a portal to the Soul. A spirituality that is not grounded in an understanding, experience, and appreciation of the Inner Child can move people away from their simple humanity too easily. The Inner Child keeps us human. It never grows up. It only becomes more sensitive and trusting as we learn how to give it the time, care, and parenting it so richly deserves.

CHAPTER VII

THE PARENTAL SELVES

Properly speaking, the parental sub-personalities belong among the Heavyweights, for heavyweights they are. As we shall see in the next chapter, however, they occupy a unique and central position in our interpersonal relationships. In this chapter we would like to introduce you to some archetypal parental sub-personalities currently common in this society. We are well aware that parental sub-personalities differ from society to society and from one epoch to the next. We would like to start with the Nurturing Mother. Her basic grounding, although she probably does not know it, is in the philosophy of child-rearing popularized by Rousseau. In this system, the mother must be present, loving, giving, and supportive at all times so that the child will grow up brave, trusting and self-confident. A woman must similarly provide this abundance of nurturing to all those around her or the society will crumble. The early Freudian views of femininity and the importance of self-sacrifice in child-rearing give further support to this particular sub-personality.

THE NURTURING MOTHER

The Nurturing Mother is a most seductive sub-personality. It makes women feel good, and indispensable (a lovely feature for the Vulnerable Child within), and it is pleasing and comforting to those around it.

"Why," might one ask, "is there anything wrong with this?" There is nothing wrong, as we have said before, when there is an element of choice, when there is an Aware Ego present that can choose whether or not to do something for someone else. It is the same with the Good Mother as with any other sub-personality; the Good Mother is fine as long as it is not in complete control. It is the Nurturing Mother/Obedient Daughter combination that predisposes one to physical illness because the natural instincts are ignored when these patterns are in control.

When the Nurturing Mother is in operation, the woman has no choice but to give and give until she is depleted. She finds herself boxed in by dependent children, a demanding husband and needy friends. She finds herself rescuing others, cheering them up and supporting them unstintingly. Their needs are always greater than hers—in her estimation. The example of Marilyn in chapter one is a perfect illustration of this.

A Nurturing Mother will give to everyone—even to the therapist who is being paid to pay attention to her. This was touchingly illustrated by Pat who came in for her session, sat down, looked at the therapist and said, "How are you doing? You look a little tired today. Is there anything the matter?" Now, this is a hard one to resist! It's so tempting to say, "Yes, I'm a little tired" and to launch into a long conversation. But this temptation was resisted, with great effort, we might add.

Therapist: Now that certainly sounds like your Nurturing Mother Voice to me. Much as I'd love to have her take care of me, you're the one paying for the session so how about changing chairs and we'll talk to Mom. (Pat moves over to another chair and begins)

Nurturing Mother: Things haven't been going too badly for Pat, and I noticed you looked a little tired. I feel the need to see how you're doing. It's very uncomfortable for me to think that something might be troubling you, and Pat would just be talking on about her own little problems. (Note: All of Pat's problems are little ones according to this sub-personality.)

Therapist: But that's why Pat is here—to talk about herself, not to take care of me.

Nuturing Mother: I know (shrugging) but it makes me uncomfortable if anyone around her is uncomfortable. I always come in and make them feel better. That's what I did in group. I was really good. I knew just what everybody needed and I helped them a lot. I even helped the therapist sometimes. People really like having me around.

Therapist: I'll bet they do. But what happens to Pat?

Nurturing Mother: (Contentedly) Pat's strong. She can take care or herself and of everybody around her too. She likes having me around. As I said, people like me and want to be near me.

Just as the Pusher can be balanced by the energies of the Do-Nothing, so can the Nurturing Mother energies be balanced by the Selfish sub-personality. Pat's Selfish Voice sees the situation quite differently.

Selfish: I wish she'd stop giving, giving, giving all the

time. It makes me sick to my stomach! She's always available, always understanding. She'll take her son wherever he wants to go and, as far as I'm concerned, he's old enough to take himself. Then she spends hours and hours on the phone listening to her unhappy friends complain. Does she *ever* ask for anything? No! Does she ever complain? Never! Does she ever just cut a conversation short and say "I'm busy?" Never! As far as I'm concerned, she's a damned fool. And as for group, she could have taken a little attention for herself once in a while and asked for something. Instead, she made herself a damn assistant leader, for no pay, and didn't get any support at all.

As Pat's Awareness separated from the Good Mother, and this was greatly speeded up by the comments of the Selfish Voice, Pat was able to make conscious decisions. She didn't become selfish, she just became discriminating in her choices. The change was particularly apparent several weeks later when she came in and announced to the therapist, "You look a little tired and my Good Mother wants to take care of you, but I have so much to talk about today, that I want to start right in with myself."

When a woman is identified with an overly Nurturing Mother, other family members automatically identify with childlike sub-personalities. These will vary from family to family. For instance, Mildred is similar to Pat in the way she identifies with the energy pattern of Nurturing Mother. She is loving, giving, and always available. As a result of this, her daughter, Ann, has grown up to be rebellious and selfish, very much the opposite of her mother. The quality of their relationship is evident in their phone calls. When Mildred lovingly telephones Ann, Ann keeps the conversation very short. "Okay, Mom, I have to go," she says and she hangs up the phone. Her mother is crushed by this behavior over and over again.

It is Ann in this situation who comes for therapy. She is upset because she realizes that there is something wrong in the way she relates to her mother. When Ann visits her mother's home she will often take personal items that belong to her mother, without asking and without obtaining her mother's consent. These are often items that she really does not want. Mildred, although she may experience an initial burst of anger, immediately goes into her usual Mother mode and becomes quite loving, concerned, and caring again. When questioned about her feelings, she might respond: "What does it really matter? . . . I love her so much . . . It isn't worth the trouble . . . She'll learn someday."

Let us now consider what this experience is like from Ann's standpoint. The Nurturing Mother dominates the relationship. Ann has never experienced any sense of limitation. Her father leaves all child-rearing matters to the mother. The overly Nurturing Mother cannot set limits. Thus Ann is constantly being thrown into the roles of Guilty Daughter, Grabby Daughter, and Rebellious Daughter. She is never able to be herself with her mother. She never gets a realistic reaction from her mother, who also cannot be herself with Ann. Ann alternates between rejecting and fervently loving her mother.

In her work with her therapist, Ann has the following dialogue.

Therapist: Why did you take the perfume from your mother if you didn't want it?

Ann: I didn't . . . It's like something takes over in me
. . . I know it sounds silly, but that's what it's like . . .
like it isn't me.

Therapist: Could I talk to the part of you that takes
over and that wants the perfume? (Ann moves over) So,
who are you?

Taking Voice (Ann): I'm a thief. I really can't help it. I
feel like I have to steal from my mother. I know that
she'll never say anything . . . anything. I wish she
would. I wish she'd stop me once. I really can't stand
the way I am, but I can't help it. Then I feel guilty and
I hate that. I really hate her when I feel like that.

Therapist: What happens when you feel guilty? What's
the next step?

Taking Voice: Then I just want to get away from her
[Ann's mother] and I hate myself more. And her
mother gets more loving. I really love her, but I can't
stand her. I wish one time she'd slap me hard. She
never stops me and I can't stop myself.

Ann has become identified with a mode of being that
is specifically archetypal. As the daughter of a woman
who is identified with the Nurturing Mother, she becomes identified with the archetypal role of daughter,
first conforming and then rebelling. Ann had been a
Conforming Daughter until adolescence, at which time
the Rebellious Daughter took over and the hostilities
commenced. It is to be noted that not *all* daughters of
women identified with the Nurturing Mother will react
as strongly as Ann did.

Ann and her mother are caught in an archetypal
drama that is highly predictable and mathematically
precise The challenge for each of them is to develop an

Awareness that can help them to separate from these stereotyped ways of feeling, thinking and responding.

We would like to give another example of how the situation looks from the standpoint of the daughter of a woman who is identified with the Nurturing Mother. The therapist is talking with the part of Shawn (the daughter) who can never keep any secrets from her mother.

Compulsive Talker: Sometimes I'll come home from a date and my mother is waiting up for me. She doesn't say anything to make me talk, but I find myself spilling my guts every time we're together. My friends don't tell their mothers everything. I feel like I have no privacy.

Therapist: . . . and you have no choice?

Talker: None. I'm afraid not to talk. I think I have a lot of anger in me.

Therapist: You mean there's another part of Shawn that is angry?

Talker: Yeah. She's afraid for it to come out.

Shawn feels that she loves her mother, but she feels trapped. The loving, nurturing, protective side of her mother is very strong and has crystallized in Shawn a part that has become bonded to it. This part is the Compulsive Talker, a part that has become so powerful that it has entirely taken over Shawn's relationship with her mother. Thus, Shawn shares intimacies, and the relationship looks close; but beneath this apparent closeness, there is anger and resentment.

The term "Bonding" refers to the fact that the two archetypal patterns, Nurturing Mother and Compulsive

Talker, have joined together without the benefit of an Awareness level. Shawn has begun to be aware of this bonding, and of another set of feelings; she has begun to be aware of the resentment that lies beneath the closeness. This does not mean that she does not love her mother or that she will never talk to her again. Our hope is only to help her to become aware of the conflicting feelings so that she has a *real* choice in what she says and what she does not say to her mother.

THE GOOD FATHER

Equally as seductive as the Nurturing Mother, is the Good Father. Who can resist a combination of "Father Knows Best," "Marcus Welby," John Walton and King Arthur? Our culture has developed an impossible ideal for its fathers as well as for its mothers. A Good Father is steadfast, responsible, loving, understanding, helpful, and gently humorous. He always knows the right thing to do and he does it without fanfare. He can set right any situation from a flat tire to a broken heart. And he never gets tired or needs helps. What a burden!

Good Fathers surround themselves with helpless children. The Good Father who does his daughter's homework might still be writing her term papers for her in college. The Good Father who takes care of everything for his wife will get midnight phone calls well after his divorce when the dishwasher overflows or the pool heater breaks. Just as the Good Mother bonds in with the needy, the Good Father bonds in with the helpless. Just as the Good Mother is loved by all around her, so is the Good Father.

A Good Father is a handy thing for a woman to have around. Just ask someone who is married to one. They shoulder all the responsibility, financial and emotional, and they usually do much of the maintenance work around the house. In fact, they do so much that many times their wives become infantalized and have trouble taking care of themselves. The Helpless Daughter bonds in with the Good Father, and all other sub-personalities atrophy.

The Good Father finds himself trapped by his compulsive need to be responsible for everyone and everything around him. He finds himself surrounded by people who leave decisions up to him or who do not bother taking care of details because they know that he will. He is indispensable. But at what a cost!

Just as a Nurturing Mother will trouble herself about the psychological needs of the therapist, a Good Father will unobtrusively put a new bottle of water in the therapist's waiting room. What a delight.

Bob's Good Father was firmly bonded in to his ex-wife's Helpless Daughter. Bob was trying to make vacation plans, but his Good Father kept getting in the way as the vacation was discussed.

Therapist: (to Bob) Wait a minute, I'm confused. I thought that you were going to stay at the ski resort until Sunday and now you're planning to come back on Friday. Let's talk to your Good Father again. (Bob moves over)

Good Father: I think he should come back on Friday. Angela (his ex-wife) has had a bad cold and she might need him to help with the children over the weekend. If she feels better, she wants to go to Palm Springs and he'll need to take care of the dog.

Therapist: Can't she get a baby-sitter or send the dog to a kennel?

Good Father: (horrified at these suggestions) No, I couldn't let her do that. I'd feel too guilty. Bob couldn't have a good time.

Therapist: You certainly make it tough for Bob to take a vacation. He was really looking forward to this one. He hasn't taken one in a year.

Good Father: (Virtuously smiling in a superior way) He'll have plenty of other chances. Right now he's needed here.

Actually, the Good Father's version of being needed doesn't necessarily correspond to the situation. In this case, the Good Father had the last word. Bob came home early from his vacation. Angela felt better and went to Palm Springs with the children. The children refused to leave the dog at home and Bob's sacrifice went totally unnoticed. Needless to say, the Good Father disappeared and the Negative Father took over.

THE NEGATIVE FATHER

As the Good Father convinces us to do more than we would do if we were making conscious choices, the Negative Father is building up an equal and opposite energy. After Bob's sacrifice of several prime days of skiing went unnoticed, the Negative Father came out in full force.

The Negative Father, in this instance, was judgmental and punitive:

Negative Father: I don't like the way Angela is handling the kids. She's mean to the older one and she's spoiling the younger one. I keep telling the older one not to listen to her. That's the best way I know of handling the situation. "Just ignore your mother" I say. Then we wink at each other. (When Bob was not in his Negative Father, he was quite comfortable with Angela's child-rearing).

Therapist: I'll talk to Bob about that a little later. In the meantime, I see that you're really angry at Angela. What else has you upset?

Negative Father: The way she spends money. She seems to think I have an unlimited supply. (Here, too, we have an alternation of the Good Father and the Negative Father without an intervening Aware Ego. The Good Father automatically paid *all* the bills and the Negative Father got angry.)

Negative Father: She uses up all the money Bob gives her within a week. And then she charges things on her credit cards and sends him the bill. He pays them all and I'm furious. Now she wants money to fix the roof of the house. She says that there's mildew on the walls in a few places and it really smells. *I* decided not to let him pay for that one. I don't think she should be in the house anyway. It's too expensive. Thank God, he lets me draw the line somewhere.

Until Bob learns to take the decision making power away from his Good Father, he is doomed to seesaw between giving too much in the Good Father and withholding and punishing in the Negative Father. This is often a difficult step forward in consciousness because others have a tendency to pull for the Good Father. As one of our children, Claudia, asked pointedly, "Isn't there some way of locking in Hal's Good Father and keeping it there forever?" No, Claudia, there isn't. If you get the Good Father (and Hal's is one of the most delicious), the Negative Father is never far behind.

THE NEGATIVE MOTHER

The Negative Mother has been shown in all her glory as the witch of the fairy tales. She destroys or she devours. The Nurturing Mother makes all kinds of sacrifices and, as in the case of the Negative Father, the Negative Mother is rarely far behind. The Nurturing Mother understands all and accepts all until her opposite appears.

Karen came to therapy because she was feeling depressed and irritated. She had been a nurturing mother and supportive wife for years, and now everything about her husband and children irritated her. Her sex drive had disappeared totally and she felt despondent about her life. She was surprised to discover the variety of sub-personalities that flourished in this apparently arid desert of her life. But none released more energy than the Negative Mother.

Therapist: How about talking to the part of you that is always irritated?

Karen: I don't see what good that would do, that's what my problem is. I'm trying to get over this irritation and back to my old good-natured self.

Therapist: It sounds like somebody in there is afraid of your irritation. Don't worry, we don't want you to become an impossible bitch. All we want to do is to give your irritated voice a chance to speak so that you can figure out if there's anything she can do to help you.

Karen: Okay. All the other voices have been helpful. But you're right. I *am* afraid of this one.

(She changes her chair, assumes an irritable and angry expression and the Negative Mother begins to speak:)

Negative Mother: Everything any of them does irritates me. Everything. The way they talk, the way they look. I just feel like making them change or pushing them away. I'd really hurt them if I could. Sometimes I feel that I could even murder someone. I get so angry. (pause) I just wish they'd all disappear and leave Karen alone. I can't stand any of them to touch her. If her husband kisses her, I want to shove him away. When her children hug her, I want to hit them. They all drive me crazy!

Therapist: It's no wonder that you frighten Karen. Tell me, what are some of the things that drive you crazy?

Negative Mother: They're always grabbing and she's always giving.

Therapist: What do you mean by that?

Negative Mother: When her son's car stalls because he's run out of gas, she's off to rescue him. Immediately. I think she should let him sweat it out a bit. Let him be late for his date and let his date be angry. But no, Super Mom here drops everything she's doing and is off for an hour to do works of mercy. It makes me sick! (with disgust)

Therapist: You don't like it when she takes care of everybody?

Negative Mother: You've got it! Big Mama here takes care of everyone. Madame Martyr, I call her. I couldn't care less if she never did anything for any of them again. And she needs to support that husband too. He gets nervous and she loses sleep. Super Mom can't let him keep his insomnia to himself. She has to get up and worry with him. And she's so understanding. I'm not. I just get angry. But she doesn't let me react. She smiles prettily and stays helpful.

Therapist: How do you come out?

Negative Mother: When she's not looking. I'm the one who makes those nasty comments about her husband when they're out socially. She doesn't know why she does it, but it's me. Somehow Super Mom doesn't have the same power in a social setting. And (smiling) if she has a couple of drinks, I can get pretty sharp. I know just how to get to him.

Therapist: Oh, so it was you. She was wondering who did that. How do you come out with the children?

Negative Mother: I let them know how hopeless I think they are. Super Mom is always trying to encourage them. You know, she builds up their dear little egos (sarcastically). I just let them know how they're doing things wrong. How ugly and stupid and not nice they are. I'm pretty subtle though. Sometimes it's just a look or a shrug. Mostly I criticize and push them away. I can't stand clinging.

Therapist: It sounds as though with this Super Mom around, Karen gets nothing much for herself. Everyone else comes first.

Negative Mother: You bet. She's been trying to read the same novel for six weeks. I'd have her lock her bedroom door and read for two hours a day.

Therapist: That doesn't sound like a bad idea.

Negative Mother: Do you mean that? Really? Nobody ever thought I had a good idea before (suspiciously)

Therapist: Well, sometimes a woman needs some time off from being Super Mom. What else would you have her do?

The therapist spent additional time with this Negative Mother. Karen had become so identified with her Nurturing Mother that all choices were immediately decided in favor of other family members. Karen's Pusher and Critic drove her on to do more and more for everyone else and criticized her for her selfishness if she dared to think of herself. The Negative Mother was under great pressure. It was disowned, but it was full of reactions.

As we listened to the Negative Mother, she was encouraged to go over specific instances where she felt Karen had made unconscious choices. This previously disowned Negative Mother came up with new ideas and creative solutions to old problems once her initial bitterness wore off. Karen was able to listen to her opinions and suggestions and to choose more consciously what she would and would not do for others. She became less depressed and irritable as these energies were released, and she no longer felt trapped by her Super Mom subpersonality. And her Negative Mother, now that Karen listened to it, was no longer daemonic. It no longer came out unexpectedly to take vicious jabs at Karen's family.

The Negative Mother appears for a good reason. It appears, as does the Bad Father, to balance a system that is unbalanced. When a woman doesn't listen to it, she finds herself, as did Karen, making nasty remarks to her family, talking about them with her friends, and feeling trapped, extremely irritable, and hopeless.

With the introduction of Awareness, the trap is sprung and the system can go through a natural balancing process. We feel discomfort for a reason. Our Negative Mothers and Bad Fathers are angry for a reason. If we listen to their sides of the story, we have a chance to restore the natural balance of energies.

We might note that sometimes, although this is less common, the Negative Mother or Bad Father predominates and the other side gets ignored. Then the Nurturing Mother and the Good Father become angry and irritable and they bring forth their demands for more concern for the well-being of others. Here too, with the introduction of Awareness, the system gets balanced out in the other direction.

THE RATIONAL PARENT

The Rational Parent is more often seen in men than in women and, sooner or later, it bonds in with some form of the emotionally reactive child in the other person. They dance a most delicious dance together. A typical interchange sounds like this:

Carol: (from an Aware Ego) I was really upset yesterday when you ignored me and made plans for the holidays. I felt left out. I'd like to talk about it.

Ted's Rational Father: (Cool and collected) What do you mean you were upset?

Carol: Upset, you know, *hurt*. I felt left out.

Rational Father: (Somewhat distant) I don't understand. Why should you feel left out?

Carol: (beginning to feel uncomfortable) I felt left out because you left me out. You didn't ask me how I felt.

Rational Father: (with a bit of disdain) You're overly upset over this. What seems to be the problem? I don't understand.

Carol's Rebellious Daughter: Nothing's the problem. I thought we were going to plan our holidays together. Since you planned yours by yourself, I'll go to Club Med in Martinique! (and she stomps out of the room).

It is almost impossible to resist the power of the Rational Father. He is always cool and in command. The more rational he gets, the more irrational the other will sound. The thing to remember about Rational Fathers, is that they are as trapped as we feel when we're talking to them. If one can maintain objectivity and, above all, humor, there is a chance of breaking the spell. If not, enjoy! There's nothing like a Rational Father to provoke a wild display of passion in a rebellious Angry Child, and that can be great fun. Once a woman was so infuriated by the Rational Father in her boyfriend that she said "I'm so angry that I could bite through this little branch." And she did. They were both instantly freed because this was so funny that they both burst into gales of laughter. Her action was unexpected and shocking, causing the Awareness level of each to be automatically alerted. Thus, it was two Aware Egos rather than a Rational Father and and Angry Daughter who were interacting.

CHAPTER VIII

THE CONSCIOUSNESS MODEL

The Dance of the Selves

THE ARCHETYPAL ENERGY FLOW WITHIN US

We have talked a great deal about the different parts of us, about how we might identify with them or disown them, and about how each has its polar opposite which operates either consciously or unconsciously. Each of these parts, as we have said, is a distinct energy pattern. Until now, we have concentrated upon the way in which these energy patterns behave as individual subpersonalities within ourselves. Now we will broaden our Awareness and move into the area of interpersonal relationships. This chapter will be concerned with the way in which these energy patterns interact with others in the world around us.

Let us review briefly the essence of the developmental process. We are born into this world as very vulnerable children. We remain in this position of vulnerability for an extended period of time. The first energy pattern that develops to protect this vulnerability, and this happens fairly early in life, is the Protector/Controller, the major sub-personality in the Parental Control pattern. This Protector/Controller becomes the guiding agent of the personality and utilizes other parts to create its protective screen. It becomes what most people think of as their Ego. As the years pass, the move from vulnerability to power accelerates. It is not fun to remain vulnerable. One must control one's environment, and so the Protector/Controller becomes ever more the authority as it organizes its team of Heavyweights and parental patterns that we discussed earlier.

As we look at the many energies or sub-personalities discussed thus far, we see that they represent opposites on a power/vulnerability continuum. We call the power pole the parental side and the vulnerability pole the child side. In all of us, our energies are constantly moving between these two sides. This archetypal and continuous energy movement can be conceptualized as follows:

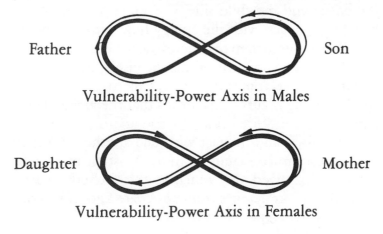

Father   Son

Vulnerability-Power Axis in Males

Daughter   Mother

Vulnerability-Power Axis in Females

FIGURE 1

This energy flow between power and vulnerability is
going on within us all the time. Generally, it is happening without our Awareness. We cannot stop it, because
it is an archetypal process. It is interesting to note that
these represent a balanced system of energies. The Son/
Daughter side which represents lack of control, and vulnerability, is every bit as large as the Father/Mother side
which represents power and control. We may not always
be aware of this balance because of our tendency to
identify with one end of this power continuum and to
disown the other. As our Awareness increases, however,
both the archetypal movement of energy and this balance within each of us become more and more apparent.
We will see what effect this Awareness has upon our behavior later in our discussion.

ENERGY PATTERNS IN RELATIONSHIP

Now that we have an understanding of our own intrapsychic energy flow between the parental side which has
the power and the child side which does not, let us see
how this interacts with the energy flow within someone
else. When our archetypal energy flow comes into direct
and constant contact with someone else's, as is the case
in a primary relationship, such as marriage, an archetypal bonding occurs. This means that the archetypes of
parent and child are drawn to one another with mag-
netic intensity and interact with one another in a most
marvelously unconscious fashion. Most primary relationships are lived very much at this archetypal level
without any interference from an Aware Ego. Let us diagram this archetypal bonding pattern:

We see clearly in Figure 2 how the archetypal bond-

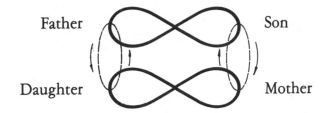

Father · Son

Daughter · Mother

Archetypal Bonding Between a Man and a Woman

FIGURE 2

ing works energetically. The energies of the man continue to flow between his father side and his son side; the energies of the woman continue to flow between her mother side and her daughter side; but something new and powerful is added. The mother side of the woman bonds powerfully with the son side of the man and the father side of the man bonds powerfully with the daughter side of the woman. Thus, the parent within each of us bonds with the child in the other and the child within each of us bonds with the parent in the other. This attraction is energetic; it is inevitable. The parent-child bonding occurs independently of sex or age. The same kind of bonding will occur, to one degree or another, in *all* important relationships.

The energy involved in this bonding is that energy which bonds us and binds us to the familiar. It is analogous, in anthropological terms, to the endogamous principle in a primitive tribe. Endogamy would be that principle which requires the young man to marry within the tribe. The opposite energy would be the exogamous principle. This is the principle that requires the young man to marry outside the tribe, to cross the river to wed a stranger; it encourages adventure, exploration and expansion.

The Introduction of Consciousness
to Archetypal Bonding

Thus far, we have been talking about relationships as they are lived, without consciousness, on a purely archetypal bonding level. It is possible, however, to become aware of these archetypal bonding patterns. As Awareness is brought into this system, so that the Awareness level begins to witness the father-daughter and mother-son aspects of a relationship, the Ego can now take advantage of this new information. Thus, we introduce consciousness to the archetypal bonding that operates in relationship. Let us see how this would look in a diagram.

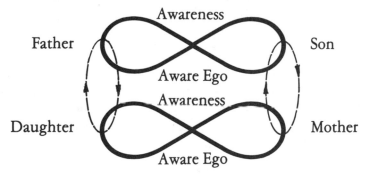

Archetypal Bonding with Consciousness

FIGURE 3

We can see in Figure 3 that our three conditions for consciousness are being met. We have here the dance of the sub-personalities: Father to Daughter and Mother to Son. We have an Awareness that is separate from this archetypal bonding, and is witnessing the interplay of energies. Lastly, the Aware Ego is outside of the energetic bonding, aware of what is happening.

In introducing Awareness to the archetypal bonding, we find that two changes occur in the bonding pattern. First, there is a change in the mathematics of the Father/ Son and Mother/Daughter axes. They diminish perceptibly. The "dance" between them becomes less automatic and it lasts for a shorter period of time. A bonding that might take a month or so to dissipate when there is no Awareness, may dissolve within a few days or a few hours.

Secondly, since the Awareness and the Aware Ego are both points outside of the bonding system itself, the individuals involved in the relationship are able to meet at these levels at the same time as their sub-personalities are embroiled in an archetypal bonding. This is very significant in relationship, since it provides some measure of objectivity.

It is interesting to note that there seems to be an equivalence of energies in each of the four parts of the archetypal bonding patterns. We like to think of this bonding as a "dance of the sub-personalities" that would be somewhat like a minuet by Mozart, perfectly balanced and flawlessly performed. The more one looks at these patterns from a position of Awareness, the more one is impressed by this balance. If one could quantify them, some sort of Pythagorean model for the interaction of sub-personalities might emerge.

BONDING PATTERNS IN RELATIONSHIP

A Classic Archetypal Bonding

Let us now look at some concrete examples and see how these ideas apply in primary relationships. We will start with a thirty-six-year-old business executive who is very much identified with the father archetype and is cut off from his vulnerability. This doesn't mean that his vulnerability isn't operating. It just means that it is operating unconsciously. His Vulnerable Child is being taken care of in some relationship—perhaps by his wife, or perhaps by his efficient office manager. Our executive, Larry, simply does not know about it. One day, he receives bad news about his business. He feels quite anxious and vulnerable but this does not last long. Let us look at this in our diagram. If we imagine that Figure 4 is a race track, then we would see Larry spending his days driving very slowly around the Father turn, because he has been trained to live in that Father mode, and quickly past the Son side. When the bad news comes, he feels vulnerable. To avoid experiencing this vulnerability, he speeds up, races at about 2,000 miles per hour around the Son curve to get back to the more familiar Father side. Feelings such as vulnerability, dependency, weakness, anything other than being in charge, are quite reprehensible to this power side. He comes home later that afternoon to find his wife, Rachel, reading a story to their four-year-old daughter.

Now Rachel is a daughter type of woman. She is a perfect mother to her daughter and a daughter to her husband. She loves Larry very much, but from her Daughter side she is a guilt machine. On the Mother side, she is *always* responsible. If a meteor fell from

Father   Son

FIGURE 4 (Larry)

space and hit her husband on the the arm, she would find a way to make it her responsibility. Bonding patterns characteristically behave in this way, daughter and mother archetypal energy patterns interchanging with amazing rapidity and intensity.

To return to our example, when Larry opens the door, Rachel immediately feels guilty. She doesn't know why, but she does. What has actually happened is that Larry has arrived home in the sub-personality of the Punishing Father. He has raced away from his earlier feeling of upset and vulnerability and has done what most men do with great expertise. He has gone into a deep freeze. His mind is sharp and he is utterly without feeling. Rachel's Guilty Daughter comes out to meet this Punishing Father.

In bonding patterns, the Father will have his Daughter and the Daughter will have her Father. It is like two elements in chemistry coming together. Hydrogen will have its oxygen. Oxygen will have its hydrogen. That is the nature of bonding in relationships. Larry does not deliberately set out to be mean and to be the Father to Rachel's Daughter side. Larry actually does not exist as a conscious human being at this point. There is only the Punishing Father and this archetype must be joined with its polar opposite. Larry, as the Punishing Father, walks in the door and immediately Rachel is in the Daughter energy. She senses that something is wrong and, as the Daughter, feels guilty. She asks Larry, still as the Daughter, because there is no Rachel around at that moment: "Is anything wrong?"

We can learn to tune into these Father/Mother/Son/Daughter patterns. It is rarely the content of the conversation that matters. It is the vibration, the sound of the voice, the inflection. One *could* say "Is anything wrong?'' from an Aware Ego, but Rachel does not do this. Guilty Daughters will ignite and intensify Negative Fathers, and this is just what Rachel does. From that Punishing Father place, now more negative because it is being fed, Larry replies curtly "No." He then goes into the bedroom to change and then makes himself a drink, pointedly not making one for her. War games are ready to erupt, and then full-scale war.

Rachel puts the child to bed and comes back into the living room. Larry's Father side is intensifying its heat. The archetypal energy is flowing now with all the rage and aggression that Larry could not release at work. He says to Rachel, "Do you *always* have to read to that child? Don't you *ever* do anything else? Every time I see you, you're with her." Underneath this, of course, is his vulnerability. He is frightened. His job could be lost and they could lose the house. From his power side it is impossible for him to think of Rachel working. He wouldn't want it. Now, however, Larry's Inner Child is unsure because if Rachel worked, he would feel safer. Larry isn't aware of any of this, so he is thrown more strongly back into the Father archetype. It is all quite predictable, very much like a Greek tragedy.

In her position as the Daughter, Rachel's feelings are hurt. She doesn't know what she has done wrong. Finally, as Larry intensifies his attack, she gets angry. Now, as Rebellious Daughter/Angry Mother, she says venomously, "If you would ever come home early enough to do something with her, I wouldn't always have to be the one reading to her. I'm sick and tired of you and your business. You're a rotten father. I never see you. You come into the house like a dark cloud."

In reaction to this Angry Mother, Larry of course is deeply wounded. Since he has no access to these feelings of hurt, he shifts ever more deeply into the Punishing Father until some grand explosion occurs. Eventually there will be a kind of "making up." This can happen a thousand times with no change in consciousness occurring. For consciousness to change, there must be an awareness of the energetic bonding that is taking place between them.

Larry and Rachel have had this dreadful argument over a matter that has nothing to do with the real issue. This is a fairly typical example of how we behave when we are gripped by an archetype. We are inflamed with passion, feel positively righteous about our positions, say the same things time after time, and never realize that we, as Aware Egos, do not exist. If Larry were aware of his vulnerability, he might come home and say something like, "Rachel, I'm terribly upset and need to talk. Could you put our child to sleep a little early?" He would communicate his need in some way. It is highly unlikely that they would have had an argument. People rarely react to an expression of vulnerability with anger.

From her side, if she were not so identified with the Daughter role, Rachel might have said to her husband, from an Aware Ego, "Look, I know that you're upset. I'll be with you in a moment and we'll talk." Remember, it is rarely the content of the statement, but rather the vibration or energy pattern through which it is expressed, that matters.

If one person is locked into the archetype and the other is able to disengage from it and becomes able to speak with something of an Aware Ego present, he or she generally tends to induct the other into some level of Awareness. This is generally, but not always, the case. The experience of being trapped in the archetypal "minuet," recognizing it and then stepping off the "dance floor" despite the other person, feels like being released from prison.

The Dream Process Enhances the Development of Awareness

Lois and Phil have been married for many years. They basically have a happy marriage, although with the passage of time, Lois has experienced increasing dissatisfaction as she becomes less of a daughter to him. She is particularly unhappy about her inability to say "no" to him when he wants to have sexual relations and she does not. At such times, her Guilty Daughter usually requires her to say "yes." One evening this happens and she is very aware of how much she is going against her real feelings. Although she says "yes," her Awareness level is now operating. That night she dreams she is having sexual relations with her father and wakes up feeling horrified.

So long as Lois continues to say "yes" to Phil in the Daughter energy, they remain bonded. He is locked into the Needy Child and the Guilt-Inducing Father. She responds to the Needy Son as Mother and to the Guilt-Inducing Father as Daughter, though the Guilty Daughter is her predominant feeling.

It may seem strange to our readers that we use capital letters to describe these energy patterns. We do it deliberately to emphasize the autonomy and reality of these parts. We capitalize "Phil" as a proper name. When the Guilt-inducing Father is operating, "Phil" ceases to exist. What was "Phil" is now "Father." Only as Awareness enters does Phil again emerge, or possibly only then is he born for the first time.

The dream of Lois further activates the Awareness

level which has already begun to emerge. Her unconscious is now making a clear statement to her. It is saying something like this: "My dear Lois, it's time you realized that when you say yes to Phil, as Daughter, it is the same as though you were having sexual relations with your father. You were always Good Girl to your father and were always pleasing him. Now you continue to be the Good Girl and to please your husband. I (the unconscious) am not interested in whether or not you have sexual relations. What does interest me is that you stop behaving like the Pleasing Daughter that you have been all your life. I would like to see you make real choices in these matters."

Needless to say, we have put in our two cents along with the statement of the unconscious. One of the sad things about such bonding patterns is that Phil can never feel fully satisfied with this type of sexual experience because at some deep level he senses that the woman is not there. If the Daughter makes love, then Lois, the woman, cannot be there. Being there, wherever "there" is, means having a real choice as to whether or not you *want* to be there.

The Denial of Negative Feelings in Archetypal Bonding

A woman consults a therapist because of an increasing sense of constriction in her life. This has reached a point where she is almost afraid to leave her home. She is constantly fearful of her husband dying. A few days before she called for her first visit, she had an anxiety attack when her husband left her alone in a restaurant in order to make a phone call.

After a few visits, during which an acceptable level of

trust was established, the therapist asks to talk to the part of her that wishes her husband dead so that she could be free. She is quite shocked at first, but is able to move into that part and explore it. From that moment on, a profound change occurs in her life. It quickly becomes apparent that she has denied her negative feelings toward her husband and her marriage. By doing so, she has become more and more of the Daughter and, eventually, the Victim Daughter. Thus, she relates to her husband as a Daughter most of the time and, in order to balance this, she is a full-time, always-understanding Mother who is unable to say "no" to her children. This identification with the Victim Daughter/ Martyr Mother leads to an ever-increasing sense of entrapment, a feeling that may well lead to physical illness. Sometimes this can be of a very serious nature, because death might be more attractive than the feeling of imprisonment that comes from being locked into this particular archetypal dance. And all of this can go on without the woman having any idea of what is happening.

The discovery that there is a part of her that hates her husband does not end their marriage. The marriage has ended, from our perspective, many years before. What this discovery does is to create a new possibility for the marriage. It gives her the chance to experience many different parts of herself that are operating in relation to her husband and to the marriage. There is now an Awareness level operating outside the bonding patterns. Her husband has not yet developed an Awareness level, but she has something to work with, and most of the symptoms that were troubling her clear up fairly quickly even without her husband's awareness.

"It Takes Two to Tango"

A man is standing at the door waiting to go to a dinner party on a Saturday night. His wife is dressing; it is 8:00 P.M. and the party is scheduled for 8:00 P.M. He asks with great irritability, "Why can't you get home on time? What do you do that's so damned important you can't be more considerate?" The wife, already feeling like a Guilty Child, tries to placate him: "I had the most interesting afternoon. I was at the museum and I met Anna and her husband. She's a Docent there now. . . . " and on and on.

In that voice, she wishes to quiet the angry waters. However, the more the Daughter placates, the more the Father rages. After all, right is on his side. She *is* late. She is *always* late. Why can't she be on time? As the Father, he is filled with righteousness. The Father has her nailed for the 342nd time. This husband has played out the same archetypal bonding over and over again, never realizing that his delicious rage is locking him into a prison which he is creating for himself.

What can we advise our friend at the door? We do not have solutions for such situations. What we offer to him is the possibility of stepping back into an Awareness level and, from there, beginning to appreciate the fact that he and his wife are in a special kind of dance with one another. It is not just her dance; they dance it together. The Angry Father or Angry Mother would have us think it was the other's dance alone. We never dance alone! Never! Never! Never!

When we become aware of a Father-Daughter or Mother-Son pattern, we always see that it is a dance involving two sub-personalities, one from each side. It is most difficult to see where this dance starts. But if our friend can begin to step out of his Father-Daughter dance, and if an Aware Ego becomes available to him, then he has options that he did not have before. He may be able to let his wife know how embarrassed he is and how vulnerable he feels when he is late. He might share his feelings of inadequacy at parties and how they are exacerbated when he is late. She may then share what it was like growing up with her father who was very punctual; how she hated having dinner at 6:00 every night and going to bed at 9:00 on the dot. Thus, what for years has been a repetitive, non-redemptive melodrama becomes a meaningful sharing, as the Awareness level comes into operation and witnesses the archetypal drama, and the Aware Ego comments upon it.

The Avoidance of Archetypal Bonding

John and Mary are on a holiday with their children. John is preparing for a major lecture and is somewhat nervous about it. It is Monday morning and the lecture is Wednesday night. Mary suggests that the family go into town sightseeing. John has three or four more hours of work remaining and they are leaving the following morning. Despite this, he thinks that it would be nice to spend some time in town with the children. This decision is not a real choice, however. It is the choice made by his ever giving Good Father, a part of John that frequently takes over in his relationship with his family.

This Good Father is always doing things that are nice, that are pleasing to the family. The family, we might add, is quite fond of the Good Father. He is over-responsible and has a very difficult time allowing John to take care of his own needs. He does, however, do a marvelous job taking care of everyone else's needs. In the situation we are describing, John is feeling quite vulnerable at the prospect of the major lecture that lies ahead of him. Because he is unaware of this vulnerability, he shifts into the more comfortable energy of the Good Father and thus makes everyone happy. The reality is that the others would have been very happy going into town without him. The Responsible Father just loves to see himself at the center of everything and indispensable to the rest of the family.

After a few hours in town, John's anxiety begins to reassert itself. At this point, since he is still not in touch with his vulnerability, his Good Father begins to move into the irritable, Negative Father. He becomes tired and edgy. The archetype of the Father shifts dramatically from positive to negative.

Mary has had some experience with archetypes and bonding patterns in this relationship. She knows the warning signs and she suggests that they go home because he seems tired and probably is anxious to get back to work on his forthcoming lecture. John feels relieved, but the archetype has taken over and, even though there is some Awareness operating, it is too late for him to free his energies. The rest of the day he is edgy and makes semi-critical comments about a variety of matters. Mary, recognizing the Negative Father in action, recognizing also that she is not in any way responsible, artfully avoids engaging this Father side.

Once an archetype has been activated and takes over one person in a relationship, it is a Herculean task not to be influenced by its energies. The Father will have his Daughter. The Daughter will have her Father. An

Aware Ego gives us a chance to make some choices about being bonded in this manner. Such is the situation with Mary as she avoids John's attacking Father. This is easier said than done because the power and intelligence of the attacking Father is rather awesome to behold. That night, Mary has the following dream:

Dream of John Throwing Matches

I am with John. He is throwing lighted matches at me. I keep dodging them. Then he gets angry with me and wants to know why it is that I keep dodging his matches. He says that I shouldn't be jumping around so much because it is irritating him.

John's anger over the fact that Mary is dodging his matches is a beautiful portrayal of how the Negative Father operates in relationship. It demands a Daughter response from the woman. It wants her to feel guilty and apologetic. It would love to see her reduced to tears; perhaps it wants the big scene, a passionate argument. Only in this way can the tension be reduced. It is by moving into the power place that the man can dominate totally, that the man (from the place of the Negative Father) can fully eradicate the nagging anxiety of his inner Vulnerable Child.

If John were truly in touch with his vulnerability, he would be able to say to Mary something like: "You have to excuse the way I am today. The fact is that I'm damned anxious about this lecture and I can't seem to get on top of it. I'm really sorry about my irritability." The lack of awareness of one's own vulnerability is the basic factor in many of the bonding patterns between people. When we do not know our hurt, or pain, or fear, we unconsciously race around to our power sides to feel better. This is true of individuals and—more dangerous for our planet—*it is also true of nations*.

Adolescence Breaks a Bonding

Jordan and his daughter, Nancy, had a good relationship in the years preceding Nancy's adolescence. He was a loving father, although perhaps a little too identified with her since she was his only daughter. (We have noticed that the degree of identification with children is generally inversely related to the intensity of relationship that exists between the husband and wife.) Jordan's marriage was less than fair, and Nancy hooked into a special place in his heart because of a certain depth that was missing in the marriage itself. Thus, Jordan was identified to a considerable degree with the good and loving Father.

With Nancy's adolescence, there was a shift. When she came home a little late one evening, after being out with a group of friends, her father started scolding her in a way that he never had before. He warned her about becoming a tramp and, whereas prior to this time they had been very affectionate with each other, all outer forms of touching were suddenly ended.

Nancy was heartbroken. She did not know what had happened. She had not done anything wrong, yet she was feeling guilty. Soon, however, this guilt turned to anger. She would pay him back for his withdrawal. She began to give him the "cold treatment." She began to stay out later. From the Loving Daughter she became the Rebellious Daughter. Her father became more punitive and more withdrawn.

Jordan had lived an essentially bonded relationship to his daughter. One of the aspects of bonding in relationship is that many feelings between the two people never reach awareness. Resentments, sexuality, reactions that would have a generally separating effect are locked up as compressed energy within the bonding pattern. It is not unlike two molecules that bond together. When the bonding is broken, enormous energy is released. So it is in interpersonal relationships. When bonding patterns are broken, a great deal of energy is released. Usually, anger is a part of the energy.

The feeling of betrayal that is so common in relationships is basically a function of bonding patterns. It means that we have locked into someone on the parent/child axis. This person does something that hurts us deeply—he or she breaks the bonding by some bit of behavior—and suddenly we are feeling injured, betrayed and very angry.

Jordan and Nancy were bonded at the level of Good Loving Father and Good Loving Daughter. At yet another level, Nancy was Mother to Jordan's Vulnerable Child. This is a very common phenomenon in parent-child relations. Sometimes at very young ages, a child can become the parent to the real parent.

What is it that happened between Jordan and his daughter Nancy that made such an idyllic relationship turn negative so quickly? First of all, Nancy's budding adolescent development was stirring in her father his latent sexuality. This is perfectly normal under any circumstances, but where a marriage relationship is not deeply nourishing, there is a sensual energy that moves from the marriage to one or more of the children.

This latent energy suddenly begins to stir in Jordan. His training, quite unconscious and quite subtle, requires him to kill these feelings. After all, how can a father feel sexual toward his daughter? He must kill his sexuality. He must kill this set of sensations within him. Since he is not aware of them, since this energetic is so disowned, a part of him takes over that becomes critical and judgmental toward the daughter's blossoming sensuality. The negative Judgmental Father has taken over from the Good Father. From the daughter's standpoint, it is like Dr. Jekyll and Mr. Hyde. She does not know what hit her.

There is another critical factor in this transformation. Nancy has played the mother to Jordan's little boy. She would get his slippers and give him the newspaper and do many things that made his Vulnerable Child feel very good. This is exaggerated in many families because most people do not know about their inner vulnerable children and hence do nothing to feed them and take care of them. With the emergence of adolescence, Nancy is less available and takes care of him less. He misses her. His Inner Child is hurt because she is not around as much. If his vulnerability is unconscious, however, how can Jordan deal with these feelings? He cannot. If they were available to him he might say something like—"You know Nancy, I really miss you, and I'm even a little bit jealous of all the fun you're having." Please understand that we are not suggesting that he should say this, only that these feelings would be available to him.

Since these feelings are unconscious, Jordan is forced still farther into patriarchal consciousness where he becomes increasingly judgmental, bitter, lonely and frustrated. It is in this condition that he finally seeks help.

What Jordan had to become aware of was his own sexual response to Nancy, and his guilt reaction over this response. He had to learn about his Vulnerable Child and how he had never been aware of it, let alone taken care of it. He had to learn that he had feelings of jealousy in regard to Nancy and her new friends and her new freedom. He had to learn about his feeling of boredom in his own life. He had to look at his marriage and where it was that his needs were not being met. He had to look at where he had been living a "form" in his marriage and how he and his wife had not been connected at any essential level for many, many years. Only in this way could Nancy be freed and could there be a possibility of a *real* relationship between Jordan and his daughter.

Bonding Patterns Kill Love

Janie is a woman in her forties who has a very responsible business position. Her mother is quite elderly and has been ill for many years. Janie feels that she is totally responsible for her. Whenever her mother feels ill, she phones Janie who is then responsible for going to pick her up, taking her to the doctor, taking her back home and then going back to work. Janie has been doing this for many years.

Janie's Mother side is bonded to the Daughter side of her real mother. Since she is identified with the Mother pattern, she is, of course, required to take care of her mother in a prescribed way. She *must* pick her up. There are no other options available when there is no Awareness that is separate from the archetypal identification. Janie feels enormous resentment toward her mother. She dreads the ring of the telephone because it might be her mother. She does her duty from the place of the Mother, and then lives with the deep resentment

that prevents any kind of genuine connection from occurring between herself and her mother.

Janie's real mother is feeling increasingly vulnerable
and abandoned. She knows nothing of her own Inner
Child, so she cannot nurture herself. She senses her
daughter's lack of concern. Becoming ill and using her
illness are the only ways she can get the attention that
her Inner Child, as well as other parts, crave. So she
dances the Victim Daughter dance with the Responsible
Mother side of her real daughter. The deep tragedy of
such bonding is the loss of any possibility of real contact
between the two people. After all, there can be no real
contact unless there is some semblance of an Aware Ego
existing in one of them.

Janie was asked whether she had ever considered the
possibility of hiring someone to drive her mother to the
doctor. Her mother's medical needs were real, and she
did have to assume some responsibility for seeing that
these needs were met. This idea had never occurred to
her. She had done a considerable amount of work on
herself and so, in this situation, her Awareness level immediately separated from the Mother side and she was
able to see the pattern that she was in.

Living in an identification with an energy pattern is
like having tunnel vision. We feel trapped. We are
unable to perceive options. We literally see only that
which is directly in front of us. The separaton of Janie's
Awareness level from the Mother pattern gave her the
real possibility of choice. She might choose to hire
someone. She might decide that one of her siblings
needs to help. She might decide to continue the same
arrangement she had before. What she actually does is
neither our business nor our concern. Our job is to help
her to have real choice about this matter.

"There's No Reason for You to Work, Honey"

Frances and Barry have been married for over twenty years. She begins to have the feeling that she needs to work and she mentions this to her husband. He tells her that this is really not necessary. "There is more than enough money and, besides, with the tax situation as it is, we wouldn't realize any real money from your working." Frances gives up the idea of working.

A few weeks later she mentions to her husband that she wants to take a night school course at UCLA. Again, very reasonably, Barry tells her that he is worried about her driving at night. "There have been so many nasty things happening lately. I really feel concerned about having you drive at night."

Barry is very convincing in his communication and it is obvious that Frances is still ready to be convinced rather easily. Six months after this conversation, Barry leaves Frances for another woman, one with whom he has been involved for a considerable period of time. Frances is enraged, bewildered, crushed, hysterical, devastated and puzzled. How could he have done this to her? How could she have done this to herself?

Frances and Barry have lived a tightly bonded relationship. He has been the Father who has brought security to her very Vulnerable Inner Child. She has had the conditioning of so many women in contemporary society, a conditioning requiring that they be taken care of by the man. It is a patriarchal conditioning that essentially disempowers them for being able to take care of themselves in the world.

Father-Daughter bonding is often reflected in the handling of money in these relationships. Barry was in complete charge of the finances and Frances had an account into which he put money. Since he was an attorney, Frances was prone to leave to him the control of all worldly matters. She was essentially on an allowance and if she wanted more money than was contained in her household account, she had to ask for it. Barry was a Beneficent Father, and so he rarely said "no" to her requests. Whether Beneficent Father or Ogre Father, Father is Father and the issue is one of control.

On the other side, the Mother side of Frances has been bonded to the Vulnerable Child within Barry. This is something he knows nothing about. She is a full-time mother both to her own children and to him at an unconscious level. However, anyone looking at their relationship would see him as the dominating agent.

When Frances came to Barry with the idea of working, his vulnerability was activated. The Child side of him needed her to be safely at home in the Mother role. The fact that he was involved with someone else made no difference to his Inner Child. Anything that Frances might do that would separate her from the bonding pattern threatened his vulnerability. Since he knew nothing about this, he moved into the Controlling Father and very rationally explained to her why these potential moves on her part made no sense.

We may assume from her side that the Voice in her that initially brought up the possibility of working and going to school was still on the Daughter side. Had there been an Awareness that was disengaged from the Daughter, she would have had a very different set of options that were available to her. It is quite likely that she would not have remained so acquiescent. It is strange to think that people who have lived together for so many years could have so little essential contact with one another. Yet, this is the situation for many of us. The understanding of bonding patterns literally changes the nature of relationship. To experience and be aware of the multitude of energy patterns that enter into a relationship is to live the relationship at an entirely different level than it has been lived before.

"I Want a New Car"

Charles and Ann have been married for twelve years. They live a fairly typical Mother-Son and Father-Daughter bonding pattern. One day Charles says that he would like a new Porsche. Ann immediately becomes negative, upset and very rational. She points out how much money they owe, how this would raise their payments. Charles tells her that he has figured out that with the trade-in on their car, the new payments would only be $300 or $400 a month more than they are paying. She gets angrier yet and tells him that he is a spoiled brat and that he is always wanting things. He is hurt, but leaps to the side of the Angry Father and explodes in rage at her "bitchiness."

Let us analyze this situation up until this moment. The part of Charles that first said—"I would like a new Porsche"—was the Son side of him. The Son in him was, in effect, asking permission of the Mother. True to the dance, Ann immediately becomes the Mother and starts to criticize and rationally explain the stupidity of this idea. Still in the Son, but beginning to shift to the Rational Father, Charles explains that he *has* thought about the money. Ann becomes enraged. Really though, there is no Ann and there is no Charles. They have danced this dance a thousand times over a thousand issues. The Negative Mother now comes out in full glory.

Charles shifts from the Son who wants approval to the very negative, Dominating Father. Since Charles handles all the money in the family and since Ann is essentially on an allowance, he screams at her that he will do what he goddam pleases and that if he wants a Porsche he'll have a Porsche. He does not need her approval anyway.

One of the wonderful things about these bonding patterns when they move into full-scale warfare is the degree of righteousness that one feels. The other person is clearly wrong and deserves all the punishment that can be meted out. Ten minutes later, when the energy patterns have released the two warriors, it is as though a hurricane has raced through the house and is now gone. Each wonders what has happened because the issue that had burned so brightly and with such intensity is no longer an issue.

Once Charles enters into the Heavy Father, Ann gives up. She withdraws into the Daughter and feels dead. She is no match for this powerful Father when he explodes in his full glory. She has been defeated. It always ends the same way. Before she began to work on these issues she did not even guess at the rage that was buried in her and, as a result of that repressed rage, she felt suicidal from time to time.

Later that night Charles wants to make love. The storm has passed and, for him, it is as though nothing has happened. She is dead inside and from the place of the Compliant Daughter, she gives in to his demands. His Vulnerable Child is hurt deeply by the sexual act because she is not really present on any meaningful level. Since he does not know about his Inner Child, he goes back into the Angry Father, berating her for her frigidity, and off they go, back to the battlefield again.

The patterns of relationship that we are describing are not abnormal. They are perfectly natural examples of bonding patterns in relationship. We do not offer solutions as to how people should behave and what they should say in these situations. We do know that as we experience more of the energy patterns within us, as our Awareness separates from parts with which we identify, and as we discover the parts that we disown, a change takes place.

One key element of this change is the ability to communicate vulnerability. If Charles had been able to speak about his vulnerability, matters would no doubt have gone differently. Charles felt vulnerable because he was not related to his Business Voice which he constantly forced Ann to carry for him. She was regularly thrown into the Rational/Practical Mother who needed to set limits. It was an energy that she enjoyed, and yet it became tedious to find herself there over and over again.

Living in these patterns is, quite literally, like being in prison. The same patterns emerge and are lived automatically and repetitiously, not unlike the dogs of Pavlovian fame. An Aware Ego is far more flexible. It is able to embrace power and vulnerability and to use both in personal communication. When we do not need to control the other person, the nature of these personal communications is dramatically shifted.

What we recommend to people is that they begin to pay attention to their interactions and see if they can become aware of these bonding patterns. If you find yourself repeatedly in the same kinds of interactions, then you may be sure that you are locked into a bonding pattern. Step back into the Awareness level and see if you can begin to tune into the quality of energy that you are bringing to the relationship. Recognizing that you are locked into one of these archetypal melodramas is the first step in bringing about a shift in the way you relate to others. Without recognition, without that first step of Awareness separating out from the interaction, nothing else can happen.

ENERGY IS NEITHER GOOD NOR BAD

There is one final consideration in the consciousness model that is relevant to the issues we are discussing. Energy is energy. It is neither good, nor is it bad. The way it is used by us is the critical feature. If Power energy is utilized by the Critical Father, we are going to have a very mean person. If Power energy channels through the Son side of someone, we are going to see an angry, rebellious Son with a serious authority problem. If Power is used by an Ego that has Awareness, then we have a person who knows how to be powerful without, at the same time, needing to control or dominate people. The common denominator for energies that are used by either the Mother/Father or the Son/Daughter archetypes is domination. An Aware Ego can use power without needing to control anyone else.

If Spiritual energy is used by the Father side of a man, we have a Spiritual Guru. This Guru will have disciples and will require obedience. That is the nature of the Father. Spiritual energy channeling through the Son or Daughter side of a person creates the Disciple. The Disciple is required to surrender and, in turn, insists upon control from the Father or Mother side of the spiritual leader.

The way in which spiritual energies cause bondings to occur also leads to what we call transference in psychotherapy. It is the Son/Daughter side of the client that bonds to the Father/Mother side of the therapist. This is, in our view, an inevitable concomitant of the therapeutic relationship. What the therapist has, hopefully, is an Awareness of this bonding process. This Awareness will allow the therapist to make choices along the way that will enable the client to become empowered as quickly as possible.

Spiritual energy that channels through an Aware Ego is simply experienced and used with Awareness. It does not require disciples or dependent clients and it is not used for purposes of control. It simply "is." The stronger the Parent-Child bond, the stronger the transference or the ardor of the disciples, and the more issues of control and domination exist. *People with Aware Egos* tend to avoid situations where they would be controlled by others. Similarly, they are less and less motivated by a need to control or dominate others.

The primary point we wish to make is that any energy pattern, if brought through an Aware Ego, can be positively used. Even Victim energy, once we are aware of it, gives us significant information about the situation we are in. Conversely, the usually positive heroic energy as expressed either through the Father or the Son side can require us do do foolish and even dangerous things. When utilized by an Aware Ego, it provides us with that special kind of fearlessness that allows us to make courageous choices in life about how we wish to live and what we wish to do. Wisdom channeled through the Parental archetype gives us tremendous control over others. The disciple students will conform or rebel. But wisdom used by an Aware Ego is just wisdom. There are no sticky wickets of control and domination connected to it.

What we are saying here is, in one way, no different from what we have been saying throughout this book. We must honor all the energy patterns. They are all fine. We must experience them and become aware of them and gradually develop an Ego that knows how to use them. With such an Ego, the most frightening daemonic energies, the most sensitive vulnerabilities, the most profound spiritual and psychic energies can be expressed in our lives. We are talking about an evolving Ego, one which is always in the process of increasing its Awareness. It is in this way that we learn to bring to our personal relationships more and more of our Selves.

IN SUMMARY

We wish to emphasize again that archetypal bonding is normal and inevitable. No amount of consciousness work can make it go away. Despite our most intense efforts, these patterns will re-appear in a hundred different guises. Consciousness does not mean that we are "centered." Consciousness does not mean that we are "clear." Consciousness means that we experience the energy patterns, have access to an Awareness level and are able, increasingly over time, to utilize an Aware Ego. It is only this definition that allows us to embrace our Selves totally.

CHAPTER IX

EMPOWERMENT IN WOMEN

THE FEMINIST MOVEMENT AND THE EMPOWERMENT OF WOMEN

Let us now look at some major changes in our culture with our newfound Awareness. Until the sixties, there were certain energy patterns that were so universally disowned by the women in our culture that they were hypothesized not to exist. The prevailing cultural norm, supported by both legislation and by the psychological theories of the time, made it almost impossible for women to own their aggression, their anger, their power, their need to dominate, their selfishness, their competitiveness, their destructive feelings, their ambition, their need to excel, their insensitivities, their sexuality, their promiscuity, their intellectuality, or their objectivity.

The feminist movement focused the spotlight upon the forced disowning of many of the energy patterns that lead to power. It raised questions regarding the disempowerment of women and there was encouragement for women to start to embrace many previously disowned energy patterns.

216

Let us look at Helen, for example. She was a pleasant and charming young woman from a middle-class Midwestern background. She married appropriately, had three children and was at home caring for them as docile as could be until she read *The Feminine Mystique*. Suddenly, her professional ambition was no longer a disowned self. She would no longer listen to charges that to pursue her own career would be castrating her husband and doing untold damage to her children. She integrated her disowned intellectual energies, she stopped over-identifying with her self-sacrificing sub-personality (which was greatly encouraged as the *sine qua non* of child-rearing in those days).

Helen no longer disowned her "unfeminine" competitiveness and ambition, and she set out with humor, compassion, and self-awareness to carve out a career for herself. This she did with great success. By integrating the energies that were still taboo to the dominant culture, she became empowered. The integration of these energies resulted in a rewarding and absorbing career which equalled, and finally eclipsed that of her husband. However, 20 years later, they are still married, with three successful and happily grown children.

It is interesting to note how threatening disowned energies can sound before they are allowed to enter into our lives. In the early '60s psychological disaster was predicted for Helen's course of action. Energies are disowned because it is feared that they will disrupt the equilibrium and lead to chaos. Actually, the reverse is true. *It is the disowning of the "chaos" that exists within each of us that causes disruptions in our surroundings because these disowned energies operate unconsciously.* Instead, the integration of these energies leads to an enrichment within ourselves and in our surroundings.

WARRIOR ENERGY AND THE GUILTY DAUGHTER

The warrior or Amazon energy is one that has been disowned in women for millennia. It was a great relief to Ellen when we first spoke with this fearless part of her:

Therapist: (After Ellen has changed chairs and the Warrior is now present) My, but you look different from Ellen. You're taller, straighter and your eyes have quite a sparkle to them.

Ellen: You bet, and I'm not afraid of any of them— not her husband, her lover's wife, none of them. Just let them try to make her feel guilty when I'm around. Let them try. They'll be sorry. She did what she did and I'm not about to let her apologize. I'm proud of her. I'll make them all cringe. (Warming to the task) If they confront her in public, I'll just tell it all, just like it was. I won't spare any details and they'll be sorry they ever tried to make her the patsy. I'm tired of her always being apologetic and taking the blame for everything. (Eyes gleaming) In fact, I'd like it. Yes, I'd love to see the looks on all their faces when they see me stand up for her. Those holier-than-thou bastards. None of them are any better than she is; and they won't judge her . . . not while I'm around. No way! I'm just here to protect her and I don't give a damn about anyone else.

The Warrior energy has been unavailable to women until recently. It was considered unfeminine, castrating, or worse yet, some form of devilish possession. One can see clearly, however, how necessary it is for self-protection and how powerless a woman can be if this energy is disowned. Without it, Ellen was a guilt-ridden victim of the accusations and judgments of all and sundry.

With it, she was capable of defending herself in an appropriate fashion with an Aware Ego. She did not identify with the Warrior and go out looking for a fight. She just took care of herself.

Before she gained access to her Warrior energy, Ellen had been identified with her Guilty Daughter—again an energy pattern encouraged in women ever since Eve. It was women who were responsible for the expulsion from Paradise and, up until the time that the feminists drew attention to the entire belief system springing from this, women have, to a greater or lesser extent, lived the Guilty Daughter. Eve was guilty of curiosity, of independent thought and of wishing to expand her horizons. How dreadful! She might be thought of as one of our earliest consciousness seekers, if one were to look at her behavior in another context.

At any rate Eve was punished for her disobedience and she gave rise to millions upon millions of Guilty Daughters. This archetypal energy is quite concerned about upsetting the "collective." It worries constantly about what people will think. For hundreds of generations, mothers have asked their daughters, "What will people think?" when their daughters want to live in any way different from the accepted norm.

Ellen's Guilty Daughter, for instance, had been terrified that people would find out about her affair and judge her. She was in a panic lest people talk about her. She kept saying, "But I want Ellen to be a good girl, I'll die if people think bad things of her. And, my God, what would her mother and father say? They wouldn't be able to lift up their heads in public. They'd be *so* embarrassed. I'd die, I'd just die!"

It is quite apparent that the Guilty Daughter does not have much clout. Anyone can judge her, anyone can shame her. She is an ancient, powerful archetypal energy, and it is time for women to dis-identify with her. But again, we must caution that this does not mean that they should identify with the opposite energy— perhaps a Judgmental or Avenging Mother—and blame everything on men or religion or the culture.

It is time to step back to a position of Awareness. It is time for women to stop identifying with the energies that keep them disempowered. It is not *just* the people on the outside! It is these sub-personalities as well, the ones within, that keep women locked into the powerful judgmental patriarchy century after century. It is time for women to become truly empowered from a position of consciousness and to accept full responsibility for themselves and their actions. In a way, women are more likely to reach for empowerment than men. They still do not have access to traditional power and are forced to move ahead from an empowered position (power plus vulnerability) rather than a power position (one identified with archetypal parental energies) because in many areas access to the power of the collective is denied them. Because of this, many women do not develop the same kinds of Heavyweight sub-personalities as men.

EMPOWERMENT VS. POWER IN WOMEN

The need for consciousness and for the development of a strong Aware Ego in women is nowhere more important than in the corporate world. It was truly fascinating to watch this process unfold for Elizabeth. She had been reared in a Latin country by an extremely dictatorial father. She left home after she finished school and came to America by herself to start a new life.

Elizabeth was ambitious, very ambitious. She was

brilliant and she was a hard worker who could spend 16 hours a day researching diligently to cover all possible details. She accepted responsibility and was willing to make important decisions even though much was at stake. She was truly courageous. But she was a woman, and, as a woman, she was constantly encountering obstacles in the field of finance. It was unquestionably a man's field, although she soon surpassed most of the men in her company.

As a woman, Elizabeth was keenly aware of her feelings. She did not want to sacrifice her sensitivity and her vulnerability for corporate success. She wanted to keep her relationship with her husband alive and she knew that if she disowned her sensitive, practical, intuitive energies, she would lose much richness from her life—to say nothing of losing her beloved husband.

Watching her move up the corporate ladder was like watching a balancing act of the most delicate precision. She needed her power voices to help her with demands for promotions and raises. But if she began to identify with her power side, her way would become blocked. The men in the company, their Vulnerable Children activated, would back off in fear and ally with one another against her. Then her vulnerability and insecurity would come forth. If she let these take over, she might lose credibility and she would have to work hard to regain previously won ground.

Elizabeth proceeded with great care. She became expert at differentiating between her power voices and true empowerment. She worked from an Aware Ego, only making big moves when she knew she was empowered. When she felt the archetypal power energies or vulnerable energies taking over, she withdrew whenever possible.

As could be expected, power was withdrawn from any

position that she won and was moved elsewhere. If she had been attached to power rather than to empowerment, she would have been angered or embittered or discouraged. She could easily have polarized against the system as a Rebellious Daughter. However, her first priority was her consciousness process and so she continued her relentless movement, deepening the empowerment and broadening her Awareness. Since it was empowerment and not power that she was after, every experience was a lesson and every move exciting. Her authority and responsibility and her actual power in the company expanded until she was on the highest management level. But she was able to remain free of the basic power structure and was not intimidated by the corporate politics. Because she came from a position of empowerment and not of power, she remained unentangled in the Father-Son bondings of the corporation and she was able to be herself, to behave with more freedom than anyone else on her level.

The Killer Who Protects

Warrior energy is needed by all humans, both men and women, for self-protection. Needless to say, women are seen as life-givers and healers, and the thought that they might have any destructive energies spreads panic among the population. We feel that a part of the intense affect surrounding the issue of abortion is that it affirms the woman's wish and ability to destroy life as well as to create it. We have not noticed equial fervor to deny men the right to destroy life in wars. Men are expected to have a destructive voice; it is to be regretted and tamed, but it is there nonetheless. Women are not similarly endowed as far as Western culture is concerned.

To be denied access to the destructiveness in oneself is to be denied another major power source. Sadly enough, it also causes all of the destruction to be projected onto men. It is the men who use these energies to protect their women, their children and themselves. It is the men who will destroy life or property if they feel this is necessary.

We want to be clear that we are not advocates of destruction, neither for men nor for women. However, both men and women need to be in touch with the part within themselves that could kill if necessary. When this is not owned, it leaves us victims. It leaves our vulnerable children, both within and without, unprotected. And it is projected—onto another sex, another race, another nationality, another belief system. It is only when we have an Awareness of this Killer Who Protects that we can truly experience the richness and beauty of our vulnerability.

It is interesting to note that this voice has been so thoroughly repressed in women that it rarely assumes the form of a female as a sub-personality. It is far more likely to be a jungle cat, a graceful feline killer. Let us listen to one of these tell about itself.

Jaguar Voice: (eyes narrowed and alert, body tense and ready to spring) I watch everything. I have sharp eyes and I know all about danger. I love danger. I love to fight. I love to hurt others. I love the taste of blood. (Smiles triumphantly) What I don't like are people who pretend they're good and pure. Nobody is and I know it. I can see the part that's like me in everyone and I know how to protect Kim from getting hurt by it.

Therapist: You sound so strong and so alive.

Jaguar Voice: That's because I am. When I'm not around, Kim is a sweet, spiritual weakling. She's so nice that everyone loves her, but everyone can push her around. She can be fooled by people who pretend to be earnest. I can't stand that. I like people who are more like me. When they cop to the killer in them, then I can trust them. (Rolling her eyes upward) Spare me from those who think they're pure in heart. I love the ones who know they're not. You know, I love to walk the streets in N.Y. Everybody there knows about me and I come alive. I look around and I see the me in their eyes. We all say, "OK, you'd better watch out. I'm not kidding." And I love it, (stretching) I just love it.

Therapist: How do you feel about the people in Kim's discussion group?

Jaguar Voice: I can't stand them. They're all so nice. Her nice part comes out and everybody does a sweet little dance. (Sarcastic) I'd like to shake them up. I'd like to growl and show my teeth. I'd like to break up all that niceness. It's saccharine and boring and I don't trust it. It makes me uncomfortable. It only *looks* safe. It isn't.

Therapist: What about her best friend?

Jaguar Voice: I wish she's let me out with her and I wish she'd let me tell her to stop being a scared rabbit about life and people. I wish she'd let me tell her to get off her ass and fight for what she wants. You have to fight for everything that's worthwhile. I want to sink my teeth into all those people who are passive and good and waiting for "the universe to provide." (Growls a bit and moves around as if she can't contain her annoyance.)

Therapist: What would you want her to do about her boyfriend?

Jaguar Voice: Tell him to stop feeling sorry for himself and go get a job. Tell him she's tired of playing Mommy to a puppy. And most of all, let me at him when he starts getting snippy with her instead of always being so nice and understanding. He won't be so snippy when I'm through with him.

Therapist: You don't sound afraid of people.

Jaguar Voice: I'm not. I'm ready for anyone who would hurt Kim or anyone she loves. And I don't give a damn if people don't like her. And I'm not nice. I'm definitely not nice (with determination).

The Killer Who Protects (for Kim, her Jaguar) had been disowned for Kim's entire life and she had been identified with her Nice Girl. The Nice Girl has been highly valued in Western society, and it is still highly valued in the Middle and Far East. The Nice Girl subpersonality is encouraged, at least in part, because she helps everything to function smoothly and she certainly makes people feel good. Kim's Nice Girl was quite upset by her Jaguar:

Nice Girl: But nobody is going to like Kim if she follows those suggestions and everything could get disrupted (sounding much younger and weaker than the Jaguar).

Therapist: How do you see that happening?

Nice Girl: (smoothing her skirt and sitting properly) First of all, I *like* her discussion group. The people in it are nice and don't hurt her. It's safe and *I* have a good time. We joke and we laugh and we're thoughtful. We're considerate of each other's needs and feelings. (A little teary) I like it when people are considerate of Kim, and if you're not nice to them, they won't be nice back. *I* know that.

Therapist: (kindly) So you're really worried about what would happen to Kim if her Jaguar came out?

Nice Girl: Yes. I'm afraid that her discussion group will turn into an encounter group like she was in in the '60s, and everyone will be confronting each other and being mean. That would be awful!

Therapist: I see. How about talking to her girlfriend?

Nice Girl: You're supposed to be a support and a comfort to friends. I think that your job is to make them feel better and not to get them worried. I'm afraid she'll just upset her girlfriend. And then, what if her friend stops being nice to her? I don't want Kim to get hurt and the only way to avoid getting hurt is to be really nice so nobody will hurt you (looking very earnest).

Therapist: What about her boyfriend?

Nice Girl: Well, that really scares me too. (looking concerned) I'm afraid he'll leave her. I think he likes her because I'm around so much of the time. I make things really nice for him. I'm very tuned in to his feelings, and I'm always considerate and easy to be with. He doesn't like tough, confrontive women. He tells her that a lot. He likes gentle, peaceful, nice women. He says they're attractive and feminine. He says the other kinds are uncentered and bitchy. I agree with him. She won't be as likeable without me.

We can see how for each disowned power voice, like the Warrior energy in Ellen and the Jaguar Voice in Kim, there is a Voice such as the "Guilty Daughter" or the "Nice Girl," that has kept the woman disempowered. These disempowering voices are still supported by the culture. It is the gradual introduction of feminist counter-culture thinking that has made it possible for women to begin to dis-identify with them.

THE DANGER OF IDENTIFYING WITH
OPPOSITE ARCHETYPES

The danger here is that these Warrior energies, when first released, are so heady and powerful that it is difficult not to identify with them as completely as one had identified with the disempowered "nice" voices of the past. This was what happened to the militant feminists. They broke the archetypal identification with the passive victim only to become identified with the Warrior archetype, the opposite energy. This is often a necessary step in order to thoroughly break the hold of the first archetype. It can also be a basic step in the consciousness process.

A woman who moves from identifying with her vulnerability, her neediness and her passivity to identifying with her Warrior, her impersonality and her sexuality, has not necessarily moved forward in consciousness. She may feel more comfortable as top dog rather than bottom dog, but, then again, she may not. She may feel alone and unloved. Whichever way she feels, she is still identified with one set of energies and totally disowning its opposite. It is in the evolution of consciousness, the development of Awareness, the introduction of an Aware Ego, that the true forward movement takes place. Vulnerability cannot be left behind any more than the Warrior. Both men and women need their vulnerability and sensitivity in order to feel truly a part of life, and their warriors to be sure that they do not become victims to life's difficulties.

THE COMPETITOR AND THE LADY

Another energy that has been denied to women is competitiveness. Competitivenes has long been considered a male attribute. The femininity of any woman was greatly diminished if she admitted that she really loved winning. "A real woman doesn't want to win; she wants to support her man so that *he* wins."

Susan's situation was very typical. As a child, she had been quite competitive and an outstanding athlete. However, Susan was raised to be a lady and, as such, she soon learned to make light of her interest in competitive athletics. She was permitted to play tennis in a ladylike fashion; that is to say, she could not try too hard and she could not look as though winning mattered. Her ladylike voice put it this way:

Lady: Tennis is a social game. (In a prim voice) I don't want her out there like her husband, furiously competitive. It just doesn't look nice. It's not appropriate in him and it's certainly not appropriate for her.

Therapist: How do you feel about her winning if she doesn't look too competitive about it?

Lady: If she's modest and she apologizes. You know, if she says that it's just been a lucky day, then it's all right with me. She has to keep smiling pleasantly and under no conditions whatsoever may she look triumphant.

Therapist: So it's OK if she wins so long as it looks like luck or an accident?

Lady: Yes, that's right.

Therapist: What about her trying to improve her game?

Lady: That's unacceptable. She is allowed to play with the girls a few times a week, but it should remain essentially social. They should talk a lot, and be nice, and giggle, and make excuses when they miss the ball. She should never get grim-looking. It's not attractive.

Susan's Competitive Voice had been totally disowned, and her athletic activities came under the control of this Lady-like Voice. But, as we have said before, our disowned selves have a way of attracting similar energies, and her husband was very competitive. Susan knew about disowned selves and wanted her own competitive sub-personality available.

Susan: I'm tired of playing tennis while I listen to that Lady-like Voice. I'd love to see what my Competitive Voice has to say.

Therapist: OK—let's hear from it.

(Susan changes her seat and she sits taller and looks stronger as the following Voice emerges.)

Competitive Voice: Those ladies she plays with drive me crazy. I want to play. I want to improve. I want to win. Susan is so worried about offending people and about looking unfeminine, that she never pays any attention to me.

Therapist: You've got a lot of pizzazz. Tell me, what would you have Susan do?

Competitive Voice: I'd have her leave the social ladies and go to play with people like me, with women who take their game seriously. They don't joke, they don't socialize. They're there to play tennis and that's all. (This Voice looks very determined and unsmiling in contrast to Susan who always looks pleasant and usually has a faint smile on her face.)

Therapist: No nonsense for them.

Competitive Voice: You bet! I'd have her go way up among the serious players. I'd have her tell the others— she can be as nice as she wants about it, I don't care —that she wants to improve her game and that she's looking for more competition. They'll understand. And, if not, I don't care. Her current group is a waste of time.

But Susan's Lady-like Voice had difficulty with this and Susan needed to take that Voice into consideration as well when she changed her tennis playing patterns. The power and excitement of the Competitive Voice helped her to extricate herself appropriately from her regular doubles games and she then went on to really stretch herself. She was so excited to have reclaimed the exuberance and power of using her body to its utmost.

Women learn to disown their competitiveness in all areas at a very young age. We know of one woman who had been verbally facile as a child. Her mother had called her away from a game of Anagrams with a little boy and suggested that she lose so that he would not feel bad. The girl was hurt and confused but, because she did not want to make anyone uncomfortable, she obediently lost the game. With some women, such as this one, learning to lose is easily remembered although not as easily overcome. With other women, the culture taught them this lesson more subtly. This lack of competitiveness, this proscription against winning and against striving for excellence has done much to keep women disempowered. These, too, are energies that the feminists have tried to make available to women.

Susan needed her competitive energies released so that her natural abilities in athletics could surface again and be enjoyed. She needed to experience and to enjoy the mastery of the game in order to re-empower herself. This led to a deep empowerment in other areas of her life. Until this voice was released, Susan was always hesitant, as though she took in half a breath and waited for permission to take in the other half. Now she could breathe fully and naturally. Now she could stretch to her limits without fear of disapproval from within or without.

THE IMPERSONAL VOICE AND THE PLEASER

The ability to be objectively and dispassionately rational is another quality that has been forcibly disowned. Women were supposed to be feeling creatures. A woman lacking in emotionalism was seen as "cold-blooded." In men, the term "cold-blooded" is usually reserved for murderers. Women's hearts are supposed to be forever warm.

It is hard to make conscious choices without allowing input from an impersonal, rational sub-personality. Without this, a woman is a victim to her emotions, swayed this way and that as her feelings move her. The Impersonal Voice can provide the navigator she needs to steer her through emotionally turbulent seas. This is particularly neded when she is trying to make conscious choices regarding intimates such as mates or children.

Sylvia, for instance, was in a very destructive relationship with a man. He was handsome, charming and accomplished, and she loved him passionately. There were times when their relationship was absolutely idyllic. He would speak adoringly to her, bring her gifts and be totally and unabashedly romantic. When he felt insecure, however, he would attack her viciously, blaming her for everything that went wrong in his life. She was at the mercy of her emotional reactions to his words. When he felt good, she felt cherished and magnificent; when he felt bad, she was desolate. At the time of this Dialogue, she was feeling desolate. There was not an ounce of impersonality, or objectivity in their relationship. Her Impersonal Voice was desperately needed to bring this in.

Therapist: Let's talk to the part of you that's not emotional about Roger. (Sylvia changes chairs and immediately looks more calm.)

Therapist: (quite calmly and objectively) Tell me please, what have you noticed about the relationship between Sylvia and Roger?

Impersonal Voice: (coolly, with composure and some real authority.) I think that it's very bad for Sylvia. It's as though she's a yo-yo and he's pulling the string. She's always in an emotional reaction to him.

Therapist: Really? How does that work?

Impersonal Voice: When he's feeling good about himself, like he was last week, her brings her flowers and little presents and they spend hours talking and going for romantic walks and making love. So she felt great all week. But when he feels bad, like last Friday, when his boss reprimanded him, he comes back home and blames it all on her. He tells her it is because of their relationship that things aren't going well at work. It's because he spends too much time thinking about her or wondering if some day she'll betray him. Then he's angry at her, and she feels terrible and guilty. It never occurs to her that *she* hasn't done anything. She never evaluates his anger rationally. He tells her to feel awful and so she does.

Therapist: Why do you think she isn't more objective?

Impersonal Voice: (calmly and non-judgmentally) She's afraid that he'll tell her that this proves she doesn't love him, that another woman would care more about his feelings, that she's too hard and unfeminine. She's really afraid that he won't see her as soft and feminine and lovable if she's too cool in her analysis of the situation.

Therapist: So her upset at his anger, her emotionality, is proof that she's very feminine and that she really loves him?

Impersonal Voice: Yes. That's just how it works. He even went so far as to get angry with her when she was able to finish an important report at work, and to present it very successfully to the management committee during a period when they were having terrible fights. (Smiling) I might point out that it was *I* who helped her do that. At any rate, Roger was angry that she could remain so level-headed. He said that it just proved that she didn't love him.

Therapist: What conclusions to you draw from all this?

Impersonal Voice: I feel that any relationship in which Sylvia is expected to disown her power, her objectivity, her needs, and her own common sense is not good for her. I realize that she loves Roger, but I think she's in for real trouble if she stays with him. She's better off leaving him now than later. If she stays with him much longer, she's going to disown me completely and doubt her own sanity.

Therapist: Since she loves Roger so much, how do you suggest that she do this?

Impersonal Voice: First of all, she needs to keep me around. That means that she has to let me talk with you

more. By the way, Roger never likes her to discuss anything about him with anyone but himself. That's because he's afraid she'll be letting me out. Then, she
should spend more time with her friends from work.
They will also help me to get stronger. Since so many of
them are men, I can come out more there. Lastly, I
think she should spend time with her friends and family, so that her Vulnerable Child will be cared for,
because she's going to feel pretty lonely.

You can see how helpful this Impersonal Voice can
be when situations are deeply emotional. Without it, a
woman is lost. With it, she can plan to deal with difficult situations. It can assess the current situation, suggest the best course of action, warn of future difficulties
and suggest plans to cope with them. In making these
plans, this voice is not concerned with the feelings of
others.

Therapist: But what about Roger: Won't he be upset?

Impersonal Voice: (Again cool, but not punitive.) Yes,
he'll be upset, but I'm worried about Sylvia. He'll have
to take care of himself. I expect he'll pursue her for a
while, and then find another girlfriend. That will upset
her a lot and she will have to be very cautious and
thoughtful when that happens.

Therapist: You don't seem to value feelings very much.

Impersonal Voice: No, I don't. I just look at them as I
look at any other factors. I see what role they play. I see
where they're helpful and needed and when they confuse basic issues.

This last juncture is where the Critic can emerge if
one is not careful. When women become empowered,

when the power voices are integrated, their Inner Critics are likely to accuse women of losing their femininity and to warn them that "no *real* man would ever love a woman like *that!*"

For Sylvia, however, it was not the Critic, but her Pleaser which acted in opposition to this Impersonal Voice. It was the Pleaser with whom she had been identified during the preceding years, and so it was the Pleaser that objected to these new ideas. (Needless to say, Roger loved her Pleaser.)

Pleaser: I still think that the relationship can be saved. If she only would listen to me, I'd make it work out all right.

Therapist: And how would you do that?

Pleaser: I'd find some way to make him happy, so that he wouldn't pick on her so much. He only does it because he is insecure. That's what he says and I agree with him.

Therapist: How could she make him secure?

Pleaser: He's had a tough life. She could prove to him that she loves him and that she'll stand by him no matter what happens. She could always be available to him. Always put him first. If he needs her to give up her other friends, she could do that. That would prove she really cares. She could stay home all the time she wasn't at work, so that she'd be available whenever he called. She can find plenty of things to do around the house. She can also dress the way he likes her to dress, and stop wearing makeup and perfume. He's so insecure that when she wears makeup and perfume and looks good, he's afraid other men will be attracted to her.

Therapist: Sounds a bit like entering a nunnery.

Pleaser: Well, her sexuality *does* scare him, so I don't think she should flaunt it. She should also clear out all souvenirs of the past. You know, burn her old love letters and that sort of thing.

Therapist: Kind of erase the past?

Pleaser: Yes, that's it. And not be so close to her family either. I'm afraid that they threaten him too.

Sylvia's Pleaser would have her move into a fully archetypal behavior. She would follow the lead of Ruth in the Bible, a much praised woman who gave up her friends, family and homeland to be with her new husband Boaz—laudable, but disempowering. We often see the opposite archetype these days. The archetype of the Independent Woman who will not sacrifice anything whatsoever for the relationship. One way, one loses oneself; the other way, one loses one's relationship. Either way, one loses. An Aware Ego is desperately needed to negotiate sticky wickets such as these.

THE PATRIARCHY WITHIN

Perhaps the greatest impediment to the empowerment of women is the inner Patriarch. We would like to present one final example of an excerpt of a Voice Dialogue session to illustrate this Voice. Rita was a 29-year-old woman who had a great deal of anger toward men. She felt that she had been treated shoddily in many relationships where men were involved. The degree of her anger was an indication that a disowned self was operating in her. The facilitator asked to talk to the part of her that hated women. She was quite shocked at the idea but eventually she moved over to another seat and the Dialogue began.

Facilitator: I wanted to talk with you because I had the feeling you must be very strong in Rita, considering her negativity toward men.

Woman Hater Voice: You were smart to catch me. I prefer remaining anonymous.

Facilitator: Why is that?

Woman Hater Voice: I can do more damage this way. So long as she thinks the problem is out there, she never looks inside and she can never find me.

Facilitator: Exactly how to you feel?

Woman Hater Voice: I don't like Rita and I don't like women generally. I find them entirely too emotional, and I can't stand weakness. Did you listen to her describe all the crimes perpetrated against her? She's a victim, a wimp. I can't stand her. Why can't she think like a man? Why can't she stand up for herself? She's just like all women; she's devious when she does try to get her way—she sneaks and manipulates—nothing straightforward about her.

The issues relating to women and power are both objective and subjective. To ignore the objective arena is to be out of touch with objective reality. To ignore the introjected patriarchal voices, however, is to ignore a different kind of reality. This last is the reality of an inner saboteur who detests women. Without knowledge of both the inner and the outer patriarchs, one is always charging windmills, consigned forever to the circular wheel of anger and rage. The Awareness that these disempowering voices live inside as well as outside gives the Aware Ego an opportunity to deal with the objective problem with greater clarity. The disowning of the introjected patriarchy, as with any other energy pattern, will pull the most negative patriarchal energies into one's life and will leave one powerless to deal with them.

CHAPTER X

OUR LOST
INSTINCTUAL HERITAGE

Reclaiming the Daemonic

DEFINITION

In this chapter we will be dealing with instinctual
energies that have been disowned because of family up-
bringing or repressive patterns in the culture. When
these natural energies, such as survival, sexuality and
aggression, are disowned over time, they cycle back into
the unconscious and go through a significant change.
Since we cannot destroy energy, they do not disappear.
Instead, these disowned instincts begin to operate unconsciously and attract additional energy to themselves.
They become engorged. They soon lose their natural
flow and they become malevolent. At this point we give
them a new name; we now call them daemonic energies.

When natural energies are repressed in this way and
they turn daemonic, natural aggression becomes an out-
of-control, killing rage and jealousy becomes a feared,
uncontrollable passion. Natural sexuality can become

fearsome after it has been repressed and combined with
other disowned instinctual patterns. Unfortunately,
these daemonic energies are now likely to break through
in our lives and, when they do so, they may well be
destructive and vicious. Then the Protector/Controller
is able to tell us how bad these energies are, and can use
this unacceptable behavior as proof of the danger in-
herent in them. These energies now get buried deeper
and deeper. So it is that a Protestant minister has the
following dream in the course of a workshop:

Dream of Drunk Penis

I'm trying to wrestle a huge drunk penis into a cold
shower.

Sexuality and sensuality are natural energy patterns.
If, for a variety of reasons, these energies are considered unacceptable, then they become daemonic. In this
dream we have a condition in which natural sexuality
has been disowned and is now distorted. It appears as a
drunk penis, out of control, and enormous energy must
be expended to bring it under control again.

It takes tremendous energy to keep our instinctual
life buried. The longer and the deeper it is buried, the
more daemonic it becomes, and the more energy is required to maintain the burial. Much physical illness and
many exhaustion patterns are a function of the disowning of these energies.

The profound fear that lives in many people is that if
we let these energies out, there will be total chaos in the
world. We wish to make it absolutely clear that we
are *not* recommending that people "let these energies
out." What we are recommending is a process that

allows all the patterns to express themselves safely, including the energies of the daemonic. These do not have to take over in this process. If, however, we do not allow these parts to speak with us, if we continue to disown them, then they will continue to become engorged, they will be projected, and eventually they will break through in us, and in the world around us, and we will all dance to their tune.

People often wonder why we use the word *daemonic*. It is frightening to many; it conjures up visions of monsters and malevolent creatures. It conjures up images of Satan. We use the word *daemonic* to establish a clear discrimination between natural instinctual life and repressed or disowned instinctual life that has become distorted. We work with the energies and voices of the daemonic in order to help restore them to their natural state of being. In this way, they can be used to support us in life, as they were meant to do.

Working with daemonic energies is one of the most difficult aspects of the Voice Dialogue process. It is what most of us fear, whether as subject or facilitator. However, there are many avenues into this area, and in the following section we would like to give you some examples of how to approach this material in the dialogue format.

First, however, let us see how the unconscious, itself, views the issue of daemonic energy patterns. These patterns come up in dreams and visualizations in very striking ways and it becomes abundantly clear, as one studies this material, that the Intelligence behind the dream process wants these instinctual energies honored and embraced.

The Daemonic in Dream and Vision

Natural Sexuality Becomes Daemonic

Agnes has done a great deal of psychological work. She is aware of energy patterns, and of daemonic energies in particular. She has decided to learn more about her own daemonic energies and what they represent in her life. She has the following dream after making this decision.

Dream of Man Turning to Snake

It was early morning at the beach and I was with Tom. We went into the ocean and it was dark. We were embracing and rolling sensually in the water. Then the tide brought us back to shore. It was daylight again and we left the water. I went back to my hotel room. I knew he would follow. When I closed the door behind me I got frightened about what would happen next.

At that point, I called on an actress to help me. She went into the shower. I walked in so I could watch the shower on all three sides. She then told me that she was frightened and couldn't finish this love scene with Tom.

Then we both decided to view an image of her completing it. After we visualized the lovemaking, Tom entered the shower and, as he closed the door behind him, he became a wild beast. He had a serpent's tail, clawed bird's feet, a beak with teeth and claws on the end of his wings. He devoured the actress, tearing and shredding her. He had cloven feet, like Satan, and after he consumed her they both disappeared.

This dream provides us with a clear example of how daemonic energies become daemonic. Agnes is with

Tom in a sensual way at first. Her Control side fears this sensuality and gradually the sensuality is disowned. So she calls in the actress, the part of her who can act rather than be fully present. Then, even the actress is afraid and now they use their powers of imagination to distance themselves still farther from the primary energy pattern of sensuality.

It is at this point in the process that a remarkable transformation occurs. Tom becomes a monster. A few seconds before, he was the carrier of ordinary sensuality. However, as this energy pattern is more and more deeply denied, it changes from a natural sexuality to a vicious Satan-like beast, who shreds and devours the actress. That is how the energies of the daemonic develop. They are our natural instincts disowned over time. Now, in the life of Agnes, these energies are requiring that they be examined and embraced. If they are not, they may well do her damage. Such dreams are portents, compelling warnings from the unconscious that it is time to embrace a Self that has been disowned.

It is very important to learn not to confuse action with energy. Sensuality is an energy. It is a certain kind of experience. What we do with this experience is up to us. It is possible to learn to honor an energy pattern without having to become that pattern in life, without being *required* to live it. The Dialogue process can allow Agnes to experience the total sensual continuum within her. Then it does not have to go sour and turn against her. If Agnes learns to embrace the sensual side, it does not have to become daemonic; she could have had a delightful time with Tom. Our inner Satans are essentially a function of our fears relating to our impulse life. Embracing these selves does not mean opening them to the world and living them out. Quite the contrary, we have a better chance of containing them when they are allowed expression than when they are continually "denied oxygen" and the opportunity to breathe naturally.

The tragedy of denied sexuality that turns daemonic and breaks out of the unconscious, causing total disruption, is a favorite theme of novelists and playwrights. *The Blue Angel* is a prototype of this tale. A meek professor, totally out of touch with his instinctual nature, falls madly in love with a dance hall singer. We watch him as he becomes more and more debauched. Finally, there is nothing left. His life has been totally destroyed by this uncontrollable passion.

Our Pagan Heritage

Josie was an older woman who had denied her sexuality, along with a variety of other threatening parts of herself. She described her daughter as the "bane of her existence." Such a description of someone close to us is a sure sign of a disowned pattern. The night before she had lung surgery for cancer, she had the following dream:

Dream of Black Bull

I am standing at the front of my home and I see a large black bull standing in front and facing me. I think to myself—"this bull wouldn't charge." Then it charges and I run to the back of the house as the bull runs after me, wrecking my home.

The bull is a magnificent image for expressing our more primitive instinctual energies. For society to evolve, the bull must be tamed to some extent. It is our primitive, pagan heritage. We have not only tamed the bull, we have dismembered it and buried it deep in the earth. It will have its revenge, however. If we do not meet our bulls and lions appropriately, they will meet us quite inappropriately.

Josie had never met her bull. She disowned her sexuality and much more of her natural instinctual nature. Interestingly enough, and not at all unusual, people described her as being bull-like in her mannerisms, something of which she was totally unaware. There is little question in our minds of the havoc such denial can produce in the physical body.

Embracing the Daemonic

Marvin has disowned his negativity for many years. He has within him a very caring and loving side and a part that is a real searcher. Because of an illness, he is forced to look in new directions and during this period he has the following dream.

Dream of the Killer

I'm with a man who is a killer. I don't want to be with him, but I have no choice. He commits a robbery and kills people in the process. I am an accessory. We spend time with many of my friends and they see me with this killer and realize that I'm going to be tainted by him.

In the last scene, he comes toward me to kill me. I have a shotgun. He taunts me, dares me to kill him. I shoot and the gun misfires. He laughs and again comes toward me. This time I fire and blow his head off. Then I hear police sirens. I think that they will never believe me when I tell them what happened. I am a killer now and they won't know why.

When an energy pattern is ready to be integrated, it appears in dreams in a variety of different ways. Basically it demands entrance; it demands submission. The phone calls of our dreams, the people chasing us, the people trying to break into our homes—these are all energy patterns of different kinds trying to make contact with us.

The killer in Marvin, this symbolic expression of his daemonic nature, wants recognition. It insists on recognition; it is quite persistent, as it gives Marvin a second chance to be a murderer. Marvin can no longer maintain the disowning process through the authority of his more loving nature. He now must learn to embrace both patterns, his daemonic as well as his loving parts.

Over the next few weeks Marvin began to appreciate the implications of this dream. He began to realize how much this energy was disowned. He then had the following dream:

Dream of the Horse and Racetrack

I am at a racetrack and a race is going on. A very large horse is in the lead. Suddenly he leaves the track and comes racing after me. I am very much afraid and I start running. The horse is breathing down my neck as I awaken.

In this dream, a transformation of energy has already occurred. The killer energy has been honored to some extent. It now appears as a powerful horse. The horse is still chasing him, but it is, nonetheless, a horse rather than a killer. Daemonic energy is gradually being transformed into the powerful, natural instinct that it was before it became daemonic. It is this transformation that is the goal of the work with these energies.

Sally provides us with another beautiful example of how daemonic energies develop and how, at a certain point of the consciousness process, the disowned energy pattern presents itself to us, insisting that we look at it, however repugnant it may be. She has the following dream:

Dream of Cruel Sultan

I dreamt I was an emissary from an Emperor of some country, making contact and hopefully arranging an alliance with a Sultan or Emperor of a large country in the Middle East. It was about 800 A.D. I was with the Emperor and he decided to take me for a tour of his palace. After seeing all the beautiful aspects of it— fountains, gardens, etc., he took me to the dungeons and prisons to show me how he dealt with people who were criminals or wrongdoers. He was very impersonal about his treatment of these people, felt he was fair and equitable in his handling of punishment of criminals. He showed me people being punished from the mildest forms, such as whipping for some minor infraction, to tortures and death by torture that ran a gradation from awful to revolting and ghastly! I, the messenger/emissary, was horrified and appalled at the Emperor's cold-blooded indifference to the suffering of the tortured and dying people. He was proud of his system of punishments, feeling he was fairly assigning punishments. When I asked him how he could not be affected by the pain of his victims, he was suprised I should ask and just answered that human life was of small importance, and very expendable; that the lives of these people just didn't matter. I was shaken and revolted by his

callous indifference to the incredibly horrible way he
was torturing people to death. And then I woke up,
feeling revolted, shaken, and appalled at the scenes of
torture and dying, and of the cold-blooded Sultan I had
just witnessed in my dream.

Sally was raised in a patriarchal family tradition that
was highly impersonal and rejecting of feeling. She
made up her mind early in life that she was not going to
be that way, and so she became the opposite, a totally
loving and caring human being. Her impersonal side
and her negative feelings were buried. Over and over
again in her life she met situations in which individuals
embodying daemonic energies attacked her from the
outside. Again, it is the law of the psyche, the law of
the universe: What we disown, life brings to us, over
and over again, until we can step back into our Awareness and recognize the teaching brought to us in these
repetitive, unpleasant life experiences.

Her unconscious now brings this negated energy to
her. She meets the cruelty of the Sultan. He is not just
cruel, he is impersonally cruel. He is everything that she
has chosen not be be, by virtue of being identified with
her loving self. There is nothing wrong with being loving. The issue lies in being identified with this pattern
to the exclusion of our instinctual heritage. The problem is in *trying* to be loving and ignoring all other feelings. This is like building a beautiful home on top of a
rattlesnake pit. We are unaware of the snakes writhing
beneath us until one day someone gets bitten, or we
ourselves are poisoned.

Projection of the Daemonic

Some years ago we were consulted by a young college student who was involved in fairly extreme action groups directed against the administration of his college and authority in general. He was in danger of being dismissed from college for his violent activities. This was in the era of the late 1960s. The night after the first meeting, he had the following dream:

Dream of Frankenstein

I am in a place in the country and I see Frankenstein. He is very frightening. Then I am at dinner with a family that I don't know, and Frankenstein is sitting next to me. I must learn how to eat with Frankenstein.

What does it mean for this young man to learn to "eat with Frankenstein?" It means that he must learn to live with his own daemonic nature. He sees himself as pure of thought and spirit, fighting for the right cause. In this process, however, he has lost contact with his own "inner monster." He does not know about his self-righteousness, his own dictatorial nature, his own inner killer. All this, living in its disowned state and gathering energy in his unconscious, is projected outwards. Then it is the University president who is Satan, or it is the Governor who is Satan or it is someone outside of himself who is Satan.

The outer person may well embody some of these daemonic qualities. Nonetheless, when we load this outer person with all of our own disowned energy, we drive the other person more and more deeply into these very energy patterns. This process of pushing someone into one's disowned daemonic energies is often seen in families where one child in an otherwise "good" family becomes the "bad" one who acts out everyone else's unacceptable impulses.

The whole meaning and purpose of working with daemonic energy patterns is to be able to reclaim and to take responsibility for our own lost instinctual heritage. So long as it remains unconscious, it is projected, and thus it is that our enemies remain outside of ourselves. Since we do not know what is unconscious, because the unconscious *is* unconscious, we do not know what is projected. Thus, our "reality" is that we are good people living in an evil and chaotic world.

We cannot solve this issue for you any more than we can solve it for ourselves. What we can do is show you a process, together with a theoretical structure, for embracing our totality as human beings. We can try to create for our readers the sense of excitement we experience in the adventure of discovery when we begin to embrace our Selves.

It is easy to embrace the "goodies." It is not so easy to embrace the "baddies." Daemonic energy patterns are among the most difficult to embrace. Here, particularly for people with any kind of spiritual orientation, the medicine is generally bitter.

THE EXPLORATION OF DAEMONIC ENERGIES
UTILIZING VOICE DIALOGUE

We have seen that daemonic energies are simply natural instinctual energies that have been repressed by the requirements of the society in which we live. Natural instincts may range from simple assertiveness to fairly primitive energy patterns. By definition, they do not become daemonic until they move into a condition of repression or disownment.

Working with these energies is an integral part of Voice Dialogue. One must always recognize the Controller's fear of this system of energies. The Protector/ Controller wants things controlled. Anything that is out of control tends to be frightening. The Protector/Controller must therefore be brought into this process from time to time. If not, he may fear imbalance and stop the exploration altogether.

We must remember, too, the place of the Vulnerable Child. The Child often fears the expression of daemonic energies because of the fear of abandonment, on the one hand, or some catastrophic expectation of retaliation on the other hand.

Aside from these two patterns, there are many other parts of the personality that have been conditioned by society to negate daemonic energies. There is the Rational Voice, the Pleaser, and the Spiritual Voice. With all of this going against them, it is no wonder that daemonic energies constitute one of the most profoundly negated psychic systems with which we have to deal.

The more energy we have to spend holding back these energies, the more drained we become, physically and psychically. The African Bushmen have a saying that one should never go to sleep on the Veldt because it means there is a large animal nearby. When we first heard Laurens van der Post make this statement, we were struck by its psychological implications. Exhaustion and fatigue, more often than not, are a function of strong instincts (animals) that are being disowned.

We know one woman who found this Bushman statement to be literally true. She discovered she had disowned her anger so totally that when she was deeply angered by her husband, she experienced, not anger, but an overwhelming desire to go to sleep. When she learned that this drowsiness was a substitute for her natural aggression, she began to search for her anger whenever she felt overwhelmingly tired. As soon as she became aware of her Anger Voice and what it wanted, the drowsiness disappeared.

If the lion in us wishes to roar and the goat bleats instead, we must pay for this in one way or another. This payment will vary. For some it is depression, a loss of energy and enthusiasm, a growing unconsciousness. For others, it can be uncontrollable, seemingly irrational behavior, where one risks one's life, fortune, profession, or marriage. In its most extreme form, the price may be a breakdown of the body which leads to illness or even death.

On a broader, more planetary level, the disowning of daemonic energies contributes to the "monster pool of the world." *The darkness of our world cannot be solved by love, unless that love is an expression of an Aware Ego that can also encompass these daemonic energies.*

If one locks an animal in a cage over a period of many years, the animal becomes wild. When the door opens inadvertently, the animal comes out raging. This proves to the jailer that the animal is inherently dangerous. One rarely stops to think that the danger is, at least in part, a function of the imprisonment.

So it is with our instinctual life. The part of us that is fearful of instinct helps to put our instinctual life in a cage. There it becomes daemonic. There it becomes the vicious snake creature, the cruel Sultan, the killer, or Satan. Periodically it breaks through in vicious ways. The "Jailer of Instincts" within us tells us that this viciousness is proof that the animals inside of us are bad. If we listen, then back into the cage goes our animal/instinctual nature.

It requires great courage to allow the voice of the daemonic to speak. There is much there that is unacceptable to traditional values. The challenge is to allow this power energy to speak while at the same time honoring the part that is fearful. The Protector/Controller fear of the daemonic is legitimate. There is enormous power for destruction in the daemonic energy structure. The longer and more powerfully it is negated, the greater its potential destructiveness.

There are many ways to work with this kind of energy. Voice Dialogue is one of the ways that we consider to be effective and safe if the facilitator has an adequate awareness of these energies. Let us look at some examples of how the Dialogue process is used with daemonic energy patterns.

Beginning the Dialogue with the Daemonic

Entering into Voice Dialogue with daemonic energies requires real choice on the part of the facilitator. We might ask one person to talk to the daemonic or to Satan and this request would initiate a good experience. Another subject might be totally put off by such a request and it would send the Protector/Controller into a spasm of contraction. Here are some possible leads for entering into Voice Dialogue with these energies.

May I talk to the part of Sue who would like to be able to do what she wants whenever she wants?

Might I talk to Selfish Jim?

May I speak with the not-nice Ruth?

May I speak with the part of Ralph that would like to rule the world?

May I talk to the part of Lorna that would like to be a hooker?

Might I talk with the part of you that would like your wife to be dead so you could be with other women?

May I talk to the Angry Voice?

May I talk to Dirty Harry?

Might I talk to the part of you that feels like killing insensitive people?

May I talk to the daemonic in you?

May I talk to the Voice that you think of as Satan?

May I talk with the part of you that wants to kill your father?

May I talk to the Hell's Angel?

All of these are lead-ins to disowned energy patterns that usually are related to repressed instinctual energies. They are difficult voices for the vast majority of people. As facilitators we must be able to shift in our work with people so as to be able to ask for the part that works for that particular subject. The way in which the Voice is invited to speak must be strong enough to evoke the disowned energies but not so strong that it threatens the subject's Protector/Controller.

Another approach in this general category is to ask for the Voice that has fantasies or daydreams. This often elicits very powerful and interesting materials relating to repressed instinctual energies. It is also one of the easiest ways to reach fantasy material since most people have great difficulty in communicating their daydreams and fantasy life.

Power

Georgine loves to wrestle with men verbally. She is a feminist. She waits, like an Olympic wrestler, for a false move on the part of the man. He makes a statement that she is waiting for, something that shows his chauvinistic tendencies. She pounces. She bites into his leg and will not let go. Her facilitator notices this pattern and decides to move into Georgine's disowned power, the power that her feminist projects onto the male chauvinists.

Facilitator: Georgine—you feel like a bulldog when you go after these men. I don't imagine that your relationships last very long.

Georgine: I've had so many men I can't count them anymore. I used to be their victim, but no more. I know how they treat women. Now I go for the jugular. It's the law of the jungle—kill or be killed. If they can't handle it—tough.

Facilitator: Could I talk to the bulldog? (Georgine moves over) Well, you certainly have powerful jaws.

Bulldog: You recognized me—I'm surprised.

Facilitator: Well, she keeps you disguised with her feminist teachings, but a bulldog is a bulldog.

Bulldog: I love biting in deeply and not letting them go. I love watching them squirm. I'm so grateful for Georgine's mind. She's a genius, you know. And I use

it. I use her mind to kill her adversaries. The more assured they are, the more I love it.

Facilitator: Do you work alone or with someone else?

Bulldog: I work with her sensuality. We dress smash-
ingly—soft clothes—light perfume—soft blouses—no
bra. We drive them crazy. She (sensuality) spins a web
and then I bite and I bite hard.

The Bulldog and Sensuality have developed an alliance. They became powerful out of the need to protect
Georgine's Vulnerable Child. The reality, of course,
is that the child is totally isolated and fearful. The
protection is no longer real, though it served its initial
function. She has been the real victim of patriarchal
consciousness. She is still the real victim, albeit from
another direction. It is now her own Inner Patriarch who
keeps her isolated.

Georgine's daemonic energies channel through this
Bulldog and the sensual part of herself. She kills from
the combination of these two spaces, and with each killing she becomes more and more isolated. Her dreams
are filled with images of orphanages and crippled children and have assumed nightmarish proportions.

The daemonic energy pattern here is more subtle. In
her job situations, in her interpersonal relations, Georgine is relatively disempowered. She is not able to bring
a natural assertiveness and expansion into her life. Her
aggressive energies come out via this one channel.

Sensuality

Sandra, for years, has been plagued by a repetitive
nightmare of being chased by wild animals, particularly

catlike animals. She begins therapy and in an early dialogue session, the facilitator asks to talk to her cat nature.

Cat Voice: She doesn't know me or like me.

Facilitator: Why not?

Cat Voice: She's afraid of what would happen if I were around.

Facilitator: Well, let's imagine that you were around all the time. What would you do? What would happen?

Cat Voice: I'd preen a lot. I'd take hot baths all the time—hot sudsy baths with smelly things in them. I'd eat when I wanted, not when others wanted. I'd never, never cook for anyone, unless I wanted to cook. Then I'd make sure the man was with me while I was cooking and I'd make sure he was making love to me all the time. That's another thing, I'd make love all the time. I'd never stop. I'd use all kinds of exotic oils and I'd massage myself all over.

Sandra has grown up in a conditioning process whereby she has identified herself with being a proper lady. In her marriage, she is Mother/Daughter. Her sensual Aphrodite nature has long been eradicated from her Awareness. She must not be selfish, sensual, or self aggrandizing.

Her unconscious, fortunately for her, maintains its pressure. Over and over again, her cat-like nature appears in nightmare form, chasing her like the aggressive demon it has become. A few nights after the Dialogue, she has the following dream:

Dream of Lion

I'm again walking down the street, a very familiar feeling. I'm aware again of the fear reaction and the sense
of being followed. I know the cat is there. I start to run.
Then I stop. I am tired of running. I turn around to
face my pursuer. It is a lion. It comes racing up to me
and then stops and licks my face. Why have I always
been so afraid . . .?

Since Sandra has been identified with a Good Girl/
Pleaser psychology all her life, it is no wonder that
her natural instincts have been negated. Since they have
been rejected, they have become enraged. Since she has
refused to look at them, they have grown in power
and authority. This has made it even harder and more
frightening for her to face them and to listen to their
demands.

What is remarkable about this whole process is that
when we have the courage to look at our disowned
parts, they change. The raging lion licks our face. He
does not need to take over our personality. He only
needs to be honored, to be heard, to be allowed to
speak.

Inner Critic

Daemonic energies often express themselves through
the Inner Critic. It is amazing to watch the transformation that occurs when one asks to speak with the
Critic in a passive individual who lives life in essentially
a victim psychology. The Critic starts to speak and the
bedraggled subject sits up straight, looks at the facilitator with a direct and unwavering stare, and begins to
speak in a strong, self-assured voice. Suddenly we see real
power. Unfortunately, this power and all the available

aggression and related instinctual energies have turned daemonic and are directed against the subject. It is as though the natural channel for these instinctual energies has become blocked through the disowning process, and the daemonic system in its growing power turns and moves against the subject. This may happen through an Inner Critic or a Pusher whose energies are clearly killing the person. It may happen also through these energies invading the physical body itself and causing some kind of physical illness.

This redirection of instinctual energies can be seen in Nan. She has had cancer surgery, a radical mastectomy. Shortly after the surgery she has the following dream:

Dream of Satan

I am in a room high on a hillside. Around the room are lush green meadows and trees but I cannot get out of my prison. In the prison with me is Satan dancing around a fire.

In her earlier life Nan drank a good deal and, when she drank, her more expressive Dionysian energies emerged. This is not at all unusual in drinking problems. If our more expressive nature is blocked, then alcohol becomes one of the primary ways of releasing these energies and getting rid of the stress reactions that build when they are disowned.

Unfortunately, when Nan gave up drinking, she became sober in every way. Her extraversion was disowned along with a number of other expressive and sensual energy patterns. Her instincts turned against her and one avenue of their expression was her Inner Critic, which developed in power in the same way as a runaway tumor gains in destructiveness.

In her dream, Nan is locked up with Satan. That is

the tragedy of the disowning process. We literally become victims of that energy which is denied. We become the prisoner alongside those energies which we are trying to imprison. If we think of Satan as the mythic expression in Western culture of our disowned instinctual heritage, then making him our enemy only empowers him, only empowers the daemonic energies to a much greater degree. If we see in Satan a figure that must be honored, along with all the other energy patterns, then Satanic energies can transform and begin to serve us in our lives. When they are recognized and honored and given the opportunity to speak, they transform into our natural instinctual heritage.

Because of the deep level of repression of these impulses in Nan, her insides have turned against her, ragefully. Her Inner Critic has become daemonic and she is paralyzed in her ability to express herself in life. From our study of many cancer patients, there is little question in our minds that of the many causes of cancer that exist, this denial of our natural instinctual heritage is a major etiological factor.

This tendency for disowned energies to turn against the person is an important consideration in the Dialogue process. Whenever we deal with a voice that carries this quality of energy, we know that we have the daemonic at hand. However, we also have the possibility of reclaiming and rechanneling these energies.

Loretta has a very strong Inner Critic. She, herself, appears rather passive and disempowered. The following is an excerpt from a Dialogue with her Critic.

Facilitator: Why do you hate her so? It sounds like you want to kill her.

Critic: I do—I would—I hate her. The trouble is if she dies I can't torture her anymore.

Facilitator: But why do you do it? Is it just for fun, or are you like a cassette tape that just repeats itself automatically?

Critic: She's weak. I despise weakness. I despise her. If she would ever stand up for herself it would be a miracle.

The rage, the passion, the vindictiveness of the Inner Critic cues us in to the underlying energy. Disowned daemonic energy becomes like a cancer in the individual psyche and in the collective psyche as well. It will work to destroy the individual organism and it will work to destroy us collectively until we learn to deal with it.

The Satanic Voice

John is considering a serious career change. He has been a practicing attorney for twelve years. Following the rather nasty breakup of his marriage, he becomes involved in a spiritual process which leads him to feel that he must give up his law practice. His Spiritual Self, with the support of an outer Spiritual teacher, has told him that he needs more time for his spiritual development. His meditations have led him to a number of profound experiences, but he feels an inner doubt about so radical a change. He has a number of friends who feel he has become too one-sided and so he seeks help to find more of a balance.

After an initial period of discussion, the therapist asks to talk to John's spiritual voice. This voice speaks at great length about John's spiritual process, how much

he has changed, the need for time to devote to more
introverted pursuits. The voice is quite positive and
supportive and points a clear direction for John's life.
The therapist then asks John if there is another voice
they might speak with, one that is the opposite to the
Spiritual Self. What emerges is the voice of Power, what
John refers to as his Satanic side.

Therapist: (to Satanic voice) How do you feel about
John's decision to give up his law practice?

Satanic: I resent it and I reject it. That son of a bitch
has rejected me all his life. Then he gets into this spiritual trip and I go down another 2,000 feet into the
earth.

Therapist: Why are you so angry at the spiritual side?
It has some very good ideas and John has been helped
considerably by it.

Satanic: I'm angry because I'm left out. Whatever I'm
not part of is crap. His marriage was bullshit because I
wasn't a part of it. I'm glad his wife nailed him. He
deserved it. He was always the angel and she the bitch.
That's because I was buried. I'm telling you something—his blood is made of saccharin.

Therapist: Have you always been this angry with John?

Satanic: Look, wise up. I'm angry because he ignores
me. He's Mr. Nice Guy. So long as he tries to act like
Jesus Christ, I will do everything I can do to defeat him.
All I want is to be acknowledged.

Therapist: What would it mean for John to acknowledge you? I mean this in a very practical way. What
does acknowledgment mean?

Satanic: Right now he thinks I don't exist—that I'm not real. Before he got into this spiritual stuff he just rejected me. Now he's learned that I'm supposed to be transmuted. How would you feel if every time you expressed yourself someone tried to transmute you into something better or higher? It's insulting.

Therapist: Well, I'm still not sure what it would mean on a very practical level.

Satanic: I don't like his passivity with his wife. She controls everything in regard to the children. He thinks that by being nice, everything will get better. Well, it's not getting better. It's getting worse. And before he signs the final property settlement I suggest he listen to me. Mr. Nice Guy is giving her ten times too much. I also don't like some of the people in his group. I'd like him to listen to me, to take me seriously, to honor what I have to say.

John's Satanic voice is like a caged animal. It is filled with the power and energy of being rejected all his life. His marriage ended in disaster, in part because he forced his wife to carry the daemonic side of himself. Since John had been unable to show his anger, negativity or selfishness, it became necessary for her to express these points of view. Conversely, as she became more identified with these patterns, he was thrown ever more deeply into the identification with his peaceful and loving parts. It soon became apparent to everyone that his wife was the bad one and he the good one. How often our mates and partners live out our disowned selves!

John had slipped very easily into the spiritual mode. It was a natural way of expressing his very loving and positive nature. The problem was that his Awareness was identified with the Spiritual energies. Furthermore, the spiritual Voices were identified with his previously existing "nice guy" mode, which precluded all expressions of power, anger, negativity and selfishness. It is no wonder that this Voice was enraged.

It takes great courage to face one's disowned daemonic patterns. The energies of these selves have lived in isolation for years, like lepers shunned by regular society. We see people who embody these qualities and we avoid them if possible. They are reprehensible to us. How easy, and yet how difficult, it is to take the next step to recognize that those people out there whom we cannot stand are direct representations of our own negated parts! What golden opportunities are presented to us with great regularity, if we are ready to hear and see them.

CHAPTER XI

IN SEARCH OF HIGHER MEANING

The Spiritual / Mythic Tradition

INTRODUCTION

There was once a native farmer in Africa who discovered a very serious problem. Each morning when he went to milk his cows, he discovered that they had no milk. This went on night after night and, finally, he resolved to find out what was happening.

The next evening he hid behind his barn and began his long night's vigil. Shortly after midnight, he saw an amazing sight. Climbing down from the heavens were beautiful star maidens, each one of them carrying a bucket and basket. They came to his cows and milked them and started to climb back to the heavens from whence they had come. The farmer resolved to catch one of them and so he leaped out as the last star maiden began her ascent, caught her and brought her back to his farm.

The Star Maiden told the farmer that she would be a good and dutiful wife, but he must promise one thing: that he would never open and look into the basket that she brought with her. The farmer willingly promised this and the two of them gradually settled down to their new life together. She was, in fact, a good wife and everything prospered under her loving care.

A few months passed and one day, while his wife was in the fields working, the farmer's curiosity got the better of him. He opened the basket and started laughing because there was nothing in it. When the Star Maiden returned, she immediately realized what had happened. The farmer laughingly asked her why she made such a fuss since there was, after all, nothing in the basket.

The Star Maiden looked at the farmer with great sadness in her eyes and then spoke to him, "I'm going to leave you now and I'm never going to return to you again. I want you to understand, however, that I'm not leaving you because you opened the basket when I asked you not to do so. I am leaving you because when you opened the basket, you saw nothing there." And, with that statement, the Star Maiden disappeared never to return again.

This lovely tale was first brought to our attention by Laurens van der Post in his book, *Heart of the Hunter*. It beautifully portrays the mystery of things of the spirit. They are not generally visible to the parts of us that are not of the spirit. Our ordinary minds cannot help us to perceive what is in the basket. Matters of the spirit are so often experienced without words, without form. The form is a later imposition to help us to communicate these experiences to others.

In working with the spiritual dimensions of consciousness, this is an essential realization for those of us who
wish to facilitate these energies in people. Words may
not be appropriate. Many times such work is silent and
energetic and quite beyond anything that words can describe. In a book such as this, however, we are using
words. Our task is to bring to you the vibration, the
feeling, the sense of what these spiritual/transpersonal
energies bring to us and mean to us.

In this chapter we will be dealing with those energy
patterns that bring spiritual meaning into our lives.
Every energy pattern brings a certain kind of meaning
to our lives. Spiritual and transpersonal energies bring a
very specific kind of meaning to us. Vast numbers of
people on our planet experience an emptiness in themselves, a yearning for something, they know not what.
Too often, in the more traditional disciplines, these
feelings are translated into purely personal terms. Diagnostic labels may be used to describe this sense of emptiness, this lack of fulfillment and this constant search
and yearning for something unknown.

There is no question about the fact that a sense of
emptiness and yearning may be evidence of a pathological condition which is connected to personal and developmental issues. Spiritual energies, however, are real.
The longing for higher meaning and a higher purpose
in life is both real and legitimate. Personal psychological work *cannot satisfy these needs*. A sense of higher
meaning and purpose can come only from a different
kind of experience.

Spiritual energies, or ideas that are grounded in spiritual reality, give us this kind of meaning. It is the experience and the awareness of these energies that permit
us to see the richness that lies in the basket of the Star
Maiden. Rather than relegate these yearnings to some

diagnostic label, let us treat them with the respect they deserve. The need for higher meaning and purpose is as much an instinct as are sexuality and thirst. This drive for higher meaning is exploding in our world today.

In striking contrast to those who might view the quest for spiritual energies as pathological, there are growing numbers of consciousness seekers who see the experience of these spiritual energies as being identical with consciousness. To our view, as we have stated earlier, consciousness and spirituality are not identical. The consciousness process requires an awareness of energy patterns, and an experience of the different energy patterns. Spiritual energy is only one of these systems of patterns, albeit a most influential one.

For the spiritually oriented person, this differentiation between spirituality and consciousness often does not exist. If the spiritual process is seen as being identical with consciousness, there is obviously no rationale for trying to discover the disowned energy patterns that are not spiritual. There is no basis for dealing with repressed instinctuality, power and emotions. This is dramatically illustrated in the following dream. Ethel, a woman minister in her seventies, remembers vividly this dream she had when she was 15:

Dream of the Snake She Loved

I'm in a forest and I see a beautiful, large snake. It wraps itself around me and I am filled with love for this snake. There are many young baby snakes around. We are at the edge of the forest and people come from the village with hoes and shovels to kill the snakes. They start to kill the babies. My snake tells me that it must leave me and return to the forest. Otherwise it will be killed. I am filled with a deep sadness at the loss of my beloved friend.

Ethel met her "snake" in her early adolescence. It was the early acknowledgment of her natural instinctual heritage. The society of which she was a part was not ready for it, neither the outer society nor the societal introject within herself. The snake, this remarkable symbol for our instinctual heritage, returned to the forest, back into the unconscious. Ethel became a minister, a very fine and beloved minister. Her vision of consciousness, however, became spiritual. There was no room for the other side, for the snake energy. This is the essential problem when we identify spirituality with consciousness. The snake energy, in its broadest sense, is lost.

The primary challenge of spiritual development is not spiritual development, *per se*. That part is relatively easy to facilitate and discover once someone is ready. The real challenge, from our perspective, is the ability to disengage the Awareness level from the spiritual value structure with which it has been identified. Then the Aware Ego can do what it needs to do to embrace the selves that have been left out of the picture, while it continues to embrace the spiritual/transpersonal energies so meaningful and nourishing to all of us. Let us now see how these spiritual energies manifest in dreams and visions.

SPIRITUAL ENERGY IN DREAM AND VISION

Dreams and visions from the spiritual realm are among the most profound experiences that the unconscious can bring to us. Our first example is that of Doris, a woman in her mid-thirties who was making a significant transition in her personal therapy. She had been dealing with personal issues for some time when suddenly she found herself beginning to be concerned

with other kinds of issues. There was something lacking. She thought about the issue of meaning in her life.
What was the ultimate purpose of her life? She began
to read books that had a bearing on these new kinds of
questions. It was during this period that she had the
following dream:

Dream of Funnel

I am outside in the yard. I look ahead of me and see an
amazing sight: there is a tall, cylindrical pillar made of
tiny, glitter-like particles moving from the ground to
the heavens. The movement is intense, with a tornado-
like force although it doesn't spin, but rather rushes
straight up. Suddenly I notice that "things" are being
swept up into the force of particles—patio table and
chairs, dishes, clothes, and other mundane items of daily
life. I stand there watching in awe.

This dream provides us with a powerful example of
the sanctification of matter, a very beautiful religious
concept. The unconscious is providing Doris with a
linkup between the earthly and heavenly planes. It is
helping to move her in her daily personal life to a feeling of the unity of spirit and matter.

The danger to an individual when these spiritual
energies begin to be experienced is the potential split
between spirit and matter. These energies are so seductive that many spiritually identified people lose their
connection to earth, to instinct, to their physical bodies.
Our challenge is to learn how to live spirit on earth, and
not see spiritual energies as something split off from
life. They are here, with us, in all of our life, in all our
relationships, in all our actions.

We now present a series of dreams and visual meditations from a different subject. Siri was in her late thirties when she discovered that she had multiple sclerosis.
This drove her into an ever deepening exploration of
her inner selves and her system of interpersonal relationships. In a series of visual meditations, she tapped
into some very deep spaces within herself that came as a
total suprise to her as well as to her therapist. In the initial guided fantasy Siri experienced, for the first time,
the voice of her inner wisdom. This was a profound experience for her, and the tranquillity it evoked stayed
with her for a considerable period of time.

Visual Meditation: Wisdom in the Desert

I have been walking a long time on the desert and I
have lost my way. I am thirsty and I look for water. I see
a mountain in the distance and I make my way to its
foot in hope of finding a stream. I find none, but hear
the sound of an underground stream. I dig, trying to
reach it, but it is too deep. I begin to climb the mountain in search of its source. There is no path and the
mountain is very steep. I am able to make my way
through a small, winding cleared space to the top.
When I reach the top I find others also there, footsore
and weary, as am I. We speak, as with one voice, to an
old man we see standing by a deep well. We thirst, we
thirst. The old man takes cups made from a hollowed
gourd and passes them to those there. The greedy grab
for the largest cups and he readily gives each the cup he
wants. When all have cups, the old man begins to
speak:
    "There is much you would ask of me, but you need
not ask, your questions are known to me. You would
ask me, what of life? I ask you, what is life but a school

of living? And you, but children in that school? Of each
child a certain amount of knowledge is required before
he may pass from that school. Those that learn not can
only fail and must repeat the term. Those that learn
readily pass on to higher schools. You ask much, but
these two things you ask the most and only of them will
I speak now. You ask, what is death? What is death,
but a step from life to life? Yet the body faints at the
sight of it, and the mind trembles and fails in fear of it,
but the soul, knowing that which comes, runs joyfully
to meet it. It faints not, nor is it afraid."

When he had spoken, all looked at their cups and
found they were filled. The greedy bent to drink
quickly, that their cups might be filled again, but they
found their cups were porous, as a sieve, and the water
had leaked onto the earth and been absorbed by it.
There were those there that feared thirst and they, too,
tried to drink quickly, but they were seized by trem-
bling and their water spilled over onto the earth and
was absorbed by it. Those remaining knew the ways of
the desert and knew a man who thirsts must quench his
thirst slowly and they quietly pondered in their hearts
on that which they were to drink. To them, the old
man spoke again, saying: "Drink deeply of this cup
that you may thirst again." When all had drunk, each
found himself again alone on the desert and none knew
the secret way to the place whence he came.

The voice of the spirit, whether in dream, vision
or Voice Dialogue, always has a very special energy
connected to it. It is uplifting. It is non-judgmental.
Things may be pointed out, but there is never admon-
ishment. It is as though one is taken to another level to
view the personal issues with which one is wrestling.

Siri's outer situation remained quite unchanged. Her
inner attitudes—those that determined the nature of

her perceptions of her personal life—were changing dramatically. This spiritual point of view, the experience of transpersonal reality, provided a new context, a new meaning, a new vessel in which to contain the life process. She was being taught, on an inner level, in a way that was very new for her.

A few weeks after this first visual meditation, Siri had a second experience:

Visual Meditation: The Old Magician

I am waiting by a dusty roadside. I see an old man approaching far down the road on my left. He carries a heavy pack on his back. When he reaches the place where I am waiting I step into the road to walk with him. The road leads into the forest. After walking deep into the forest we see a small squirrel dart into our path. The old man catches it and cuts it open and removes something from it. I do not see what it is, but the wound is closed quickly by the old man who has hands as sure as a surgeon's. The squirrel is then released.

We go on our way through the forest again. As the sun begins its descent we see a small thatched cottage and enter it. A very old man with a long white beard is in the one room that makes up the interior of the cottage. He is sitting in front of a great cooking pot on the hearth. My companion opens his pack and takes from it the object he removed from the squirrel. He hands it to the old man who seems to be a magician. The old magician drops it into his black cooking pot and after a moment it is transformed into a bluebird which flies from the pot. It flies to my traveling companion who places it on my shoulder. He then leads me back to the road and disappears. I am a little hesitant about resuming my journey alone as I do not know the way, but from time to time the little bird flies on ahead and then returns and shows me the way to go.

In this vision, we have the emergence of several archetypal figures. We have the Wise Old Man/Magician/
Alchemist. We have an Inner Guide. All of these are
archetypal patterns that can be elicited in the Voice
Dialogue process. The deeper the facilitator's understanding of archetypal motifs, the deeper is the potential for the Dialogue process. To what depth and what
degree such material can be elicited varies with different
subjects and different situations. What is important is
that the Dialogue process and deeper visualization processes can be used together. Voice Dialogue thus becomes a wonderful tool to use in relation to dreams and
visual imagery of all kinds, at both the personal and
mythic levels.

In working with dreams and visions that are related to
spiritual energies, the decision on the part of the facilitator is always the same—whether to work at a non-verbal level or whether to see if the "spiritual voices" wish
to express themselves in verbal ways. Non-verbal meditative processes will most likely take people into deeper
experiences of transpersonal reality. In this book, our
focus is more on the energies that we can reach through
the Dialogue process and some levels of visualization. It
is important for a facilitator to learn to be comfortable
with non-verbal spaces. Otherwise we remain locked
into verbal modes of communication and significant
levels of transpersonal awareness remain unavailable to
us.

The material that was now emerging in Siri's process
was interspersed with extensive work on the personal
level. Many of her parts had been disowned in her
growing-up process and much territory had to be reclaimed. Her deepest conflict was what she experienced
as the never-ending war between her spiritual and

earthly natures. Instinct had been disowned. Spirituality, until now, had been a system of rules and regulations about behavior. Now she was experiencing her
spiritual / transpersonal nature in a very direct way. She
was also beginning to understand the real meaning of
instinctual reality and how her fears had blocked this
from being expressed in her own life. She then had the
following dream:

Dream of Red Serpent and Dove

A large, red serpent was coiled on a slab of stone with
its head tipped up and its mouth open. A dove flew
straight down from heaven and directly into the snake's
open mouth and was swallowed. I was grieved because
I thought it was awful and then suddenly the snake
convulsed and the wings of the dove protruded from
each side of the snake and the two became as one and it
flew away. In the sunlight it was difficult to know
whether it was a snake or a bird in flight. It flew straight
up toward the sun. It looked like a rayed snake.

Here we have two very different energy patterns, the
snake and the dove. What first appears as a tragedy to
the dreamer ends up as a remarkable transformational
symbol, a union of heaven and earth, of spirit and matter. It is not as though this problem is solved once and
forever by Siri. It is simply a union of opposites that is
occurring within her at a very deep level, that is helping
to heal an ancient split that belongs to each one of
us. As individuals move into the consciousness process
more deeply, this question of how to embrace heaven
and earth, the dove and the snake, becomes increasingly
relevant.

Our final example was again in a meditative state and

it provides us with a remarkable picture of the depths that we are capable of reaching in the symbolic process. It directly followed the dream of the "rayed snake."

Visual Meditation: Be Still and Know that I Am God

The image of the rayed snake keeps coming to mind and I stop my thinking and concentrate on the image. It grows larger and larger until it fills the room. It is dark red and the six rays on its back are pointed. The movements of his body seem designed to crush me and burst the confinement of the room. I realize he must be freed or he will completely destroy the house and all that is in it.

With this realization the house fades away and I am on a tiny island completely surrounded by the sea. The sea is dark and still and from the stillness the huge snake bursts forth and I try to run, but he completely encircles the island, crushing it with his great strength, and pulls me into the sea where he wraps himself around me, crushing me. I struggle to free myself and manage to free my arms, but he twists his back and the rays pierce my hands. He then turns them, like great thorns, against my head, piercing it. I feel a desperate need to free myself and fight the crushing pressure, but he seems to anticipate this and drags me deeper into the sea as if he gloried in showing me his strength and my weakness. I try to breathe and my lungs seem incapable of filling with air. The water stings my eyes and I cannot see. I know I cannot free myself and yet I cannot stop trying. Then deep inside me something says: Be still and know that I am God.

I become acutely aware of the pain the pressure brings, but the will to fight it is gone and I feel myself begin to slip into the black void of insensibility. Gradually I become aware again and the void slips away. I open my eyes and find I am no longer in the sea and the snake is gone. I am in a small oasis surrounded by the desert. There is a single palm tree in the center. At the foot of the tree a spring bubbles and a small fish emerges from the spring and, lying against the tree, begins to convulse and change form. It becomes a tiny child. A soft light emanates from around the child. I kneel before my child and see in his hand a tiny golden sceptre in the form of a cross and entwined around it is a snake. A voice speaks and says: *Understanding weakness brings strength.* I feel completely still but it is not an empty stillness. It is full, full of the things I wanted least and needed most, and I realize how little I knew of my own needs.

Spiritual energy channels through particular societies and particular cultures. Siri was a devout Episcopalian, very much committed to her faith. She had never been able to tap into the deeper regions of her soul, however, because there were so many patterns within her that blocked her access to these levels of experience. Her spiritual images were specifically Christian, as one would expect with her religious background.

The birth of this Divine Child was a most profound experience for Siri. What is remarkable is that the birth occurred after her surrender to the snake. She had *tried* to be spiritual before, but it was a spirituality that was not grounded in her instinctual process. The surrender to the Snake God is the surrender, at a very deep level, to earth, to the body, to her disowned instinctual heritage. She had been working with these different energy patterns for well over a year. Now they received their proper honor. The Voice within her spoke and said, "Be still and know that I am God." She experienced this Voice as emanating from the snake.

How, we may ask from a more traditional background,

can a snake be God? What manner of irreverence is this? *From our perspective, all energy is part of the Universal Energy Source that may be referred to as God. When the voice in Siri's vision speaks to her, it is expressing the reality that belongs to any disowned energy pattern. Each kind of energy wishes to be claimed by us if it has been disowned. Each pattern returns to us in our dreams, in the personal reactions of our friends, in our meditations—each one of them is turning to us and saying—"Be still and know that I am God. Claim me, for I am that part of the Universal Energy Source that has been left unclaimed."*

Siri was learning a lesson of profound importance. All her life she had thought of spiritual reality as consciousness. She had no separate Awareness level to view her spiritual reality. This reality, however, was filled with ideological content and training that negated her body, her emotions and her instinctual life. Now, finally, her lost instinctual heritage had returned, claiming its proper space as part of the divine source of universal energy. Once this surrender was fully acknowledged, she was ready for the birth of the Divine Child, for the birth of the child that she experienced as the inner Christ.

VOICE DIALOGUE AND THE SPIRITUAL DIMENSION

Voice Dialogue is one of a multitude of approaches that can be used in the facilitation of the consciousness process. It can be used successfully to help people gain access to spiritual dimensions. We have given prior examples of dreams and visions to demonstrate the depth and profundity of these transpersonal dimensions. Voice Dialogue can be used to reach these energies. However, it is able to do what it does, and it cannot do what it cannot do. Then other approaches must be utilized. In the following section, we will demonstrate some applications of Voice Dialogue in facilitating spiritual energies.

Dialoguing with the Higher Mind or Higher Self

Voice Dialogue creates the possibility of connecting to energies on the spiritual continuum. One can ask directly to talk to the higher mind or one can lead a person into the higher mind through a meditative procedure and then shift to Voice Dialogue. We will demonstrate both of these methods. First, however, we must make a point of clarification.

Spiritual energies are a real kind of energy. They have the capability of bringing great beauty and meaning into people's lives. What gets confusing is that spirituality becomes codified into a system of rules and regulations about how life should be lived and these are then seen as spirituality. The higher consciousness movement is no different from any other religion; we begin with experience and then we create structure to contain the experience. In this way, we can easily lose its original depth and meaning.

In dealing with the higher mind, we must be very careful as facilitators that we do not confuse an inner Pusher with the actual spiritual energy. In the examples that follow, we will illustrate these differences.

In our first example, the facilitator does an induction technique to help put Ken in contact with the higher mind. Ken is asked to close his eyes.

Facilitator: Imagine, Ken, that you're leaving this space here in this room and that you're going into an unknown space. It might be a nature scene of some kind—forest meadow, cave, mountain—or you could even be leaving the planet. It's up to you. Just let me know when you get there and describe it to me. (Pause until Ken describes space)

Ken: I'm in a meadow. It's more on the barren side, like at a higher altitude.

Facilitator: Find a comfortable spot to rest.

Ken: There's a rock and I'm leaning against it. It's quite comfortable.

Facilitator: Imagine now, Ken, that the Higher Mind of the universe wants to make contact with you. It can take any form it wishes; just let us know what comes in.

Ken: It's an old man, in a monk's robe. He's walking right past me.

Facilitator: Stop him and make contact with him.

Ken: (Ken makes contact and they look at each other) Who are you?

Monk: Why do you wish to know?

Ken: I have questions to ask.

Monk: Ask them.

Ken: Do you have anything to say to me generally about my life?

Monk: Would you listen?

Ken: Yes, I would listen. Do you have anything to say about my life and path?

Monk: You need more discipline. You are too lax, too easy with yourself. A spiritual life requires discipline.

(The voice is sounding heavily patriarchal. The facilitator steps in to work in a Voice Dialogue format.)

Facilitator: Would you ask the monk if I can talk to him?

Ken: (Ken asks) He says yes.

Facilitator: You say that Ken needs more discipline—what kind of discipline?

Monk: He is too easy on himself. He needs a regimen. He needs to know when he is going to do everything that he does in his life. He needs to know when he is going to pray and for how long. He needs to know when he is going to exercise and for how long.

The Monk has definite recommendations, but they are severe. They are Monk-like. They are ascetic. The Higher Mind has been taken over here by an ascetic Monk/Pusher who makes very stern demands on Ken. The Monk Voice is a reality in Ken's life. Here, a voice was contacted that had actually been guiding him, but without his Awareness being involved.

Now, Bernadette has a different kind of Pusher/ Higher Mind combination. Here is some of its advice to her.

Higher Mind: You are too undisciplined. You need to run every morning. Then 15 minutes meditation, every day. You need to eat properly. The junk food has to go. No bacon, no meat, no potatoes, no bread, no sugar. You'll live. You'll feel better. You need to write in your journal regularly, etc.

If Bernadette does not have an Awareness that is separate from this voice, she is going to be in a very difficult position. It is not that this voice does not have some good ideas. It is that this particular Higher Mind has become, in fact, the bearer of rules and regulations about how life should be lived. It has become an essentially patriarchal voice that throws Bernadette into a daughter position. She can never meet the demands of this voice. As a result, she loses the possibility of becoming connected to a real spiritual energy. It is very important in dealing with the Higher Mind to be discerning in determining whether the vibration is the orthodox patriarchal Father/Pusher/Critic or a genuine spiritual energy.

In the following example, the facilitator has inducted Jordan into a Higher Mind meditation. He sees a bright white light.

Facilitator: Just let yourself be with that light. Take your time and just feel the energy and see if it has anything to say to you. It may be in thought forms, not as a real voice. (There is a long pause as Jordan sits with the light.)

Jordan: The light says essentially that it is always there for me. All I have to do is turn to it. (continued silence)

Facilitator: Is there anything you want to ask of it?

Jordan: Yes. Am I on the right track? Is there anything I need to do?

Light: There is nothing to do. There is no reason to drive yourself so hard. It will all happen. Allow yourself time to be. Learn to enjoy the silence.

Here the light speaks and gives advice, but it is advice of a different kind. It is not a voice that makes Jordan feel inadequate. It says, simply, that he is fine the way he is. He just needs to learn to enjoy the state of being. The voice of the Light does not tell him to meditate or to program himself, only that it (the Light) is there whenever he wishes to turn toward it.

Jennifer has been inducted into a Higher Mind Meditation. The voice of the Higher Self comes through with some clarity about her life in a very general way. The facilitator wants to help Jennifer create a dialogue that is more specific in its nature.

Facilitator: Jennifer, would you ask the Higher Self if I can talk to it directly?
(Jennifer's Higher Mind has taken the form of an old, wise-looking woman who agrees to talk with the facilitator).

Facilitator: I appreciate that you're allowing me to speak with you. I wanted to ask you if you have any thoughts about Jennifer's marriage. It is a source of great concern to her—whether or not she should remain in it.

Higher Self: The issue is not whether or not she should remain married. The issue is the process she is in. Worrying about whether or not she should separate just wastes energy. She is doing what she needs to do now.

Facilitator: Could you be more specific? This is a very troubling issue for her.

Higher Self: The issue for Jennifer is learning how to express herself more directly. She has always hidden her

real feelings. She has lived a role rather than her reality.
Her husband knows nothing of her reality. It may be
that she will have to separate to find her reality as a person, but this is of secondary importance. Of primary
importance is learning to be in relationship in a new
way.

Facilitator: So this situation, from your perspective, is a
teaching for her?

Higher Self: Exactly. If she sees this as the teaching it
was meant to be, then she has a chance to do the work
that has to be done.

Facilitator: Is there anything else you could say about
her marriage? Things she needs to learn?

Higher Self: She has always lived her life very personally—mother—wife—friend. Everyone and everything
has come before her own being. Now that is changing.
It is naturally upsetting to her and to everyone around
her. Sometimes people confuse separation with divorce.
The issue now is separation—letting go of all forms of
living, so that new ways of living and relating can come
in. She will do whatever has to be done to help this
change take place. The challenge is not to confuse the
personal with the impersonal. She needs to separate
psychologically from her husband and children. Whether or not that means a physical separation is secondary
to the real issue.

Jennifer's Higher Self gives her a "view from the
bridge." It gives a perspective. It does not solve problems. It does not create pressure. Amazing insight can
come from such parts of ourselves. When such a voice is
contacted, a strong empowerment may take place. We
are helping the subject connect to inner sources of
strength and wisdom.

The job of the facilitator in these dialogues is two-fold: 1) To help the subject recognize the difference between the Higher Mind and the Power/Critic groupings, and 2) To help the subject develop a more aware and a more reactive Ego so that the connection between it and the Higher Self becomes a real dialogue, a true interactive process.

When dialoguing with the Higher Self, the facilitator must be aware of the possibility that its expression may be totally non-verbal. In this case, the job of the facilitator is simply to help the subject stay with the energy of the Higher Self, whatever form that may take. When the communication from the Higher Self is non-verbal, the facilitator simply supports the meditative process. A great deal of Dialogue work is non-verbal.

The Hero/Wanderer

Frances was immersed in personal issues in her life. She was constantly dealing with areas of conflict with her husband and children. She was always locked into personal issues. During one session the facilitator asked to talk to her Ulysses voice—the part of her that saw her life as a journey to be lived rather than a series of problems to be solved. The change in her was immediate as she moved over to a different chair.

Facilitator: (After a pause) Could you tell me something about yourself?

Ulysses: She was really not ready for me until now. She had too many personal issues to work through. Now she is ready to see the bigger picture, the meaning behind all of this work.

Facilitator: Is that what you stand for—I called you Ulysses, but I'm not really sure who you are yet.

Voice: The name doesn't matter. You may call me Ulysses. You may call me the planetary wanderer. I stand for the journey of life. I bring to Frances the vision beyond the personal. Why has she struggled for so many years? She was born a woman and had to solve a woman's problems. I am beyond male and female. I bring courage. I bring new energy. I create new possibilities. I stand at the top of the mountain, at the prow of the ship. I create adventure in life. Her whole marital struggle is a part of that journey. It is not just personal. The work she is doing will free her to live a life of greater adventure and purpose and meaning.

The Hero voice can be very specific in its recommendations or it can create an energy, a mood, as was the case in the preceding Dialogue excerpt.

At a different time the facilitator asks to talk to the Wise Woman in Frances. What follows is a series of excerpts from that voice.

Wise Woman: Yes, I am always with Frances, just as I am always with all women and all men. One just has to turn to me. Wisdom is available to each of us. All that is necessary is that we turn inwards and hear the voices. The marriage is a vehicle for Frances. Who can say whether she should be there or not be there. No one can make that determination. What Frances can do is realize that life is a training ground, an opportunity for growing and changing. It is an adventure in learning, all kinds of learning, but especially self-learning. Without going through what she is going through, she would never have learned about me or about her adventurous side. She would never have considered the trip she is taking next month. There is a reason for suffering if the issues of life are squarely dealt with. The other side of the suffering is an expanded being, a life that is joyful. Frances will have a life that is much more joyful. It is already happening. She is doing her work.

Wisdom Voices help us to see our lives from a different perspective. They take us to another level so that we can step out of the current personal issues and see the meaning of these issues in the context of our entire life. Thus, the personal struggle is put into a larger and wider framework.

UNCONDITIONAL LOVE

The Awareness level of consciousness, and the more Aware Ego that accompanies it, lead us to unconditional love. One does not arrive at unconditional love by trying to love unconditionally. As soon as we *try* to love unconditionally, we will disown major energy patterns —especially our non-loving sides.

The attempt to love unconditionally is to identify with the heavenly God and to love humanity from up above. To learn to embrace all of our Selves is to learn to honor, respect and love our own humanity, both earthly and heavenly. Then, as our love pores open, we learn gradually to live our humanity and to love humanity at one and the same time.

Whenever we *try* to love unconditionally, whenever we *try* to transmute energies, we are supporting a repressive process in the psyche. To *try* to love unconditionally means that we are not embracing, honoring and loving certain parts of ourselves. This is a paradox for the spiritually oriented person, who wants deeply and profoundly to change the world, and who knows at some deep level that love is the answer.

From our perspective, love is not the answer. The consciousness process is the answer. Embracing all of our Selves is the answer. Love is a natural concomitant of this process. The love that emerges with this kind of Awareness is clear, and requires no sacrifice of any part of ourselves. It is a love that incorporates heaven and earth, a love that incorporates all of our humanity.

CHAPTER XII

EMBRACING OUR SELVES

The New Renaissance

WE MUST HONOR ALL THE GODS

In ancient Greece there was an understanding that one was required to worship all the Gods and Goddesses. You might have your favorites, but none of the remaining deities could be ignored. The God or Goddess whom you ignored became the one who turned against you and destroyed you. So it was with the Trojan war. So it is with consciousness work. The energy pattern that we disown turns against us.

There is an Intelligence in the universe, both without and within us, that moves us inexorably toward an expanded Awareness and a more complete consciousness. The energies that we continue to disown will return to us in some form to plague us, to defeat us, and to cause us stress. These disowned energy patterns behave like heat-seeking missiles, launched by this Creative Intelligence, which find their way unerringly to their disowned counterparts inside of us. Thus, they *demand* our attention

289

through the discomfort they cause upon impact. And impact they do!

Our thesis in this book is very simple. There are a multitude of energy patterns inside of us as well as outside of us. They can hardly be separated because the inner patterns so strongly affect our perception of the outer ones. The task of the consciousness process is to become aware of these parts. We must learn which ones we are identified with and which ones are disowned or simply unconscious. This work extends over time; it is a never-ending process.

In mythology we see most clearly this requirement that all the deities be honored. The failure to do so has provided us with some great literary tragedies. King Pentheus of Thebes is a classic example of a leader who refused to submit to this requirement in life. Raised in the tradition and worship of Apollo, he was totally resistant to the new energy of Dionysius. Greece had become too rational a country. Apollo had reigned as a primary deity since the fall of Crete between 1400 and 1200 B.C. Now, between 700 and 500 B.C. there appeared an invader from the North. He stood for a value structure that was totally different from Apollo. His followers drank wine. They defied the rule of moderation. The worship of Dionysius was ecstatic and frenzied. These rites angered Pentheus and he was determined to stop this invador from the North. The drama was now underway.

What is the rule of disowned energy patterns? "That which we reject becomes the fate we live." The divine intelligence of the universe began to go into operation. There appeared before Pentheus, the god Dionysius. He had come with a message to the king. He declared himself to Pentheus along the following lines. Needless to say, the quotes represent our contemporary extrapolation of what was actually spoken:

"Dear King Pentheus—I understand that you don't like me particularly. In fact, from what I've heard, you positively despise me. Now that situation isn't really the greatest for either of us, but especially for you. I am in fact *here*, a new kid on the block, and you have to make peace with me because I'm here to stay. However, I've got a deal to make with you that I think is eminently fair. I will simply require that you learn my minor dance. That really isn't so dreadful. If, however, you don't learn the minor dance, then, I'm sorry to say, you will have to dance the major dance. I wash my hands of the entire affair from that point on."

King Pentheus was furious with Dionysius. This young upstart god had the effrontery to require anything of him! He had Dionysius thrown out of his castle and told him never to return again, neither to his castle nor to his kingdom.

Now it is obvious that Pentheus knew nothing of disowned energy patterns. He knew nothing of the fact that the things we hate are direct personifications of our disowned selves. He had been listening to Apollo for so many years that he thought Apollo had all the answers. He did not realize that Apollo only knew what he knew, that he was only one among many deities, each of whom knew and experienced life in a different way. But then, how could he know? This is ancient Greece and he is a player in the drama.

That night Dionysius and his train of followers went into the forest for their nightly worship. They drank and they became crazed and they indulged themselves with wild abandon. Into this scene came Pentheus, determined to put an end to this nonsense once and for all. He did not realize that his wife and mother were part of the train of maenads, followers of Dionysius. They, too, were drunk with wine. His mother saw him and, mistaking him for a lion, she threw her spear and killed him. Then she cut off his head and, impaling it on her spear, she marched into Thebes proudly announcing: "Look at the lion I have killed." So it was that King Pentheus, who refused to dance the minor dance of Dionysius, was forced to dance the major dance, as was promised.

The consciousness process does not demand that we live out each of the energy patterns with equal fervor. It simply requires that we be committed to discovering all of them within ourselves and to honoring each one. Each must have its shrine. A mental-plane, Apollonian type of man does not have to be fully comfortable with Dionysian, expressive energies. He does, however, have to honor them and be related to them so that they do not turn against him.

EMBRACING HEAVEN AND EARTH

The need to embrace both the spiritual and the instinctual energies is a particularly important issue in the consciousness process. We will use the story of Cadmus and the Dragon's Teeth to illustrate the journey of discovery and the ultimate integration of these two complementary energy systems.

In this famous story of the founding of the house of Thebes, Cadmus, his brothers and Queen Telephassa are sent from the kingdom by King Agenor to search for their sister, the princess Europa. She has been kidnapped by Zeus, disguised as a snow white bull. Nobody knows, of course, that the culprit is Zeus. After many years of wandering, Cadmus is told by his mother to go to the Delphic Oracle and there to receive instructions.

He promises to do this, the queen dies and Cadmus proceeds to the oracle.

The Pythoness, spokeswoman of the oracle, tells Cadmus that he must give up the search for his lost sister. He must follow the cow, and where the cow stops, there he will build his own kingdom.

Under the direction of the oracle, under the direction of these transpersonal energies, Cadmus sees a cow that he begins to follow and he continues his journey till the cow stops in a beautiful valley. During this journey, he has been joined by many new friends. He now sends these friends to search for wood in the nearby forest so they can begin to build the new kingdom. Suddenly he hears a terrible screaming and he rushes into the forest to find the last of his companions being eaten by a large dragon. Cadmus is crazed and slays the dragon, but it is too late to save his companions.

While he is standing amidst the desolation of this scene, alone again, a voice speaks to him. It directs him to take all the teeth of the dragon and to bury them in the earth as though he were planting crops. He does this and then steps back to watch the results.

As he watches the field, he sees sprouting up where each tooth has been planted, a gigantic warrior, fully armed and ready for battle. These are the warriors of the dragon's teeth. Directed by the Goddess he throws a stone into their midst and they begin to fight, the most ferocious fight ever seen. They fight all day and night until only five are left. These pause for a moment to rest. Then the Goddess speaks again to Cadmus and tells him to step into their midst and make them his servants. They will help him build his new kingdom. Cadmus follows her instructions and the five remaining warriors do, in fact, help him build the kingdom of

Thebes. As a reward, he is given a wife, Harmonia, who is a combination of his lost sister, his mother and Woman.

We have given a much shortened version of this amazing story to illustrate again the thesis that we are presenting in this book—namely, that we must honor all the Gods and Goddesses. The journey of Cadmus is prototypical of each of our journeys. He starts out living the injunction of his father, to find his lost sister. Then he is directed to the Delphic Oracle by his mother. He must make contact with a new reality. For us, this means tapping into energies that are beyond the purely personal. It means tapping into those energies inside of us and outside of us that can bring new kinds of ideas and experiences; new energies that are not tied to the traditional forms of our culture and our family heritage. For Cadmus, it means connecting to the feminine principle. It is his introduction to the world of the Great Mother.

Cadmus is now given a new set of instuctions. He must follow the cow. He must separate from the blind obedience of patriarchal consciousness and learn to follow a different kind of energy, something other than pure will. In following the cow, Cadmus surrenders to the direction of a higher authority. This authority is not as clearly goal oriented as his father. Its goals are not apparent. He follows the cow in its aimless wanderings until finally it stops.

It is not enough, however, for Cadmus to simply be connected to this new, higher principle. He must also connect to a different kind of transpersonal energy— the energy of earth, of the warrior, of instinctual reality. Cadmus has a special fate. He must embrace heaven and earth. He must be friends with his oracular nature (as embodied in the Oracle) and at the same time with his warrior, earth nature, as embodied in the warriors of the dragon's teeth.

Over and over again in fairy tales, we see how the hero must learn to lose his or her innocence and must connect not only to the energy of the earth forces, the instinctual matrix of our being that gives power, but also to the magical energy of the transpersonal which shows the path. Cadmus must do both, just as we must do both. We must learn to experience not only these, but the multitude of energy patterns that exist at all levels of our beings: physical, emotional, mental and spiritual. We must learn to value the power and validity of each part of ourselves, recognizing always that we know only what we know. We have illustrated many of these energies in this book. There are others as well. The voice of wisdom in us recognizes that the unconscious is always unconscious. This saves us no end of trouble.

Dreams, like myths, can give us a beautiful picture of the importance of honoring all of our parts. They can connect us to both the spiritual and earth energies simultaneously. In the following dream, Dorothy, who has been struggling with the conflict between her spiritual yearnings and her personal earthy issues, is taught a meaningful lesson.

Dream of God and Gunk

On the other side, high above the clouds in a land of filtered light, stood a young woman, in a line peopled by many. All were dressed in white that sparkled, iridescent from the silvery rays. Everyone was waiting in turn, to present his or her offering at an altar that was made of marble and had pillars on either side.

She looked at the gifts the others were bearing. The

finest of jewels, fabrics woven in gold threads, rare
herbs and perfumes all dazzled her senses. In her
hands, she carried a silver platter that was large and oval
shaped. It was filled with one mountainous glob of
gunk.

She realized with stone-cold conviction, and no little
embarrassment, that she could not possibly present this
slimy dish as her offering. Setting it down, she tried
with frantic fingers to mold it into an elegant shape. No
sooner would the oozing mass be created into a display
of flowers or an impressive castle, than it would collapse
again, into the jiggly glob of off-green gunk. She was at
her wits' end and soon to approach the other-worldly
altar.

It was her turn to step up. She decided, instead, to
step out of line, to forsake her turn, but that was not
allowed in this land. So with as much dignity as she
could muster, the tray of gunk was presented. As she set
it down, a hand from above stamped it with a clenched
fist. Before her eyes, it was transformed into a shimmer-
ing fish, colored pink with gold gills. She understood
that this was to feed the masses.

Dorothy's dream is a beautiful portrayal by the unconscious of the meaning of all the work that we do
in the consciousness process. She is ashamed of her
"gunk." She is ashamed of all the personality level conflicts and symptoms and struggles that she has to go
through. She loves spiritual reality and she wants to present a special gift at the altar, not a plateful of "gunk."

Yet, each of us must bring that plateful of "gunk"
to the altar. We are each of us exactly who and what
we are. We cannot "gussie it up." Whatever it is that
we are, we are. We must live our reality, and become
aware of it at the same time. We cannot eradicate parts

of ourselves because some other part feels that they should not be there.

Dorothy was learning, from a place of Awareness, to accept all of herself. It was out of this developing realization that her dream emerged; that new energies of a transpersonal nature had the chance to evolve and to transform the "gunk" into a food that could feed other parts of her psyche and, possibly, even people outside of herself.

It is sometimes painfully difficult to honor all the parts. As Jung once said so aptly, "the medicine we need is always bitter." Well, it may not be always bitter, but "gunk" is "gunk" and it is not always easy to accept patterns that seem reprehensible to us or, more accurately, that seem reprehensible to that part of us with which we are identified.

The rewards for embracing our Selves are great, however, for each claimed pattern feeds us with a new variety of energy, each of which helps to make our journey on earth more meaningful, more effective, and more joyous.

THE NEW RENAISSANCE

We like to think of the era that we are entering as an all-inclusive New Renaissance —a re-introduction to the many facets of our being. We see the New Renaissance person as that man or that woman who accepts the challenge of a life committed to the consciousness process, a life devoted to his or her own evolutionary process in all its complexity.

Voice Dialogue is a most helpful tool in this process. We are, however, selling the process and not the tool.

On a theoretical level, there should be nothing in our approach that is at odds with any existing system of growth, therapy or healing. Each approach represents an avenue to a different system of energy patterns. Our approach is one such avenue that honors all the parts and all the systems.

There is an infinite number of ways in which one may enter into and deepen the consciousness process. Each of these ways leads inexorably to the creation of the New Renaissance person. All of us are harbingers of this new breed of being. Each of us has accepted the challenge and commitment to the journey, and we need each other for support along the way.

And what is it that we have to give up when we commit ourselves to this journey of consciousness? We must give up the feeling of security that comes from living life out of only one energy pattern, or a cluster of similar patterns. Life seems so much simpler when the world is viewed through the eyes of the Protector/Controller. The moment our Awareness level separates from this pattern, we are in the paradox of the opposites. Awareness means that we must always live with the knowledge of the opposing energy patterns.

Along with the loss of security, we lose the wonderful feeling that we are always right. Being absolutely sure that we are right means that we are identified with a single pattern or a cluster of similar patterns. It is like reading an election ballot. If there is no Awareness level operating, the arguments on the "no" side of a bond issue seem entirely convincing. If we do not bother to read the "yes" side, and we cast our vote for "no," we feel secure. Yet, if we go ahead and read the "yes" argument, that also seems entirely convincing. It is rare that only one side is totally right or totally wrong. With an Awareness level operating, we are in a position to make a choice in our vote. There is an honoring of both positions, but an Aware Ego is available to balance these and to vote as it sees fit.

Once we accept the loss of security and the loss of dogmatic rightness about things, then we see the advantages. We do not have to give up any of our views, feelings, belief structures or nationalistic identities. We simply have to recognize them as energy patterns and develop an Awareness level that is separate. We do not have to give up religious, cultural or moral belief structures. We simple must be aware of what they are: religious, cultural and moral belief structures. We must be aware of them. The moment we become aware of any thought, feeling or behavior pattern, our consciousness evolves. Nothing need be sacrificed except our total identification with specific parts.

Individuals will often ask us how to solve their problems. We do not have solutions for the individual problems of people, nor for the political and economic problems of the world. What we offer is the process of the development of human consciousness. We are two among hundreds of thousands of human beings around the planet who have made this consciousness process their main priority.

In our Awareness we learn to live in the moment and we join with the silence, peace and timelessness of divinity. In embracing our Selves, and experiencing the multitude of energy patterns, we live our humanity. In developing an Ego that is more Aware, we have the opportunity of making choices that are increasingly clear. This is the essence of the consciousness process. This is both the medicine and the magical elixir that is needed to heal our planet. We believe that consciousness begins with individuals and eventually expresses itself on a collective level. A more conscious humanity will not destroy itself, nor will it destroy the planet.

We are joined to one another at the level of Awareness. In our differing Selves, we manifest our uniqueness and our differences in relation to one another. With an Aware Ego we are able to meet across national, religious, racial and other boundaries. It is in this way that we can honor the diversity and uniqueness of our fellow human beings, while at the same time experiencing the oneness of us all. May we all, with joy and compassion, become Teachers for one another as, together, we accept the challenge of embracing all of our Selves.

About the Authors . . . Hal Stone

Dr. Hal Stone was born in Detroit, Michigan, and moved to Los Angeles at age 17. He did his undergraduate studies at U.C.L.A., receiving his Ph.D. in Clinical Psychology in 1953. He served as a psychologist in the U.S. Army from 1953 to 1957, attaining the rank of Captain.

Following his army service, Dr. Stone began private practice in Los Angeles and entered the training program of the C. G. Jung Institute in L.A. He completed this training in 1961 and practiced as an analyst through the decade of the sixties. He served as a training and teaching consultant to the Department of Psychiatry and Psychology at Mt. Sinai Hospital in Los Angeles, and was one of the coordinators of the humanities program of the new school of professional psychology. During this time he also became certified as a member of A.B.E.P.P., the American Board of Examiners in Professional Psychology.

The late sixties marked a time of searching and exploration into the new modes of therapy and transformational work that were exploding on the consciousness scene. He helped coordinate a series of programs through the extension division of the University of California at Berkeley. These programs attempted to bring many of these new developments in consciousness to a larger audience. Eventually, his entry into these many new modalities led to his separation from the Jung Institute in 1970 and his resignation as an analyst in 1975.

Out of these explorations, Dr. Stone founded the Center for the Healing Arts in 1972 and served as its Executive Director until 1979. The Center was one of the first Holistic Health Centers established in the United States and it became known for its pioneering work with patients suffering from cataclysmic illness.

Dr. Stone returned to private practice in 1979. He began developing training groups in which he taught his own approach to consciousness work. He and his wife, Sidra, founded the Academy of Delos and Psychological Services of Delos. Together they developed the Voice Dialogue process. In the fall of 1983, they began to travel and teach and establish consciousness training centers around the world. During this time, Dr. Stone published his first book, *Embracing Heaven and Earth*.

About the Authors . . . Sidra Winkelman

Dr. Sidra Winkelman was born and raised in Brooklyn. She attended Barnard College, graduating *cum laude* with special honors in Psychology in 1957. She then married and moved to Baltimore, where she pursued graduate studies at the University of Maryland, earning her Ph.D. in 1962.

She moved to Washington where she spent a year with the D.C. Bureau of Mental Health, working with outpatients, both adults and children, and with federal prisoners. She then accepted a position with the Prince George's County Mental Health Clinic, where she worked with a rural Virginia population, gaining valuable experience with acting-out adolescents and alcoholics.

Upon returning to New York, she became staff psychologist at the Manhattan V.A., where she worked with inpatients. Shortly before the birth of her second daughter, Dr. Winkelman left the V.A. She then affiliated with the Lincoln Center for Psychotherapy, a psychoanalytically oriented group of therapists. She worked there until she moved to Los Angeles in the late sixties.

In Los Angeles Dr. Winkelman became interested in Gestalt methodology and in Jungian theory. She built a private practice of psychotherapy and also began work at Hamburger Home, a residential treatment center for acting-out adolescent girls, as a staff psychologist. After the birth of her third daughter, she was offered the position of Executive Director of Hamburger Home.

This afforded an excellent opportunity to introduce holistic concepts to residential treatment. She enriched the program by arranging for the introduction of an on-grounds school, intensive analytically oriented psychotherapy, a behavior modification program, an art therapist, a class in creative writing, theater games, yoga, camping experiences in California wilderness areas, atttention to nutritional aspects of life style, and athletic activities. During these years, she also served as a consultant to the California School for Professional Psychology.

Dr. Winkelman resumed private practice in 1979. She worked with her husband, Hal Stone, developing the Academy of Delos and Psychological Services of Delos. Together, they continued to deepen and expand the Voice Dialogue process which they had developed in the early '70's. While Dr. Stone taught classes, she worked with individual clients and was active in the administration of both the Academy and Psychological Services (a group of therapists specifically trained in the Voice Dialogue technique). In the fall of 1983, they began to travel together, teaching and helping in the establishment of consciousness training centers both in the U.S. and abroad. *Embracing Our Selves*, written jointly with Dr. Stone, is her first book.

For information regarding any of the national or international training activities of Drs. Stone and Winkelman, you may contact them as follows:

Until July 1, 1986:

15300 Ventura Blvd.
Suite 505
Sherman Oaks, CA 91403

After July 1, 1986:

P.O. Box 604
Albion, CA 95410-0604

The following materials may be ordered from Delos:

15300 Ventura Blvd., Suite 505
Sherman Oaks, CA 91403

After July 1, 1986:

P.O. Box 604
Albion, CA 95410-0604

Please write to Delos for current price list.

☐ Books:

Embracing Heaven and Earth
   by Dr. Hal Stone

Embracing Our Selves
   by Dr. Hal Stone and Dr. Sidra Winkelman

☐ Articles:

Voice Dialogue – A Tool for Transformation
   (1978) brochure
   by Hal Stone, Ph.D. and Sidra Winkelman, Ph.D.

Holistic Health – Holistic Consciousness
   (1978) article
   by Hal Stone, Ph.D. and Sidra Winkelman, Ph.D.

☐ Tapes (by Hal Stone):

The Dragon's Teeth (1977)
Integrating Spiritual and Instinctual Energies:
The Interpretation of a Myth

Dreams and Cancer (1977)
Exploration of the Dreams of Cancer Patients

Healing the Whole Person (1978)
Integrating Disowned Selves

The Transformational Journey (1978)
A Personal Odyssey

Introduction to Voice Dialogue (1978)
A Tool for Transformation

Integrating the Daemonic (1982)
Our Lost Instinctual Heritage

New Visions of Consciousness (1983)
Sub-personalities and Relationships

Visions and Prophets (1983)
An Examination of Apocalyptic Visions (2-tape set)